FEROZ AHMAD

Feroz Ahmad is Professor of History Emeritus at the University of Massachusetts, Boston. At present he is affiliated to Yeditepe University in Istanbul. His works on the later Ottoman Empire and Modern Turkey include *The Young Turks*, *The Turkish Experiment in Democracy, 1950-1975*, *The Making of Modern Turkey*, and *Turkey: The Quest for Identity*.

İSTANBUL BİLGİ ÜNİVERSİTESİ YAYINLARI

FROM EMPIRE TO REPUBLIC
ESSAYS ON THE LATE OTTOMAN EMPIRE AND MODERN TURKEY
BY FEROZ AHMAD
VOLUME ONE

İSTANBUL BİLGİ UNIVERSITY PRESS 218
HISTORY 25

ISBN 978-605-399-056-7
SET ISBN 978-605-399-055-0

COVER PICTURE THE MANAKIS BROTHERS - OFFICERS OF THE 3RD LIGHT INFANTRY BATTALION –
ON THE PAPERS: LONG LIVE LIBERTY

FIRST EDITION, İSTANBUL, SEPTEMBER 2008
SECOND EDITION, İSTANBUL, APRIL 2014

© BİLGİ İLETİŞİM GRUBU YAYINCILIK MÜZİK YAPIM VE HABER AJANSI LTD. ŞTİ.
ADDRESS: İNÖNÜ CADDESİ, NO: 43/A KUŞTEPE ŞİŞLİ 34387 İSTANBUL/TURKEY
PHONE: +90 212 311 64 63 - 311 61 34 / FAX: +90 212 297 63 14 • CERTIFICATE NO: 11237

www.bilgiyay.com
E-MAIL yayin@bilgiyay.com
DISTRIBUTION dagitim@bilgiyay.com

EDITED BY GÖKSUN YAZICI
COVER DESIGN MEHMET ULUSEL
INDEX BORA BOZATLI
ELECTRONIC PAGE MAKEUP MARATON DİZGİEVİ • www.dizgievi.com
PRINTER AND BINDER SENA OFSET AMBALAJ VE MATBAACILIK SAN. TİC. LTD. ŞTİ.
LİTROS YOLU 2. MATBAACILAR SİTESİ B BLOK KAT 6 NO: 4 NB 7-9-11 TOPKAPI İSTANBUL/TURKEY
TELEFON: +90 212 613 03 21 - 613 38 46 / FAX: +90 212 613 38 46 • CERTIFICATE NO: 12064

İstanbul Bilgi University Library Cataloging-in-Publication Data
A catalog record for this book is available from the Istanbul Bilgi University Library

Ahmad, Feroz.
From Empire to Republic 1 / Feroz Ahmad.
    304 p. 16x23 cm.
    Includes bibliographical references and index.
ISBN 978-605-399-055-0 (pbk.)
ISBN 978-605-399-056-7 (v. 1: alk. paper)
1. Turkey—Politics and government—1908-1923.
2. Turkey—History—Revolution, 1908-1923. I. Title.
    DR486.A36 2008

Feroz Ahmad

FROM EMPIRE TO REPUBLIC
Essays on the Late Ottoman Empire and Modern Turkey

Volume One

Contents

Preface

Kaynak Yayinlari published eight of the ten essays in Turkish translation under the title *Ittihatciliktan Kemalizme* – From Unionism
to Kemalism - in 1984. This book has gone through a number of print-
ings ever since and continues to be read. This has been gratifying for
the author for essays are often buried in journals, forgotten, and occa-
sionally resurrected by students interested in a particular subject.

I was pleased to learn that Fahri Aral of Bilgi University Press
wanted to publish my article in two volume is an English-Language edition. To the eight articles I have added two more: 'War and Society
Under the Young Turks, 1908-1918', and 'The Kemalist Movement in
India' – to make up volume one. I have left all the essays as they were
when they were originally published so as to reflect my thinking about
the topics at the time of writing. On rereading these essays after many
years, I found that my ideas about the period had not changed radically.

I would like to add a word of thanks to Fahri Aral for encouraging me to publish these essays, and to my editor Goksun Yazici for
her patience, courtesy, and careful editing of the text which, I am sure,
has saved me from numerous errors.

FEROZ AHMAD
İstanbul, 2008

Credits

1. "The Young Turk Revolution," appeared in the *Journal of Contemporary History*, iii/3 (July 1970), 19-36.

2. "Vanguard of a Nascent Bourgeoisie: The Social and Economic Policies of the Young Turks 1908-1918," was first read at the *First International Conference on the Social and Economic History of Turkey* a conference in Ankara during the summer of 1977. It was published in *Social and Economic History of Turkey (1071-1920)*, Osman Okyar and Halil Inalcik (eds.), Ankara 1980, pp. 329-350.

3. "The Agrarian Policy of the Young Turks 1908-1918" was read as a paper at *The Second International Congress on the Social and Economic History of Turkey*, University of Strasbourg in July 1980. It was later published in *Economie et Societes dans L'Empire Ottoman*, Jean-Louis Bacqué-Grammont and Paul Dumont (eds.) Paris 1983, 275-88.

4. "The Search for Ideology in Kemalist Turkey, 1919-1939" was read at the *Colloquium on the Middle East in the Inter-War Period: The Interaction of Political, Economic and Cultural Developments*, organized by the Institut fur Europaische Geschichte at

Bad Homburg, Germany, August-September, 1984. It was then published in German, "Die Suche nach einer Ideologie in der Kemalistischen Turkei 1919-1939" in *Der Nahe Osten in der Zwischenkriegszeit 1919-1939*, Linda Schatkowski Schilcheer & Claus Scharf (eds.), Franz Steiner Verlag: Stuttgart, 1989, 341-354. It is being published for the first time in English.

5. "Unionist Relations with the Greek, Armenian and Jewish Communities of the Ottoman Empire, 1908-1914" was read at the Conference on "Christians and Jews in the Ottoman Empire" at Princeton University, in 1978. It was published in volume i, *Christians and Jews in the Ottoman Empire,* Benjamin Braude and Bernard Lewis (eds.), New York, 1982, 401-34.

6. "Great Britain's Relations with the Young Turks, 1908-1914" appeared in volume ii, part 4, pp. 302-29 of *Middle Eastern Studies*, in July 1966. This was my first article published in a scholarly journal.

7. "The Political Economy of Kemalism," was read as a paper at the UNESCO conference in Paris in December 1981 to celebrate the centenary of Ataturk's birth. It was published in an anthology entitled Ataturk Founder of a Modern State, London 1981, 145-63, Ali Kazancigil, and Ergun Ozbudun (eds.) A French translation, "Ataturk fondateur de la Turqie moderne", was published in Paris in 1984.

8. Paper on "The Times (London) and the Kemalist Revolution 1930-1939" was read at The International Conference on "The Press and Modern Turkey" organized by the French Institute (Istanbul) and the Institute of Journalism, Istanbul University, May 16-18, 1984. It was published in the book *Turkiye'de Yabanci Dilde Basin*, Istanbul 1985, 155-71.

9. The paper on "War and Society under the Young Turks, 1908-1914" first read in the Seminar on War and Society, Brooklyn College, City University of New York in April 1983. It was revised and presented at the Conference on "The Ottoman Empire and World Capitalism" at the Braudel Center at State University of New York, Binghamton, in November 1984. It was published in *Review* (Fernand

Braudel Center) vol. xi, no.2, spring 1988, 265-86. In 1993, it was published in *The Modern Middle East: A Reader*, Albert Hourani, Philip Khoury, and Mary Wilson (eds.).

   10. "The Kemalist Movement and India", *Cahiers du GETC* (Groupe d'etudes sur Turquie contemporaine), no.3, Automne 1987, 12-26 (special number edited by Iskender Gokalp & Francois Georgeon).

The Young Turk Revolution

The reasons for the outbreaks of July 1908 and April 1909 in Turkey, which amounted to a constitutional revolution, were complex and varied. Foremost amongst them was the dominance of the court under Abdülhamid, the ruling Sultan. Power was monopolized by a small group around the Palace which took the major decisions of Ottoman politics, but this did not ensure stability and continuity, since grand vezir and ministers could be changed at will; during Abdülhamid's reign there were 28 changes at the grand vezir. Apart from the obvious shortcomings, such as intrigues, graft, and peculation, the inefficiency and total absence of stability, the main criticism of this system was that it gave the opportunity to participate in political life – even nominally – to very few. This, at a time when new forces were emerging, was bound to lead to trouble, and slowly the system's critics united against the Palace; when the crisis came the Sultan found himself isolated, unable to turn to or rely upon any outside interest.

The inefficiency of the system, manifesed most clearly in the country's finances, led to dissatisfaction in the army and the administration. In both these departments esprit de corps broke down, demoralized by a powerful espionage network which had become the instrument of the Sultan's despotism. The aggressive and imperialist ambitions of the Great Powers made the situation worse; there was a fear that Britain and Russia in particular were about to intervene in Macedonia, always a turbulent area, and detach the province from the Sultan's control. The meeting of the English and Russian monarchs at Reval in June 1908 seemed to confirm this fear, and this gave an impetus to the revolutionary movement.

These were some of the negative factors which prepared the ground for revolution. On the positive side the Young Turks, as the oppositionists were called, took encouragement from Japan's example of reform and progress, and from the attempts in the neighbouring countries of Russia and Persia to establish constitutional regimes. The revolution, long smouldering, broke out on 3 July 1908 and took the form of a demand for the re-establishment of the constitution of 1876, in abeyance since 1878. Abdülhamid capitulated on 23 July and announced that parliament would be convened in accordance with the 1876 constitution. The political stage of the revolution was over; but the struggle for more fundamental changes had scarcely begun.

The antecedents of the Young Turk movement can be traced back to the reforms inaugurate by Sultan Selim III and continued by his successors. The movement reached its zenith in 1876, when the Sultan was forced to promulgate the first formal constitution. But the success of the reformers proved ephemeral and Abdülhamid, whom they had placed on the throne, was able to reverse the situation in 1876 by proroguing parliament and shelving the constitution. Despite this setback, the movement did not die. From their retreats in exile the reformers kept alive the idea of constitutionalism. A new social basis was given to the movement by the changes which were slowly transforming the socio-economic structure of the empire, even though in the political field the status quo remained unchanged. Although the

Sultan viewed liberal ideas with hostility and considered them a direct threat to his authority, he realized the necessity of institutional modernization as a means of consolidating his own position and strengthening the empire. Thus, 'Politics apart, the first decades of Abdülhamid's reign were as active a period of change and reform as any since the beginning of the century ... the whole movement of the Tanzimat – of legal, administrative, and educational reform – reached its fruition and its climax.'[1]

One by-product of Hamidian reform was the creation of a new social class, distinct from the traditional elites, with interests in conflict with theirs, and with a much broader base in Ottoman society. Though representatives of this class also spoke the language of liberalism, their demands – as events were soon to reveal – were not satisfied by political change alone. The were determined to alter not only the political, but also the social and economic structure of the empire in their own favour.

In the last year of the nineteenth century another significant event occurred, namely the desertion of three members of the royal family to the ranks of the constitutionalists in exile. Damad Celaleddin Paşa, the Sultan's brother-in-law, fled to Paris, taking with him his two sons, Sabahaddin and Lutfullah. Not only did this give a fillip to the flagging spirits of the opposition, but it seemed as if the ruling group was at last beginning to grasp the probable consequences of its misrule.

Abdülhamid's timely concession of 23 July robbed the revolution of its *raison d'être*. The demand for the constitution had been met, and the Sultan even went further to conciliate the constitutionalists by dismissing ministers and replacing them with men of standing

---

1   Bernard Lewis, *The Emergence of Modern Turkey*, 3rd ed. (London, 1965), 174-5. For a documentary account of the revolution see I. H. Uzunçarşılı, '1908 Yılında İkinci Meşrutiyetin Ne Suretle İlan Edildiğine Dair Vesikalar', *Belleten*, 1956, 103-74; Y. H. Bayur, *Türk İnkılabı Tarihi*, i/II, 2nd ed. (Ankara, 1964), 59-61; and E. E. Ramsaur, *The Young Turks* (Princeton, 1957), 132-7.

and integrity. However, during the first days of constitutional rule, the situation in the empire was highly confused; law and order had broken down and the authorities were unable to function. It was on these grounds that the Committee of Union and Progress (CUP), the political association responsible for the revolution, took charge. No attempt was made to assume power; the Sultan was left on the throne and allowed to rule through ministers of his choosing. It seemed that the Committee was attempting to carry out a revolution with, and not against, the apparatus of the state, no doubt in the hope that, as they gained power and influence, the desired changes would follow naturally. In any case, they lacked the training and experience necessary to take over the administration. More significant, they lacked the social status neessary to make themselves acceptable as leaders of such a traditionally conservative society. Rather surprisingly for revolutionaries, they were aware of their shortcomings but nonetheless too conservative to overcome them. Nor were they unanimous about what to do with their newly acquired power. A minority wanted to use it to the full, but the majority had no desire to carry the revolution beyond its political stage. They had suported the CUP in the struggle against the Palace and now that the struggle was over they considered that the Committee had served its purpose; many of them broke away to form the Ottoman Liberal Party (Osmanlı Ahrar Fırkası) in September 1908.[2]

The Liberals came largely from the prosperous and conservative elements in Ottoman society, and were socially a cut above the Unionists. They wanted decentralization in government, with virtual autonomy for ethnic groups as in the traditional *millet* system, and this won them the support of the non-Turkish population of the empire. They favoured a laissez-faire economic system with minimum intervention from the government.

The Unionists, on the other hand, expressed the aspirations of

---

2 T. Z. Tunaya, *Türkiye'de Siyasi Partiler 1859-1952* (İstanbul, 1952), 239 ff.; Bayur, *op. cit.*, 134-5.

the new social class which had arisen as a result of the reforms of the last quarter of the nineteenth century. Inarticulate and lacking confidence, this class consisted mainly of professional men: teachers, lawyers, journalist, doctors, minor officials, junior officers, and of the depressed artisans and merchants of the towns. The political changes had brought no real advantage to this group, and its members were determined no carry the revolution further.

The Unionists may not have wanted to destroy the existing social structure, but they did not intend to maintain the status quo. They too laid stress on hierarchy, but not the hierarchy of traditionally entrenched privilege. While encouraging greater political and economic participation, hoping in time to break the monopoly of the ruling elite, the electoral laws they applied and their attitude towards socialism made it plain that they were not prepared to grant any power to the masses. They wanted a centralized government controlled by an elected assembly which would be independent of traditional institutions. This would mark the end of te religious community (millet) and its all-pervading influence, except in the sphere of religion. The CUP was also in favour of economic reform, particularly of a more rational organization of public finance. Many of their ideas were inspired by the past, but their concepts of political and socio-economic organization were up to date, and this automatically brought them into conflict with the conservatives.

The July revolution had created a new and fluid political situation: a delicate balance between the Palace, the Liberals (acting through the government), and the CUP. While the Committee as the vanguard of the revolution seemed to hold the dominant position, its appearance of strength was deceptive, for it was divided into factions with conflicting interests, aims, and ideas. Their refusal to take positions in the government, and their failure to create interest groups of their own, deprived their organization of firm foundations. At the same time they made enemies by standing forth as the champions of change and forcing the Porte to carry out reforms which led to large-scale retrenchment in the civil service and the army.[3] In this situation, where authority was undefined and a political vacuum existed, a struggle for power was bound to follow.

Abdülhamid made a roundabout attempt to regain power on 1 August. He issued an imperial rescript, article 10 of which gave the Sultan the right to appoint the grand vezir, the Sheikh-ul-Islam (the senior Islamic dignitary), and the Ministers of War and Marine. This violated the spirit of the 1876 constitution, under which (article 27) the Sultan had the right to appoint the vrand vezir and the Sheikh-ul-Islam, but only to sanction the appointment of the remaining ministers. The issue went beyond the constitutional; the posts were critical, for whoever appointed the Ministers of War and Marine acquired control of the armed forces and, by extension, of the empire. The Porte and the Committee sensed the danger and as a result of their intervention the offending article was withdrawn; Said Paşa, the grand vezir who had drafted the rescript, was made the scapegoat and forced to resign.[4]

This abortive attempt was the Sultan's last, and until the opening of parliament in December an unofficial truce was maintained between the Liberals and the Unionists. Both sides seemed content to bide their time, hoping to gain control through parliament. Elections were held in the autumn of 1908 and were contested by the CUP, the Liberals, and a few independents. The Committee won by a large majority. Although the Liberals failed to win a single seat in the capital, they did not lose hope. Kamil Paşa, who had succeeded Said as grand vezir and who had stood as a Liberal condidate, assured Sir Gerard Lowther, the British ambassador at the Porte, that the Committee would not be able to command a majority when parliament met.[5]

---

3   Celâl Bayar, *Bende Yazdım*, I (İstanbul, 1965), 208.
4   Şeyhülislâm Cemaleddin, *Hatırat-ı Siyasiye* (Cairo, 1917), 10-2; Ali Cevat, *İkinci Meşurtiyetin İlanı ve 31 Mart Hadisesi* (Ankara, 1960), 8; Bayur, 69-70; 72-6.
5   Lowther to Grey, no. 415, Constantinople, 12 December 1908, F.O. 371/557/43443, Public Record Office, London (hereafter cited as F.O.).

Few people took the Committee seriously. While everyone – except perhaps the Palace – was grateful to it for restoring constitutional rule, it was expected, by the Liberals and the conservative elements, that the CUP would now opt out of politics and leave the business of government to those who knew the job, namely the Porte. But the Unionists had other ideas and soon set themselves up as guardians of the constitution. They advised the Porte on policy and Kamil's political programme and his speech before parliament reflected Unionists ideas.[6] It was the CUP which mobilized public opinion, and forced the government to adopt a firm line in the negotiations following the declaration of Bulgarian independence and the annexation of Bosnia and Herzegovina. Their representatives called on foreign embassies as spokesmen for the gornment and the people, and Unionists even went to Europe to conclude an alliance with the Entente Powers.[7] In 1908 the CUP was the driving force behind the Ottoman government and the controlling factor in the country's political life.

Kamil and the liberals naturally resented Unionists activity and interference in government. But even after their defeat in the elections, they saw it as merely a temporary phase which would end once parliament assembled. Meanwhile Kamil was willing to temporize, even to the extent of appeasing the Unionists by appointing reformist ministers to his cabinet. In November he appointed a Unionist deputy, Manyasizade Refik, Minister of Justice, and Hüseyin Hilmi Paşa, former Inspector-General of Macedonia, Minister of the Interior.[8]

Although the atmosphere, when Parliament assembled on 17 December, was optimistic, the Liberals were determined to resolve the duality between the CUP and the Sublime Porte. To be sure, there was

6   Text of programme in *Sabah*, 16 August 1908; translation in Lowther to Grey, no.49, Therapia, 18 August 1908, F.O. 371/546/29298; the Committee's official programme for 1908 in Tunaya, *Partiler*, 208-10.

7   Ahmed Rıza and Nazım Bey's interview with Sir Edward Grey in Grey to Lowther, London, 13 November 1908, F.O. 800/185A *(Lowther Papers)*.

8   Lowther to Grey, nos. 408, 819, Constantinople, 30 November and 2 December 1908, F.O. 371/561/41872 and 42605.

a faction in the Committee which distrusted the grand vezir and wanted to bring about his downfall. Kamil was, after all, supported by the
Liberals, having stood on their ticket in the elections. Furthermore, he
was accused of failing to carry out his promises of internal reform, of
'slackness and inefficiency both in domestic and foreign policy, and of
an attempt to transfer the despotism of the Palace to the Porte.'[9] He
was held responsible , and rightly – for failing to reach agreement with
Bulgaria and Austria, and censured for using these negotiations to
strengthen his own postion in parliament.[10] But in spite of Unionist
attacks and criticsm, the CUP as an organization did not want to bring
about his fall.

There were practical reasons for retaining Kamil in power. An
experienced statesman whose liberal views and independent ideas
were universally respected, he was invaluable at a time when the
Young Turks were beginning their experiment in constitutional government, especially in their dealings with the Great Powers. Kamil
was also actively supported by the British embassy, and this factor
deserves emphasis because in 1908-9, and indeed up to the Balkan
wars of 1912-13, the CUP leaned on Great Britain more than on any
other Power. Unionist criticism was intended to curb, not to put an
end to the power of the grand vezir, and a deputation composed of
Enver Bey and Talat Bey called on Kamil to inform him that the
Committee as a body dissociated itself from the hostile attitude
towards him adopted by some of its members.[11] Thus when Kamil's
statement was read, he was given an overwhelming vote of confidence by the Chamber.

The Liberals interpreted the Chamber's mandate for Kamil's
cabinet as triumph for their party and a rebuff for the Committee.
Kamil's estimate of the Committee's weak position in parliament

---

9   Same to same, no. 894, Pera, 29 December 1908, F.O. 371/760/330; *Şurayı Ümmet*, 15
    December 1908.
10 İsmail Kemal, *Memoirs of İsmail Kemal Bey* (London, 1920), 324.
11 Lowther to Grey, no. 29, Pera, 14 January 1909, F.O. 371/760/2283.

seemed to be vindicated. It appeared an opportune moment to consolidate the power which was already theirs, especially while negotiations with Bulgaria and Austria were in progress.

The method of consolidating power was the same as that attempted by the Sultan on 1 August: by acquiring control of the armed forces. On 10 February 1909 Kamil replaced the ministers of War and Marine by his own nominees. The new appointments were hastily sanctioned by Abdülhamid, and the Liberals set about trying to create a political diversion by circulating rumours of a plot to depose the Sultan in whice the ex-War minister and the Committee were implicated. In Salonica it was even reported that Abdülhamid had been deposed.[12] The Committee reacted quickly, issuing a statement denying the rumours and asserting that all was well.[13] What followed was a political crisis of the first magnitude. Three ministers resigned as a protest against Kamil's arbitrary behaviour and his failure to consult with his colleagues before acting. The Unionist press denounced the grand vezir's action in the strongest terms, describing it a a coup d'état an encroachment on the rights of parliament, and a violation of constitutional principles, and demanded immediate action from the Chamber.

On Saturday, 13 February, the grand vezir was summoned by parliament to explain the ministerial changes. Kamil sent a note asking for the postponement of the interpellation until Wednesday, declaring that the changes were connected with issues of foreign policy. The deputies rejected the note, regarding it as a manoeuvre designed to gain time for Kamil to prepare public opinion and strengthen his position. A second invitation was sent and rejected. The Chamber, losing patience, passed by 198 to 8 a vote of no confidence in the grand vezir. Meanwhile Kamil had despatched his third and

---

12 Ali Cevat, 36; Bayur, 164-71; Kamil Paşa's interview in *Neue Freie Presse*, 18 February 1909, quoted in *Fortnightl Review*, 1909, 397-8.

13 Ali Cevat, 36; proclamation in *İkdam*, 13 February 1909. See also *The Times*, 15 February 1909.

final note, claiming the right under article 38 of the constitution to postpone any interpellation until 17 February. He repeated that this was necessary because of issues of foreign policy and threatened to resign if the deputies pursued the matter further. He warned them that if he were forced to resign he would publish his explanation in the press and leave the Chamber with the responsibility for any harm that might be caused to the state. But the threat came too late; Kamil had been dismissed and the following day Hüseyin Hilmi Paşa was appointed grand vezir.[14]

Kamil's fall marked a turning point in the relations between the CUP and the opposition. The Committee realized that it could not opt out of politics and relinquish all power to the Porte. A month earlier the Chamber had supported Kamil almost unanimously; on the second occasion only eight deputies voted for him. According to Kamil about 60 deputies had been intimidated by the Committee and left the Chamber without voting.[15] His defeat made it crystal clear to the opposition that they would have to utilize means other than constitutional if they were to oust the CUP from power.

In the two months between Kamil's fall and the outbreak of the insurrection on 13 April political tension continued to mount, reflected in a bitter press campaign between the opposition and Unionist journals. The Britih embassy in İstanbul and British interests in the empire, seeing in the change of government a blow to their prestige, joined in the chorus against the CUP. The opposition was quick to exploit Britain's sympathetic attitude (especially as reflected in *The Times*), and articles in the English language press 'were welcomed by

---

14 *Takvim-i Vekayi*, 18 and 19 February 1909; *İkdam*, 14 February 1909; Ali Fuad Türkgeldi, *Görüp İşittiklerim* (Ankara, 1951), 18-21; H. K. Bayur, *Kamil Paşa*, 293 ff., İsmail Kemal, 325; *Sabah*, 15 February 1909; Ali Cevat, 36-8.
15 Kamil's defence in *İkdam*, 3 April 1909; French translation in Lowther to Grey, no. 249, Pera, 6 April 1909, F.O. 371/761/13689.

large sections of the population and were reproduced with comments by anti-Committee organs.'[16] The embassy's moral, and later active, support for the anti-Unionists became a factor of substance in Turkish politics.

The Unionists knew the value of British support and realized that Kamil's fall would have an adverse effect on their relations with the British Embassy. One of their first moves after Kamil's fall was to inform Lowther that they had opposed Kamil on constitutional grounds, and would support no ministry unless it pursued his policy of friendship with England.[17] Hilmi Paşa, too, reasured the ambassador that his policy towards England would be the same as Kamil's, and that Turkey would continue to act on the advice of His Majesty's Government.[18] Lowther was not convinced, and continued to support the Liberals.[19]

The Unionists were apprehensive. In the press campaign the advantage lay with the opposition, which had a virtual monopoly of newspapers as well as the support of the English and French press. It was to the advantage of the Committee to reduce the tension and reach an understanding with the Liberals. They therefore offered a political truce and urged the Liberals to co-operate with the CUP in finding solutions to existing problems. But the Liberals were in no mood to compromise. As the price for their co-operation they demanded the dissolution of the CUP and its withdrawal from the affairs of government and the army. Their inflexible attitude was summed up by İsmail Kemal Bey, their chief spokesman. On being approached by Talat and Hilmi Paşa he declared: 'As it was the Committee and the new government representing it that had

---

16 Same to same, no. 151, Pera, 3 March 1909, F.O. 371/761/8914; F. McCullagh, *The Fall of Abdul Hamid* (London, 1910), 31, 56.

17 Hüseyin Cahit, 'Kabinenin Sükutu ve İngiltere', *Tanin*, 15 February 1909. See also 'X', 'Les Courants politiques dans la Turquie', *Revue du monde musulman*, 1912, 193.

18 Lowther to Grey, no. 53, Constantinople, 15 February 1909, F.O. 371/760/6275.

19 Lowther to Hardinge, Constantinople, 2 March 1909, F.O. 800/184 *(Hardinge Papers)*.

brought things to this pass, it was for them and not for us to seek a remedy.'[20]

The Committee and the government tried to regain the initiative through legislative measures. On 3 March a law on public meetings was passed which laid down that the authorities had to be notified of any meeting 24 hours in advance. Hilmi Paşa also introduced a bill restricting the freedom of the press, but opposition to this measure was too strong and the debate on 25 March turned out to be inconclusive. Finally, early in April, the government replaced the Albanian and Arab Palace Guard – fanatically loyal to the Sultan and the old regime – with troops attached to the constitutional regime.[21]

The anti-Unionist force were also getting better organized. The Muhammadan Union (İttihadi Muhammedi) was officially founded on 5 April; it had already made its appearance in the columns of its paper *Volkan*, in which its political programme had been published on 3 March. The Union was an extremist religious movement posing as the champion of Islamic orthodoxy; it was strongly opposed to modernization, and stood for the rule of the Sheriat, Muslim canon law, maintaining that national union must be based on the ideal of Islam.[22] In theory the Muhammadan Union should have been against the westernizing reformism of both the Unionists and the Liberals, the latter, if anything, being more 'socially progressive' than the Unionists. But as events were to show, the Muhammadan Union exploited religion as a political lever only against the Committee. Its appeal was directed to the conservative and religious elements, and through *Volkan* it exercised great influence on the tradition-bound deputies and the rank and file of the army.

Early in April the opposition stepped up its anti-Unionist activities and seemed to be preparing the ground for an insturrection.

20 İsmail Kemal, 330-31; Lowther to Grey, no. 151, Pera, 3 March 1909, F.O. 371/761/8914.
21 Cevat, 39, 44-5; Lowther to Grey, no. 223, Pera, 30 March 1909, F.O. 371/761/12788; *The Times*, 7 April 1909.
22 Proclamation and programme in Tunaya, *Partiler*, 270 ff.

Kamil's explanation, long overdue, appeared in the press on 3 April, but far from clarifying the issue of the ministerial crisis, Kamil used the opportunity to attack the Committee for interfering with his government both before and after the opening of parliament. The Muhammadan Union was founded on the 5th, and two days later Hasan Fehmi, editor of *Serbesti* and a violent anti-Unionist, was assassinated on Galata Bridge. The opposition were quick to exploit this crime for political ends. The CUP was accused of murdering the journalist and his funeral was turned into a hysterical demonstration against the Committee. The Unionists issued a circular to the press deploring the attribution of the murder to their organization; it was 'unnecessary to deny the accusation since it was no more than a calumny.'[23] On 12 April, Hüseyin Cahit published an article in *Tanin* entitled 'Unity'. He appealed to the Liberals to sink their differences with the Unionists and close ranks against the danger of reaction. There was no time for the Liberals to respond to this appeal because on the night of 12-13 April the rebellion broke out. The İstanbul garrison mutinied, overpowered its officers, and with theological students *(softas)* as its leaders marched to Ayasofya Square demanding the restoration of the Sheriat.[24] The cabinet resigned, the Chamber dissolved into chaos, and the Sultan accepted the demands of the rebels; within a day order had been restored and the CUP removed from power.

This insurrection is known in Turkish history as 'Otuzbir Mart Vakası' (Incident of 31 March) from the old style calendar then in use. To this day it arouses controversy and – around the date of its anniversary – finds an echo in the Turkish press, where is interpretation is shaped by the prevailing political climate. Generally speaking, it has been seen as

---

23 *Levante Herald*, 10 April 1909.
24 Most of the works cited above deal with this event; for a fuller bibliography see Bernard Lewis, *Emergence*, 212.

a religious-conservative reaction against secularism and modernization, while its political aspect has been given scant attention. Religion
certainly played an important part, as it must in any society whose traditions have been largely moulded by a dominant religion; but its role
tends to be exaggerated. The movement of 13 April was neither reactionary in the religious sense nor counter-revolutionary in the political. Both elements were present but, as we shall see, they were inef-
fectual and inarticulate once the CUP had been overthrown.

Even the religious fanaticism and sincerity of Derviş Vahdeti,
the founder of the Muhammadan Union, is in doubt. It has been suggested that he and his followers were no more than the tools of those
who were determined to overthrow the CUP, and prepared to use
Islam to this end. This thesis needs to be substantiated but there is
abundant circumstantial evidence in its favour. It is not clear how
Volkan and the Union were financed, especially as on occasion the
paper was distributed free of charge. Funds may have come from the
Sultan or the Palace;[25] they may have been provided by the Liberals.
There were even rumours current at the time that Vahdeti was an
agent of the British embassy who supplied him with money.[26]
Whatever the truth may be, it seems reasonable to infer that the movement was religious only insofar as the anti-Unionists were willing to
employ Islam in order to reach the audience. Otherwise, in all its ram-
ifications, the movement was political.

The insurrection was an acute phase in the power struggle
between the liberals and the Unionists. It was a conflict not between
religion and secularism, but between those forces which wanted to
retain the supremacy of religion and the Sheriat as the foundation of
their domination, and the forces of change represented by the CUP.
The movement was broad and all-embracing because all kinds of different elements had united against the Committee. The religious ele-

---

25 Vahdeti appealed to the Sultan for funds but was turned down; see Ali Cevat, 45-6.
26 Halide Edib, *Memoirs* (London, 1926), 278; P. P. Graves, *Briton and Turk* (London, 1941),
    136.

ment went bankrupt as soon as its meaningless demand for the restoration of the Sheriat was satisfied, since it had no other aims. The counter-revolutionaries lost their importance once Hilmi Paşa resigned and the Unionists were driven out. Neither had any positive alternative to offer and the Liberals took over, though Abdülhamid used the opportunity to his own advantage.

The events following 13 April reveal further the political and anti-CUP nature of the movement. Had it been religious and reactionary, the traditional alliance between the common soldier and the *softas*, so reminiscent of Janissary rebellions, would have struck terror to the hearts of the non-Muslim population of İstanbul. Yet not a single non-Muslim was harmed, let alone the socially progressive Liberals. The non-Muslim communities welcomed the insurrection as a blow against the Unionists and their policy of centralization. The *Neologos* of 14 April, a Greek language journal, praised the army for its patriotism and concluded that 'the army was inspired yesterday by its love for the country and by no other sentiment.'[27] Moreover, the rebellious soldiers were far two well disciplined for a spontaneous mutiny. They refrained from looting and exercised great discrimination in seeking out only Unionists and their supporters for violence, and in sacking only the offices of the Committee press.

In the absence of any opposition, the success of the rebellion was unexpectedly rapid. The government offered no resistance and Hilmi Paşa's only move was to despatch his Chief of Police to learn the demands of the rebels. Apart from the restoration of the Sheriat, the politically-minded and articulate rebels called for the dismissal of the War Minister and the Unionist President of the Chamber of Deputies. Other are said to have asked for the appointment of Kamil Paşa as grand vezir and Nazım Paşa as War Minister. Hilmi, who lacked the will and the resolution to face up to such a crisis, went to the Palace

---

27 The *Neologos* quoted in McCullagh, 59; see also İ. H. Danişmend, *31 Mart Vak'ası* (İstanbul, 1961), 210-11.

and resigned.[28] Mahmut Muhtar Paşa, Commander of the 1st Army stationed in İstanbul; later claimed that had the grand vezir given him the necessary orders and authority he could have crushed the rebellion with ease. If such an opportunity existed it was soon lost. The Sultan accepted Hilmi's resignation, having already agreed to meet all the demands of the rebels and to pardon the mutinous soldiers. A proclamation was drawn up and Ali Cevat, his first secretary, was sent to read it before the Chamber and the rebels in Ayasofya Square.

Abdülhamid has been absolved of all responsibility for the outbreak of 13 April by most reputable authorities.[29] No satisfactory evidence has appeared to prove the contrary and none seems forthcoming. Nevertheless it is impossible to deny that the Sultan took advantage of the situation in an attempt to restore his former authority. He made no move to arrest the movement and his prompt recognition of the *faith accompli* only encouraged the rebels. As the Sultan-Caliph, he was the traditional symbol on whom the rebellion centred and without whose passive connivance it would have stood no chance of acquiring legitimacy. If Abdülhamid did not start the conflagration he made no effort no extinguish it either. As in August 1908, he attempted to regain the initiative. On 14 April he appointed Tevfik Paşa grand vezir and, contrary to the decision of August 1908, again took upon himself the prerogative of nominating the ministers of the armed forces. Tevfik protested against this usurpation of the grand vezir's prerogatives, refusing to take office under these conditions. The Sultan stepped down, though in fact he had already appointed his nominee, Field Marshal Edhem Paşa, War Minister. Abdülhamid had avoided appointing Kamil and Nazım – whom the Liberals would have preferred , on the grounds that this would be a challenge and an affront to the CUP.[30] The more plausible reason seems to be that he wanted

---

28 Ali Cevat, 48, 90-92.
29 Danişmend, 19-1; Türkgeldi, 43.
30 Lowther to Hardinge, Constantinople, 14 April 1909, F.O. 800/184; McCullagh, 127; Abdülhamid, 138, wrote that he appointed Tevfik 'so as not to intensify passions'.

pliable and loyal ministers, and Kamil and Nazım did not meet his requirements.

The Committee had been routed and a new regime and been set up; it remained for the Liberals to establish their authority in the empire. Tevfik's appointment was a step in the right direction and explains why the liberals did not press for Kamil's appointment. Kamil was committed to the Liberals; Tevfik Paşa, on the other hand, was known to be neutral in his relations with the various factions of the Young Turks. There was a good chance that he might be acceptable to all and his cabinet was formed with an eye to conciliating the moderate element, overcoming partisanship, and winning over Macedonia, the centre of Unionist power, to the Liberal cause. Thus Hilmi Paşa was offered a post and notorious anti-Unionists like Ali Kemal, editor of *İkdam*, and İsmail Kemal (who, however, became President of the Chamber), were kept out. But this was in fact only a provisionaly government, formed to win time and enable the new regime to consolidate itself. Once the Liberals were firmly in the saddle they intended to form a government subscribing to their own views.

The new regime would no doubt have established itself had it not been for the army. But the role of the rank and file in the insurrection and their involvement in politics made it imperative for the High Command to intervene and restore discipline. The troops had mutinied, overpowered their officers and executed some of them; such behaviour could not go unpunished. The Sultan had made matters worse by pardoning the rebels. Thus the army intervened not on behalf of the CUP, but in order to restore discipline among the troops and law and order in the capital.

While the army acted mainly for professional reasons, the Committee's stand was constitutional. It rejected the Liberal contention that the constitution had not been violated and refused to recognize Tevfik's cabinet. The fiction of legality was all the more difficult to maintain after the assassination of a deputy and a minister, the sacking of the Unionist press, and the escape of Unionists from the capital to Salonica. The Committee bombarded the Palace and the Porte with telegrams of protest, denounced the Sultan as the destroyer of the constitution, and demanded the arrest of certain prominent Liberals and reactionaries.[31] Meanwhile an army was being organized in Macedonia to march against the capital. This force, known as the 'Action Army' *(Hareket Ordusu)* set out for İstanbul on 17 April, having sounded out and neutralized the other military commands in the empire. Its proclaimed aim was to restore order in he capital and discipline in the army, and the Sultan is therefore said to have welcomed its intervention; but among the Liberals the news of the advance caused panic. They decided to send out high-level deputations to meet the Action Army and to reassure the troops that all was well and that the constitution was being upheld.

Deputations wee sent but met with no success, one being placed under arrest and prevented from returning to İstanbul.[32] The political control of the CUP over the army was too firm to be easily undermined. At the request of İsmail Kemal, the British ambassador had instructed his consuls in Macedonia 'to assure the population that the constitution was not compromised' by the rebellion. By assuring the Macedonians that the constitution was in no danger, the Liberals hoped to undermine the ideological position of the CUP there. But the Unionists countered Liberal propaganda effectively and this measure failed to have the desired effect. Now, with intervention impending, the Liberals asked Lowther to send Fitzmaurice, his first dragoman, with a delegation, calculating that such evidence of active British support would strengthen their own bargaining position while undermining the resolution of their adversary.[33] (Fitzmaurice was permitted to

31 Cevat, 62; Danişmend, 32 ff.; Türkgeldi, 29-30.
32 İsmail Kemal, 343; Lowther to Grey, no. 287, Constantinople, 20 April 1909, F.O. 371/771/15582.
33 Lowther to Grey, no. 129 telegraphic, Constantinople, 17 April 1909, F.O. 371/770/14474.

go but the Liberals later decided not to take him.) This delegation was also unsuccessful and the Action Army continued its siege of the capital. Operations began on the night of 23-24 April and after some skirmishing İstanbul was occupied.[34]

The two Chambers had formed themselves into a National Assembly on 22 April and were sitting in the Yacht House at Yeşilköy, a suburb of İstanbul. They ratified the proclamation of the Action Army, guaranteed the constitution and internal security, and stated that the actions of the Macedonian army were in conformity with the wishes of the nation.[35] On 27 April the National Assembly, after receiving instructions from Mahmut Şevket Paşa, Commander of the Action Army, announced the deposition of Abdülhamid and the accession of Mehmed Reshad to the Ottoman throne.[36] This decision was endorsed by a *fetva* (religious-legal writ) extracted from a reluctant Sheikh-ul-Islam.[37] Thus ended the second phase of the constitutional revolution of July 1908.

It may be worth examining briefly the reasons for the Committee's sudden collapse on 13 April and the failure of the Liberals to legitimize their power, and to assess the overall effect of the insurrection on subsequent events.

After the July Revolution the Unionists had two alternatives: either to destroy the old institutions and sources of power and replace them with new ones, or to maintain existing institutions and exploit

---

34 Abidin Daver, 'Hareket Ordusu İstanbul'a Nasıl Girmişti?', *Cumhuriyet*, 24 April 1951; for a detailed account see Colonel Surtees (military attaché) to Lowther in Lowther to Grey, no. 307, Constantinople, 28 April 1909, F.O. 371/771/16541.
35 Proclamation of the Action Army in *İkdam*, 21 April 1909; the National Assembly's ratification in *Takvim-i Vekayi*, 24 April 1909.
36 *Takvim-i Vekayi*, 28 April 1909; Ali Cevat, 153-4; Ahmed Rıza, 'Hatıraları', *Cumhuriyet*, 3 February 1950.
37 Bernard Lewis, *Emergence*, 213; Türkgeldi, 36; Cevat Paşa to Grey no. 1, London, 27 April 1909, F.O. 371/771/15929; text of *fetva* in Ali Cevat, 148.

them for their own movement. Too conservative and tradition-bound to attempt the first, they tried to carry out their revolution with, and not against, the power of the state, in the hope that, having secured power, they could then begin to introduce reforms. But this attitude came up against the ambitious elements in their own ranks, and it also meant that the Committee could not identify itself with any real interests in Ottoman society. Consequently its support came from groups which, though numerous, exercised little power or influence in 1908-9. Gone, too, was the consensus which had been the Committee's strength during the struggle against the Palace. The CUP had built a vast superstructure, but after the revolution it failed to lay down foundations based on tangible interests, and the Liberals were quick to expose this weakness.

By its continued involvement in politics after the revolution, the Committee alienated all those elements who had been its supporters against the Palace, but who were content with the change already accomplished. They had no sympathy for the Unionist plan to carry through a socio-economic revolution. These were the Liberals, men who aspired to inherit the Sultan's powers. They became the Committee's most bitter enemies, resenting its intrusion into politics; in their eyes the Committee had played out its role once it had established the constitution.

Unlike the CUP, the Liberals were supported by interests both broad and powerful. Their ideology of 'decentralization and personal initiative' was designed to attract those element in Ottoman society whose existence was threatened by the CUP. In this category came the traditional ruling elites, non-Muslim communities like the Greeks, Armenians, and Bulgarians, Muslim commuties like the Arabs and Albanians with nationalist aspirations, foreign Powers and their economic interests threatened by the economic nationalism of the Unionists, and lastly the Palace and the reactionaries, and all those who became redundant after the revolution. The secular policies of the CUP united the opposition, Muslim and non-Muslim alike. The

broadening of the political structure and greater participation provided more opportunities for the Powers to interfere in support of indigenous groups and the Powers were mainly anti-Unionists.

The position of the Liberals was much stronger and this became
evident on 13 April. Yet they too failed to consolidate their success
and acquire legitimacy, primarily because of the attitude of the High
Command. The military was averse not to the Liberals, but to the
methods they had used to overthrow the Committee. Mutiny could
hardly go unpunished without grave repercussions; nor were the
senior officers prepared to allow the Sultan to be restored to his former position, and this is what the insurrection seemed to do.

After the insurrection the fluid political situation which had
existed since the previous July crystallized. The role of the Palace as
one of the dominant elements in Turkish politics was ended, and
though the struggle between the Unionists and the Liberals remained
unresolved, for the time being it was shelved. The military had crushed
the rebellion but they did not permit the Unionists to destroy the
opposition. Instead martial law was established and the soldier
became the guardian of the constitutional regime and the arbiter in the
struggle of the politicians. The military lacked any ideology and had
intervened in the name of law and order and to neutralize political
conflict by holding the ring. Salvation for the empire was to be
achieved on the basis of the constitution and not by the policies of one
party or the other. Thus military involvement in policies was perhaps
the most enduring legacy of the Young Turk Revolution. It marked
'the intrusion of the army into politics, leading to the twin evils of a
militarized government and a political command',[38] and its effects are
there to be seen and felt today.

---

[38] Bernard Lewis, *Emergence*, 222.

Vanguard of a Nascent Bourgeoisie: The Social and Economic Policy of the Young Turks 1908-1918

The idea that the State *(Devlet)* is omnipotent was deeply entrenched in Ottoman society and culture and this enabled the State to intervene in every conceivable field of activity. All initiatives during the periods of expansion and decline emanated from the State. Thus, in contrast to the developments in Western Europe, there was no evolution of classes strong enough to press their interests against those of the State.

It is not therefore surprising that the mono-party state in which the party (the Committee of Union and Progress-the CUP) and the state coalesced should carry out social and economic policies designed to create a new class, the Turkish bourgeoisie. For this reason, one may appropriately describe the CUP as "the vanguard party of the Turkish bourgeoisie." Before proceeding any further it may be worthwhile defining what we mean by the term bourgeoisie. Our definition is primarily political and not restricted to the functional and social attributes of that class. For in the Ottoman Empire there existed people who carried out the economic functions of a bourgeoisie, but never acquired the political power and influence of that class to mould the

State in its own image and interests. That is surely what Bernard Lewis implies when he writes: "In Turkey too there were rich merchants and bankers, such as the Greek Michael Cantucuzenos and the Portuguese Jew Joseph Nasi-the Fugger of the Orient, as Braduel called him. But they were never able to play anything like the financial, economic, and political role of their European counterparts... Despite the scale and extent of their financial operations, they were unable to create political conditions more favourable to commerce..."[1]

Thus it is possible to talk of Ottomans who engaged in bourgeois activities such as banking, commerce, and industry but not of a bourgeois class that exercised any significant political influence on the State. As the Empire declined the members of this group became even weaker. But in the nineteenth century, as the Empire was integrated in the European capitalist economy, the major non-Muslim elements amongst them linked their interests with those of the European powers. They became in essence a comprador bourgeoisie, the economic intermediaries between Europeans and Ottomans, benefitting from the extra-territorial privileges exploited by the Europeans under the capitulations. Many of them even became foreign citizens and served the interests of the foreign powers against those of the Ottomans. Such people, who are sometimes decribed as the bourgeoisie, hardly perceived the Ottoman State as their state, one through which they could enhance their position in society. Quite the contrary, the aspirations of the comprador bourgeoisie were better served the more the authority of the Ottoman State was weakened. Thus if we consider a positive relationship between bourgeoisie and State to be a necessary component in defining such a class, we must conclude that a Turkish bourgeoisie did not exist until the Unionists set about creating one. Prior to the revolution of 1908 there was no such class amongst the Muslims, and most non-Muslims did not regard the Ottoman State as their state. Moreover, until the revolution, the State represented only the

---

1   Bernard, Lewis, *The Emergence of Modern Turkey* (1968), 31-2.

bureaucratic and landed interest and seemed to have no perception of a bourgeois society.

Some scholars talk of "rising classes" among the Muslims in the late Ottoman Empire as though they were the bourgeoisie in evolution. Such elements would be more accurately described as the "depressed classes" whose position in the traditional economy was being rapidly eroded by the advance of a relentless capitalism as the nineteenth century progressed. Such people were generally backward looking and sought the protection of the State in the futile task of checking the advance of European economic penetration so as to maintain the status quo. They were hardly the entrepreneurs who usually form the backbone of a bourgeoisie. The Unionists were forced to use such people as one of the components of their bourgeoisie. But as scholars like Selim İlkin have shown, these people, who often came from amongst the guilds and artisans' associations, were too conservative to be suitable for the progressive functions the Unionists had in mind.[2] That was to be one of the major shortcomings of the new class which could not distinguish between profit and profiteering.

In the interest of historical accuracy it must be emphasized that not all non-Muslims were members of the comprador bourgeoisie. The attitude of the communities towards the Ottoman State depended on the extent to which a community was integrated into the economic sector dominated by Europe; or conversely the extent to which a community was still part of the depressed, traditional Ottoman economy.

The absorption of the Empire into a world economy was a relatively new phenomenon and so there was some overlap. Until the second quarter of the nineteenth century, the Ottoman economy was still autarchic. Thus in March 1914, a writer in *Sabah* wrote:

---

2   Private communications with Professor Selim İlkin; also the first draft of a long article, co-authored with İlhan Tekeli, on "(Kör) Ali İhsan (İloğlu) ve Temsili-Mesleki Programı" which he kindly let me read.

"Up to the epoch of machines and of steam... Ottoman finances were not in such a state [of disequilibrium and dependence]. We met our own industrial needs in our own factories in large measure. Our life was simple. This simplicity, although in comparison to western things it might be regarded as decadence, was yet compensated by the ability of the land itself to supply the greater part of our needs. Eighty years ago [i.e. in 1834], the clothing of the people was almost entirely the product of native manufacture. Though it was not rich, Turkey was then more financially stable."[3]

Which elements were able to take advantage of the economic revolution wrought by Europe and join the modern sector? The leaders of this group were those one might broadly describe as the "Levantines", people who came from Europe and the Mediterranean region and settled in western Turkey, retaining their language and culture generation after generation. Count Ostrorog, who came to know the Empire intimately, writes that the English had settled in Turkey in the heyday of the Levante Company, and notes that "some of the families are still extant; the Lefontaines, the Hayes, the Barkers, the Charnauds, the Whittals, the Hansons have no other origin... At Constantinople Moda and Bebek are well known as English centres; the same may be said of the charming Barnabut, near Smyrna, which is even more exclusively English."[4] Despite their long years in the Empire such people retained foreign citizenship, living under the privileges of the capitulations and the protection of their embassies and consulates. They never identified with the Ottoman State yet their role in the economy was most significant.

The inner core of the comprador bourgeoisie was composed of Greeks and Armenians. According to Sussnitzki these two communities dominated almost all spheres of Ottoman economic life. They cultivated the profitable cash crops (vegetables, fruits, tobacco, mulberries) in preference to cereals and thus dominated silk culture in west-

---

3 *Sabah* (n.d.) quoted in *The Orient* v/12, 25 Mar. 1914, p. 117.
4 Count Leon Ostrorog, *The Turkish Problem* (1919), p. vii.

ern Anatolia. In industry which was still not mechanized and remained restricted to handicrafts, the situation was more equal between the various communities and the Turks continued to hold their own. But in commerce and finance the Greeks and Armenians had established their supremacy. Sussnitzki describes the situation as though they had succeeded in establishing a total monopoly over that sector of the economy. He wrote: "They hardly allow other national groups the possibility of developing their own economic powers. And they often proceed as though their objective were so to divide up the market so that the two rival groups might be spared mutual comptetion..." Among the reasons for Greco-Armenian economic supremacy Sussnitzki mentions "the protection they enjoyed from foreign powers, whose subjects they sometimes were, thus becoming, thanks to the former Capitulations, exempt from taxation."[5]

Neither the Greeks nor the Armenians regarded the Ottoman State as the representative of their interests. This becomes very clear from their relations with the constitutional regime after 1908. They waged a determined struggle against it in defence of the traditional privileges granted to the *millets** which they considered to be as sacrosanct as the capitulations. They were therefore openly hostile to the national and centralized state the Unionists were trying to set up and from their point of view it is easy to understand why. Most Ottoman Greeks, with deep emotional and cultural ties to Athens, found it dif-

---

5   A. J. Sussnitzki, "Zur Gliederung wirtschaftslicher Arbeit nach Nationalitaten in der Turkei", *Archiv fur Wirtschaftsforschung im Orient*, II (1917), 382-407 in Charles Issawi (ed.), *The Economic History of the Middle East 1800-1914* (1966), pp. 120-21.

(*)   The *millet* system was the division of Ottoman society along the lines of religious communities, with a total disregard for class except within the *millet* or religious community. The non-Muslim *millets* enjoyed almost total religious and cultural autonomy and that enabled the Ottoman State to stay out of their affairs and avoid conflict with the non-Muslim population. The head of each *millet* acted as the intermediary between his community and the State. While the *millet* system continued to exist there could be no national economy as the "Ottoman nation" was divided along religious-ethnic lines which had come to represent a division of labour. The Unionists detested this division of labour and knew that they had to undermine the *millet* system in order to destroy it.

ficult to identify with İstanbul. The Armenian case was more ambivalent a small group prospered under Ottoman rule, yet in the age of nationalism it also yearned for national autonomy if not total independence. In the İstanbul community there were Armenians who supported the policy of union and progress and supported the emerging national State. But the community as a whole resisted this inevitable transformation.

In contrast to the Greeks and Armenians, the Ottoman Jews remained an intimate part of the traditional, non-capitalist, socio-economic structure. They derived no benefit from the domination of the Ottoman economy by Europe and suffered the consequences of the Empire being converted into a semi-colony. "Turkish Jews" wrote Ostrorog "in no way resemble the magnificos of Frankfurt. A few, skilled in medicine or the law, attain wealth and influence; but the majority are humble folk, engaged in small businesses, or very modest manual labour, boatmen, porters, and so forth..."[6] Sussnitzki confirms this view and notes: "The Jews were in partial competition with the Greeks and Armenians, competition which, since in contrast to their opponents they seldom enjoyed [foreign] protection, was seldom crowned with success."[7] The situation of the Jews resembled that of the Turks in so far as both communities suffered the consequences of European domination. Both communities therefore had much to gain from restoring the political sovereignty and economic independence of the State.

For that reason, the Jewish community from Salonica to Baghdad supported the Unionists wholeheartedly. This relationship between economic interests and political involvement was noted by an American observer in 1917. He wrote that "the (Deunmeh] Jews, it is claimed, differ from the other Jews of Europe in the fact that, they have made their money out of exploiting the Ottoman Empire with-

---

6 Ostrorog, *Turkish Problem*, p. 14.
7 Sussnitzki, 121, as in n. 5.

out the assistance of the European powers, and that as they look to Turkey for their future prosperity they want to see come into existence a new and greater Turkey."[8] The Turkish and Jewish harmony of interests was such that many European writers described the Young Turk movement as a Jewish, masonic conspiracy in which the Unionists were the dupes in the hands of Jews and the Dönme or the crypto-Jews. For the same reason the Zionist movement failed to find an enthusiastic response amongst Ottoman Jews who remained totally loyal to İstanbul.[9]

This was the situation the Unionists inherited when they carried out their revolution in 1908. One of the principal goals of their movement was to create a national economy and a national bourgeoisie so as to become independent of Europe. They pursued this goal with determination, and, as we shall see, with some success.

The Young Turk Revolution of July 1908 was first and foremost a political movement whose aim was to rescue the Empire from the old order and liberate it from the control of the European powers. During the first six years, until the outbreak of the First World War, the struggle remained essentially political. Only after the Great Powers had opened hostilities and were unable to intervene in the affairs of Turkey did the Young Turks abrogate unilaterally the capitulations. This gave them the freedom to implement economic policies without the interference from the embassies of the Great Powers and opened a new page in the history of modern Turkey. Commenting on the conflict between the foreign embassies and the Young Turks, Sir Andrew Ryan (the Dragoman of the British Embassy) noted: "We were no less tenacious of our fiscal than our judicial privileges. Concessions were sometimes made to the Turks, but only subject to the principle that no

---

8 Report of "an American citizen now travelling in the Near East" Jan. 21, 1918 published in Department of State, Weekly Report on Matters Realiting to the Near East, no. 8, Mar. 7, 1918, p. 8.

9 Elie Kedourie, 'Young Turks, Freemasons and Jews', *Middle Eastern Studies* VII/i (1971). 89-104; Abraham Galanté, *Turcs et Juifs* (İstanbul 1932); idem., *Türkler ve Yahudiler* (1947).

new taxes could be enforced without our consent... It was no wonder that the Turks resented the disabilities imposed upon them."[10]

But even during the years of political struggle it is possible to discern the outines of the economic policy which later evolves into *étatism*. The Committee of Union and Progress, which was the dominant political organisation of this era, explained the economic programme it expected to have implemented by the government at its first convention. It proposed: the elaboration of laws defining the relations between employees and workmen; the distribution of land to the peasants (but without encroaching on the rights of landowners) as well as credit for the peasants at moderate rates of interest; the alteration of the existing system of titles and the gradual adoption of the cadastral system; state supervision of education, with the state schools open to all races and creeds; the introduction of Turkish in elemantary schools and the opening of commercial, agricultural, and technical schools; and finally general measures to ensure the economic progress of the country and the development of agriculture.[11]

It became evident from the repressive policy of the Young Turks towards the striking railway workers in Rumelia that the elaboration of laws defining relations between employers and employees would-favour the former. But the rationale for such a policy was that the nation could not afford strikes at such a critical period of history. The concept of the nation with a national economy was also put forward, though not articulated by the Young Turks during these years. Its first manifestation came immediately after the annexation of Bosnia and Herzegovina by the Austrians. The Unionists, unable to take any counter-measures against Austria herself, organized a boycott against Austrian goods and the shops which sold them. This harmed mainly the non-Muslim merchants who tended to be the agents for Western goods and benefitted the smaller Turkish merchant. Thus it was dur-

CUP

---

10 Sir Andrew Ryan, *The Last of the Dragomans* (1951), p. 35.
11 Tarık Zafer Tunaya (comp., ed.), *Türkiye'de Siyasi Partiler 1859-1952* (1952), 208-10.

ing this boycott that the fez cap, made in Austria, gave way to the Anatolian kalpuk.[12]

It is worth noting that Unionists made speeches supporting by boycott. Members of the Liberal Union, meanwhile, addressed meetings counselling caution, arguing that it was superfluous and ridiculous to boycott shops since such demonstrations damaged local commerce.[13] Such was the economic dimension of the political conflict between the Unionists and the Liberals; not only were the Unionists partisans of a modern, constitutional, and centralized state, they had also declared themselves convinced partisans of the system of state monopoly and state control over the economy.[14]

But despite their desires for political and economic autonomy for the Empire, the Unionists were acutely aware of their dependence on foreign capital for economic growth. They hoped that the foreign powers would be impressed by their reformist activities designed to put the house in order and transform an archaic structure into a modern one. They hoped that foreign financiers would acquire confidence in the Young Turk régime and invest the necessary capital to stimulate the economy. Ironically the Young Turk revolution had the opposite effect, alarming the foreigner with its new consciousness of defiant nationalism. There were those in the CUP who were hostile to foreign investment but they were a minority. Mehmed Cavid, who become Finance Minister in 1909 and played a key role in Turkey's economic policy thereafter, represented the dominant view:

"The number of those ... who do not want the coming of foreign capital to our country is less than the foreigners believe. There are certain small-scale enterprises that can be carried by the accumulated

---

12 *Le Moniteur Oriental* and Turkish Press, 10 Oct. 1908 and ff.; Renè Pinon, *L'Europe et la Jeune Turquie*, 2nd ed. (Paris 1911), p. 274.
13 René Pinon, *L'Europe*, 275, the Press 14 October 1908. It is interesting to note that the Congress Party of India also reacted by boycotting British goods in August 1905, following Lord Curzon's partition of Bengal.
14 For a discussion of Turkish politics in the years 1908-1914 see Feroz Ahmad, *The Young Turks* (1969).

capital in the country which, of course, we would not like to have pass into the hands of foreigners... Yet, in my opinion, we must accept foreigners even in such enterprises for the sake of establishing a skill, that of management and rationalization, which we lack so badly. As important public works, these can be done only with foreign capital.. All countries in state of opening themselves to civilization will inevitably stumble and fall in their path if they seek to advance by their own force... All new countries have been able to advance only with the help of foreign capital."[15]

Niyazi Berkes in correct in noting that the Unionists saw the Empire's economic problems "in terms of the categories of the capitalist economy and as if Turkey belonged to the same economic system."[16] In a sense they were right, for in the nineteenth century Turkey had indeed been sucked into the world capitalist economy and the world the Young Turks wanted to emulate was the western world, one which had made such devastating progress under capitalism. But they were naive in believing that Europe would encourage them to develop an independent capitalist economy and that this could be accomplished by borrowing capital and know-how from those who had it. Suspicious of European imperialism, the Unionists tried to invite Japanese experts in the venture of establishing capitalism. Japanese stewardship never materialized, partly because of western opposition and partly because Tokyo was reluctant to challenge Europe so far west, thereby alienating all the Powers. But Japan remained an inspiration and its model in the Unionist struggle for independence.[17] Though the Unionists placed great significance on foreign capital they refused to accept it with strings, especially if the strings attached to the loans were political and hampered the sovereignty of the State.

---

15 Mehmed Cavid, "Neşriyat ve Vekayi-i İktisadiye" in *Ulum-u İçtimaiye ve Aktisadiye Mecmuası*, 11. No. 5 (May 1909) 129-30; quoted in Niyazi Berkes, *The Development of Secularism in Turkey* (Montreal 1964), p. 424.

16 Berkes, *Secularism*, 424.

17 Ahmad, *Young Turks*, 23, n. 1.

During the first year of the constitutional régime, foreign loans proved hard to raise in the money markets of Europe. By September 1909, the Ministry of Finance attempted to float a public loan of seven million Turkish liras. "This operation (wrote the British Ambassador) was an endeavor on the part of the Turks to emancipate themselves from the control of the very narrow banking circle [very largely dominated by Anglo-French bankers] from which they have hitherto borrowed, to obtain a loan without giving a regular guarantee, to avoid having the loan countersigned by the Ottoman Public Debt Administration, and in fact to prove to the world ... how greatly the administration of the new régime has enhanced the credit of the country. The French, Italian and German ambassadors (he concluded) thought that the operation would fail."[18]

The foreign powers interpreted this scheme as Cavid Bey's attempt to go over the head of the Public Debt Administration with the "insidious object of minimizing its importance with the aim of ultimately abolishing it."[19] This was probably a correct interpretation, for the Unionists were determined to establish their financial independence as soon as possible. But the public loan proved a failure and the following year Cavid Bey was forced to seek loans in France once more. But is Paris, the French offered terms which amounted to placing Turkish finances and the Finance Ministry under French control and that no self-respecting government could possibly accept.[20]

In Unionist circles, the French demands aroused much indignation. *Tanin* (August 13, 1910), which was the voice of CUP, expressed some of this indignation.

---

18 Sir Gerard Lowther to Sir Edward Grey, no. 723 confidential, Therapia [Terabya] September 8, 1909, in F.O. 371/763/34194.

19 Sir Adam Block to Sir Charles Hardinge, Constantinople, September 14, 1909 in F.O. 371/763/34938 (Block was the head of the Public Debt Administration).

20 Ahmad, *The Young Turks*, 75-81. The reason why internal loans were difficult to raise was because there was no machinery in the form of a "national bank". As a result people tended to hoard money.

"Turkey is weak and wants help from foreign powers. But it cannot repay their assistance with political favours and so it has to give material advantages such as concessions. We say: No! We will have nothing to do with such bargains, for they are injurious to Turkey's dignity and independence... If Young Turkey is going to live it shall live like a European state in a dignified and honourable manner.

"We have kept it on this principle so far... We follow the principle of granting concessions to those who give us the best terms, irrespective of nationality *et cetera*.

"We must warn those who consider Turkey weak and helpless and want to sell political assistance for economic gains. They are on a very wrong path. It is possible that Turkey may not raise her voice against or resist such treatment today, but very soon, Turkey will have brought her armaments to such perfection that not even the greatest pessimist will regard her as 'weak and helpless'."[21]

Despite the obstruction and the lack of cooperation from the foreign powers who continued to exploit the régime of capitulations, the Young Turks began to put their economic house in order. In September 1909 Sir Adam Block wrote that the "... praiseworthy efforts that are being made by the Ministry of Finance to improve the system of [revenue] collection, to establish a proper system of control and inspection, and to reorganize the financial staff in the capital and the provinces, are already producing results..."[22] The government's receipts for the first four months of the financial year 1909 (March, April, May and June) showed a slight increase, while the recaipts of the Public Debt Administration showed a distinct increase over 1908.

Cavid Bey's budget made no attempt to conceal the facts or to present the case in too favourable a light, as had been the practice of earlier ministers. He increased the allocation of productive departments like Public Works and Education while economizing in the non-

---

21 See also Hüseyin Cahit's article in *Tanin* (October 2, 1910) in which he recommended raising taxes instead of loans in order to preserve "rational honour" and avoid foreign control.

22 Block to Hardinge, Constantinople, September 13, 1909, F.O. 371/763/34938.

productive ones like the grand vezir and the Ministry of Foreign Affairs. Economes were realized in every direction, and in every department of the State a policy of retrenchment of the inflated bureaucracy was being implemented. Despite all these economies, budgets for the next few years continued to show deficits. Such was the legacy of the old regime which had been drifting towards bankruptcy, in spite of borrowings on the foreign market.

"In the memorandum I wrote in October of last year (concluded Block) I said that the Turkish reformers were determined to take in hand the work of financial reorganization. I can honestly state that the work has been well begun. The government, for the first time in the history of Turkey, has produced a budget based on real figures, and, for better or worse, has placed before the world a true statement of its current liabilities. There has been no attempt at concealment. The government has not only taken the resolution to work in the lines of the budget, but the Chamber of Deputies is firmly resolved to keep the government up to the mark in this respect. I am confident that the Ministry of Finance will ensure that the laws on the budget shall be faithfully observed throughout the Empire, and that an efficient control will be exercised over every Ministry, even including the Ministries of War and Marine, where the scandalous contracts for the purchase of store and materials have cost the government in the past many millions of pounds.

> "One of the chief obstacles to a proper financial system was the interference of the Sultan and the Palace camarilla. The intervention of the Palace has now disappeared completely. Besides the considerable sums which the late Sultan [Abdülhamid II] laid hands upon, the revenues of the immense Civil List properties will now revert to the State, and the hordes of favourites at Yıldız [Palace] who fattened on the country and on the unfortunate peasant has been swept away."[23]

---

23 *Ibid.*

Block then described the reform within the Finance Ministry itself, noting the lack of chauvinism in the use of foreign financial experts -M. Laurent who was preceeded by M. Joly (French), Mr. Graves (British), M. Steeg (French), Sn. Maissa (Italian), and Mr. Crawford (British) - on the reform commission. He noted that a new law for regulating the actions of the tax-collectors had been put into force and the government had devoted most serious attention to the modification of the entire tax system. Cavid's schemes had the support of the CUP and it was realized that the best way of ensuring a permanent increase in revenue was by alleviating the position of the peasantry and by taxing those who had avoided payment in the past. The Ministries of the Interior and Public Works were determined to develop the prosperity of the country by maintaining security and by opening up the countryside by improved communications, and by encouraging the investment of foreign capital for works of public utility. For all their schemes the Unionists needed new sources of revenue. The immediate and feasible solution seemed to be the increase of customs from 11 to 15 per cent and the establishment of government monopolies.[24]

Within the limits circumscribed by the capitulations, the Young Turks continued to modernize the economic structure of their society. In 1911 they passed a law on house property designed to facilitate communication within İstanbul. This new law necessitated the registration of all immovable property in the capital and a commission was set up to supply streets with names and houses with numbers. This was expected to improve communications and the business community was particularly happy about this.[25] About the same time internal passport *(vesika)* which had hampered travel within the Empire were abolished and other restrictions on movement were removed. The Government also began to draft a new com-

---

24 *Ibid.*
25 *The Near East*, vol. 1 (new style), May 17, 1911, p. 23.

mercial code and to amend the laws on property, bringing both in line with contemporary needs.[26]

In keeping with their policy to improve agriculture, the Young Turks introduced the scheme to irrigate the plain of Konya under the direction of the Deutsche Bank. A survey was also being carried out for a similar undertaking in the Cilician plain, which was expected to turn the countryside around Adana into another Egypt. The emphasis on agriculture had already begun to pay dividends and the harvest of 1910 had been excellent. But a large part of the crop had been wasted because of a lack of labour, opening up the question of mechanized farming.[27]

By 1911, observers of the Turkish scene began to speak of an economic revival. "... Under the new régime in Turkey a constitutional government has been formed, abuses and corruption have been abolished, and steps have been taken to place Turkey in the march of progress... The country already feels the impetus of the new departure. Concessions have been granted [to foreign firms] for the construction of new and the extension of old railways, for the building of highways, for the installation of telephones and electric lighting and power plants, and for the electrification of the tramways; and other concessions have been made, or are pending, the fruition of which will develop the great national resources of the country, expand its resources, establish mechanized industries and enhance the purchasing power and promote the happiness of the people.[28]

---

26 *Ibid.*, May 24, 1911, p. 58.

27 *Levent Trade Review* (hereafter cited as *LTR*), vol. i/1 (June 1911), 59-61. The increasing cost of labour −50 per cent in two years− was also encouraging the demand for mechanisation of agriculture and industry. By 1912 Turkey was beginning to use its own raw materials and produce goods like paper, glass, cloth, cottonseed oil, cement, tiles, furniture and leather. The government, in order to encourage the import of machinery, had removed customs duties on machinery. See Bie Ravndal, "Commercial Review of Turkey", in *LTR*, ii/3 (December 1912), 23-2.

28 *Ibid.*, pp. 16-7. According to the Public Works programme published in 1909, the Ministry planned to build 9,000 km. of railways in addition to the existing 6,000 km., and 30,000 km. of highways and a large number of harbours. The criterion for improving communications was

The *Levent Trade Review*'s estimate of the new régime's economic programme is rather inflated and over optimistic. Firstly, we ought to remember that most of the modernizing activity was taking place at the centre, in and around İstanbul, and İstanbul was not "Turkey" let alone the Ottoman Empire. But the Unionists were aware of this, more so because they themselves were representatives of the provincial petty bourgeoisie. It is worth remembering that their movement had developed in the provinces, especially in Rumelia, and they held their annual congress in Salonica, until the city was lost to Greece in 1912. If anything, they were suspicious of "Cosmopolitan İstanbul" just as the Kemalists would be. Thus one of their aims was to establish a firm and productive relationship between the centre and the periphery which would lead to "a wholesome decentralisation and autonomy". According to the *Deutsche Levante Zeitung* (n.d.) "The new system had already had gratifying results in local industrial enterprises and in the financial policies of the cities. Here a [provincial] governor pursues a policy of building up forests and there another that of colonization; in short another spirit is passing through the country."[29]

The outbreak of the Turco-Italian war in Libya in September 1911 followed by the Balkan Wars of 1912-13 arrested the programme

---

to be economic not strategic as it has been under the old regime. See *LTR*, vol. i/3 (December 1911), 252-6.

In February 1912 when Mehmed Cavid became Minister of Public Works he proposed the following programme for the coming decade:

(a) *Railways:* (i) the Black Sea line (French capital); (ii) Adriatic line (French); (iii) The Chester Project in Anatolia (American); (iv) Baghdad-Basra line (British); (v) line connecting Ankara with the Samsun-Sivas line (German);

(b) *Ports:* (i) Samsun and Trabzon under survey; (ii) large harbour at Dedeağaç (lost to Greece in the Balkan Wars); (iii) a small port at Kavala; (iv) Salonica to be enlarged; (v) ports at Jaffa, Haifa and/or Tripoli.

(c) *Irrigation:* (i) Contract for Mesopotamia to be thrown open to bids; (ii) plans for the Adana region as well as for the rivers Bardar, Boyana, Maritza and the Jordan.

(d) *Highways:* 9,655 miles to be constructed in four years. Cavid Bey expected the mobilization of local resources by the provincial governors for the implementation of small projects. (*LTR*, vol. i/4 (March 1912), 426. See also E. G. Mears, "Transportation and Communicaton" in E. G. Mears (ed.), *Modern Turkey* (New York, 1924), 201-37).

29 Quoted in *LTR*, vol. i/3 (December 1911), 252-6.

of economic reform. But the wars forced the Unionists to mobilize all the resources of the country, especially its human resources. They became aware of their isolation and reacted by turning inwards towards the "people" *(Halka doğru)* and arousing national conscious-ness in order to fight for the very existence of the Empire and the Ottoman State. Following the example of the French revolutionaries, the Unionists formally inagurated the Committee of National Defence (CND-*Müdafaa-i Milliye Cemiyeti*) on 31 January 1913.[30]

The economy could hardly be isolated from this national mobi-lization and one of the functions of this "unofficial" body was to raise money from the public: The Government "entrusted it with the care of placing five and a half million pounds with Treasury Bonds...", and the CND in turn called upon the Government to raise a public loan.[31]

This national mobilization coincided with the activities of a Turkish group among the Unionists, articulating its views in the peri-odical, *Türk Yurdu.* Professor Berkes notes that the "Turkists were clearer on the economic aspirations for which the Turkish Revolution should stand. Probably influenced by Parvus's socialism and inspired by the economic development of the bourgeoisie of the Turkish-speak-ing people of Russia, they developed the idea of economic nationalism and the policy of étatism in order to combat the economic bondage of the Turkish masses to the European economy, and to foster the eco-nomic growth of a middle class which would be the carrier of the eco-nomic interests of the Turkish nationality within the Ottoman Empire."[32]

---

30 See the Turkish press of 30 and 31 January and 1 February 1913 and following. In French it was known as the *Comitée de Salut Public.* See Consul General Rommily to Secretary of State, Constantinople, February 13, 1913. 867.00/484, no. 412.

31 Rommily, *Ibid.*, and *Stamboul* 3 and 4 February 1913.

32 Berkes, *Secularism*, 245. Alexander Helphand, the Russian Marxist, better known by his pseu-donym Parvus, arrived in Turkey in 1910 and remained there until the outbreak of war in 1914. Judging by his writing in *Türk Yurdu* and the Turkish press, Parvus seems to have been an influ-ential figure in the counsels of the Turkists. For a fuller but incomplete account of his life in Turkey see Z. A. B. Zeman and W. B. Scharlau, *The Merchant of Revolution: the life of Alexander Israel Helphand (Parvus), 1867-1924* (London, 1965).

At this point it is not possible to evaluate this influence of Parvus's ideas on the Unionists. His writings, all puslished in Turkish, in *Türk Yurdu* and other journals ["The Peasants and the State"; "A Glance at Financial Situation in 1911"; "Turkey is Under the Financial Yoke of Europe" (two articles); "The Road to Salvation from Financial Slavery"; "A Penny the Turks Are Most Entitled to Borrow"; "The State and the Nation"; "Financial Dangers"; "Wake Up Before it is Too Late"; "Let a Turk Take Care of Your Finances"; "A Letter to the Turkish Youth"; "The Future of Turkey's Agriculture" and his book "Turkey's Sensitive Spot: The debts of the Ottoman State and their Reform" (İstanbul 1914) undoubtedly influenced contemporary views on Turkey's relations with Europe. In Professor Berkes's words:

> "If he did not bring socialism to the Turks, Parvus shattered a persistent illusion of the Turkish intellectuals. He pointed out that Turkey was not a part of the European civilization and could not become a part of it simply through volition or even by being taken into the European diplomatic concert. On the contrary, Turkey was a target of imperialist aggression by European capitalism and well along the way to becoming an area for colonial exploitation. The economic relations between Turkey and Europe were of the nature of the relations existing between the exploited and the exploiters. The major question of social revolution was not, therefore, one of a socialist revolution. This had meaning only in the capitalist countries. It was a question of national independence and economic recovery under a democracy that would turn to the people and take measures in terms of a national economy."[33]

The Turks had long been aware of the need for national independence and economic recovery. But only around 1914 did they articulate that this could be achieved only by a Turkish bourgeoisie which was hardly in existence. "The foundation of the modern state [wrote Yusuf Akçura] is the bourgeois class. Contemporary prosper-

---

33 Berkes, *Secularism*, 425; see also pp. 335-7.

ous states came into existence on the shoulders of the bourgeoisie, of the businessmen and bankers. The Turkish national awakening in Turkey is the beginning of the genesis of the Turkish bourgeoisie. And if the natural growth of the Turkish bourgeoisie continues without damage or interruption, we can say that the sound establishment of the Turkish state has been guaranteed."[34] In 1914, especially after September 10 when they announced the unilateral abrogation of the capitulations, the Unionists began to implement a conscious policy of fostering an enterpreneurial class amongst the Turks by offering the most generous incentives.

The régime of the capitulations had been one obstacle in the way of this policy. Another, and in the long run more formidable, was the problem of overcoming "... the mentality that despised trade and industry and believed that government and military occupations are most worthy of an Ottoman Turk."[35] An American observer, with long experience in the country, commented on the conservative character of Turkish economic life, the cautious attitude of the businessmen "accustomed to a policy of wariness necessitating the holding of resources in reserve." He noted how gold was hoarded in the form of jewelry and coins throughout the Empire and how existing laws on real estate restricted the mobility of capital.[36] The Unionists intended to pass legislation which would end this stagnation, releasing dead capital, accelerating industrial and commercial activity, increasing land values, and generally contribute to the financial uplift of the

---

34 *Türk Yurdu*, No. 63 (April 3, 1914). 2102-3, quoted in Berkes, *Secularism*, 425.

35 *Ibid*. The word mentality suggests a psychological and irrevocable aspect to the problem. Yet this was not the case. The Turks were reluctant to engage in commerce and modern industry only because of their experience throughout the nineteenth century that such economic activities did not pay under the circumstances of European hegemony. It time this question may have acquired psychological overtones as a way to rationalise the division of labour that emerged. But when a State capable of challenging European domination emerged after 1908, the Turks were quick to abandon their distaste for economic enterprise.

36 Consul General G. Bie Ravndal in *Levante Trade Review*, vol. ii/1 (September 1912), pp. 138-51.

country. The new laws would extend the right of inheritance, regulate the proprietorship and transfer of land, render property belonging to pious foundations *(vakf)* and the state *(miri)* subject to mortgage, and enable corporation. Such properties tended to be leasehold and converting them into freeholds was expected to stimulate both industrial and agricultural activity.[37] By June 1914, the Government had even introduced a "Bill to Encourage Industry." The Government promised to give preference to indigenous manufactures and to facilite the operation of local factories. On the initiative of Yunus Nadi –the future owner and editor of the newspaper *Cumhuriyet*– a clause was added to the Bill binding the State to buy from native manufacturers even when foreign substitutes were cheaper by as much as 10 per cent.[38]

As this mentality, retrogressive to the development of capitalism was overcome, the question arose of creating a social group willing and able to play the entrepreneurial role. This had been virtually impossible during the first five years of competitive politics (1908-1913) when various groups were able to lobby on behalf of their narrow interests. But after the *coup d'état* of January 23, 1913 when the CUP seized power, a pattern began to evolve. With the creation of a mono-party state in which party and state were one, and in which the party personified "the nation", it was natural for the CUP to find entrepreneurial cadres from within its own ranks. But this was in no way a totally arbitary policy which utilized men unsuitable for the task. In many cases we find that, attracted by this policy, members of the small-town gentry *(eşraf)*, as well as the artisans *(esnaf)* and small merchants *(tüccar)* joined the party. In the countryside the CUP attracted the landlords and the landowing peasantry. But where such

---

37 *Ibid.*
38 *The Orient*, vol. v/22 (3 June 1914), 203. Again, as in the case of the boycotts, there is close parallel with the economic policy of the Congress Party in British India. One MP made an impassioned appeal in favour of all Ottomans swearing never to buy foreign made articles and wearing homespun cloth; he hoped that this idea would spread even to Africa. Solders, officers, government official senators and deputies were to wear homespun cloth on the penalty of a fine, and then dismissal. This was even more extreme than the Indian *swadeshi* movement.

elements were lacking the CUP tended to make entrepreneurs out of bureaucrats and professionals.

The war in Europe proved to be a great stimulus to the Turkish economy. There was an immediate and virtually insatiable demand for Turkish goods, agricultural and industrial. A summary review of the Turkish press during the war years demonstrates the Empire's concern about economic questions. Thus, alongside the articles on military and political affairs, there were usually articles dealing with the important issues in the country's economic life. One can read about the state of the harvest in a particular district or the measures being taken by the peasants, the authorities, or the specialists to combat vermin amongst the crops and cattle. The press kept the public informed about the meteorological centres being set up in the capital and the provinces, about new laws on the preservation of forests or about the founding of new Chambers of Commerce. There was frequent news concerning organisations set up to encourage this or that industry; or local trade fairs which were helping to educate and mobilize the peasantry; or the despatch to Germany of factory hands to learn modern industrial techniques, where in the past only university students were sent.

The Turks knew that they would have to mobilize all their resources, especially their economic resources, if they were to survive the war. Under these circumstances, it did not prove difficult to overcome "the mentality that despised trade and industry" and sought careers in the bureaucracy and the army. The press began to report the submission of applications to set up small factories of all kinds. *Le Moniteur Oriental* of December 8, 1914 wrote that the administrative council of the vilayet of İstanbul had discussed such applications and decided to sanction the application of a macaroni factory in Üsküdar and a brick and cement factory in Pendik. The group setting up these factories was to be provided with facilities recommended by the new law for the encouragement of industry. There were some other trading and industrial companies founded during the early days of the war. But it was only after the Turkish army had succeeded in holding back the Anglo-French assault at Gallipoli and Turkey's future seemed more secure that such firms began to mushroom throughout Anatolia.

Initally, however, the war provided a small Unionist clique in İstanbul with the opportunity to make great profits out of blackmarketeering in scarce commodities. Before the war many of İstanbul's needs had been met by imports from outside the Empire. This was true for industrial goods but it was equally true for essential foodstuffs like flour, imported from southern Russia and sugar from Europe. The war isolated İstanbul and the city survived largely because of the pre-war stocks. But such stocks could not last for ever and before long local merchants began to hoard essential goods and speculate, causing acute shortages and prices to rise rapidly. Many of these merchants were non-Muslims and the CND intervened to end their profiteering and transfer this lucrative operation – one hesitates to call it legitimate trade – to Muslim merchants. "The Committee of National Defence (recorded Lewis Einstein in his dairy on August 6, 1915) is now making money rapidly by its monopolies of sugar and petrol *et cetera*. Their declared intention is to accumulate capital which they can afterwards use to get the trade of the country in Moslem hands..." On August 17 he added "The Committee of National Defence has monopolized all commodities and doles them out at enormous profit."[39] Some days later (August 27) he noted how "The Committee ... asked the French Tobacco Régie, directed by M. Weyl to have the tobacco which the Régie sold to the army pass through their hands. The tobacco was then sold in town at great profit and not to the soldiers. The army blamed M. Weyl whom the Committee... denounced as a French spy and had him expelled from the country."[40]

In 1915, the Unionists also founded the *Esnaf Cemiyeti* (the

---

39 *Inside Constantinople*, p. 218 and p. 243.

40 *Ibid.*, 260-61. It is worth noting: (i) that enemy nationals were permitted to continue their business activities during the early part of the war; and (ii) that the Unionists were not above swindling the army, suggesting that the were not dependent on its goodwill as is often suggested. See also Ziya Şakir, *Son Posta*, 4 October, 1934.

Society of Tradesmen), an organization of local merchants, grocers and entrepreneurs, under the official patronage of İsmet Bey, the Prefect of İstanbul, and supported by prominent Unionists such as Kara Kemal, Dr. Nazım and Bedri Bey. Its ostensible aim was to control the market, by maintaining supplies and regulating prices. But in fact the outcome was just the opposite and there was an acute shortage of essential goods such as bread, sugar, oil, and petrol which were available only on the blackmarket. Cavid Bey lamented in his diary: "The Esnaf Cemiyeti-what a good idea it was and with what good intentions it was set up! But what a state it is in having fallen into the hands of thoughtless, foolish and ignorant people. Everyone is hostile to those who make a few *kuruş* through personal initiative. Everyone assists those who can only maintain their position through [political] patronage. What a beautiful basis for a society's retrogression!..[41]

By the end of the year, this economic corruption and profiteering had reached such proportions that the CUP government was forced to intervene. The sub-committee responsible for implementing the rationing of bread was said to be making TL 4,000 a day and the CUP was totally divided over the issue of profiteering: Şeyhülislâm Hayri Efendi took the lead and he was soon joined by Ahmed Rıza.[42] By the end of the year the government had introduced a law to regulate the sale of essential goods (Havayici Zaruriye Kanunu) and set up a "Commission to Prevent Profiteering", (Men'i İhtikâr Komisyonu).[43] Such was the sense of outrage in the party against the war profiteers, that Talât Bey, who was associated with their patron İsmet, was almost forced out of the CUP.[44]

1915 year was a critical year for Turkey. The outcome of the Gallipoli campaign was crucial and the British decision to evacuate the

---

41 Cavid, *Tanin*, 30 January 1945.
42 Ziya Şakir, *Son Posta*, 4 October and 12 December 1934. At this time a Turkish lira was worth almost one pound sterling or four U.S. dollars.
43 Cavid, *Tanin*, 8 February 1945 and Hüseyin Cahit Yalçın, *Halkçı*, 22-23, December 1945.
44 Cavid, *Ibid.*

Gallipoli peninsula in December had an inestimable impact on Turkish morale. The Turks were convinced that they had paid their way in the war and their attitude towards their allies changed as a result. They became more sure of themselves and demanded to be treated as equals. The victory over the British army reinforced Turkish national pride, while a year of almost total isolation made the Turks aware of their dependence on Anatolia, strengthening the concept of a Turkish nationalism based on Anatolia which was described as *Anadolu Türk Milliyetçiliği*. This newly found self-confidence and national consciousness was immediately extended to the sphere of the economy. In the very first issue of a new journal dealing with economic affairs, Ziya Gökalp wrote: "One of the factors which will give to the Turks the character of a nation and contribute to the formation of a Turkish culture is the national economy."[45] As though to symbolize this goal, the name of the Ministry of Commerce and Agriculture was changed to the Ministry of National Economy.[46]

In an interview, the minister of Trade and Agriculture explained his government's economic policy. Agriculture was to be given priority and fallow lands in the Çukurova and the plain of Konya were to be put under cultivation. Rice cultivation was to be extended and the government would provide the cultivator with seed and animals, and eventually machines. The advice of a German expert was being sought for the plantation and refining of sugar. He said that the number of Chambers of Commerce would be increased to encourage the growth of commercial activity in the provinces and Turkish merchant shipping would also be encouraged by the establishment of a monopoly over coastal trade. In future, foreign companies would have to operate under Turkish law and while foreign capital investment was considered vital for economic expansion, it had to work with Turkish capital.[47]

---

45 "Millet Nedir, Milli İktisad Neden İbarettir?" in *İktisadiyat Mecmuası*, vol. i/1 February 1916, p. 3.
46 "Milli İktisada Doğru" in *Ibid.*, 1-3.
47 "Ticaret ve Ziraat Nazırı ile Mülâkat", *Ibid.*, 6-10. The minister was Ahmed Nesimi Bey.

In February 1916, the Turkish parliament passed legislation which made use of Turkish obligatory in commercial matters and began discussing new customs tariffs which would protect local industry by placing high excise on imports. Hasan Tahsin, who was deputy Minister of Finance, explained the government's policy in a statement which is worth quoting at length:

"It is not our intention to present here a profound study of the question ... but merely to indicate the Government's motives in adopting this new method of levying customs duties... [The] following points are of special significance:

a) Objects that can be easily manufactured in this country because of the presence here of the requisite raw materials are entitled to protection and a heavy duty has been levied upon imported goods of this sort;

b) Manufactured articles where production here is capable of development are likewise taxed in order that local industries may meet foreign competition (30 % on cotton thread);

c) Agriculture in general is protected;

d) Agricultural products are specially protected (100 % on canned vegetables).

"We conclude, then, that whenever the government desires to *encourage* an article of local manufacture, it imposes on the importation of similar goods from abroad just a duty of 30 %, and that where it desires to *protect* it levies upon imports a duty approximating 100 % of their value.

"The Government decision in this connection [i.e. agriculture] is most logical. It is unnecessary to demonstrate here that our country is essentially agricultural. The amazing fertility of our immense territories, the aptitude of our citizens, all favour this conception. Is it not truly a pity to import grain from America, Russia and Rumania when we ourselves could not only produce it in quantities sufficient for our needs, but are capable of supplying other countries as well?

"In protecting agriculture *in general*, the Government has in mind as well the raising of farm products that, whether through ignorance, or principally because of foreign competition, have not been cultivated thus far, to the general detriment of our farmer who could have profitted immeasurably from their sale.

"As can be seen, the Government has committed itself neither to a policy of out and out protection nor to the other extreme of an exaggerated free trade, harmful to the development of industry and local agriculture.

"Although the system of levying *ad-valorem* customs duties is one that is easily handled, it admits too readily of fradulent practices; it is often possible to ascertain the true value of the merchandise brought to customs. Even the presentation of the original bills of lading is not a sufficient guarantee for the treasury.

"As long as the Capitulatory régime existed, it was absolutely impossible for us to do other than maintain our system of *ad-valorem* duties; it is only the abrogation of the capitulations that, affording us entire liberty of action, permits us to adopt the system of specific duties.

"Among other advantages this system offers, one must remember the facility that it affords us for the conclusion of commercial treaties in as much as it allows us to enter into negotiations armed with an autonomous tariff; in this fashion, one accords no commercial advantages to other nations unless assured that the favour will be returned.

"Upon this basis of mutual concessions, our Government will from now on be in a position to conclude advantageous commercial treaties or agreements. For example in order to secure an outlet for our production of grain, we will demand that the countries that seek to export to us the iron that they produce in abundance must lower their duties upon the grain that we send them."[48]

The new tariffs were submitted to parliament in December 1915, passed on 23 March 1916, and came into force on 14 September 1916.[49]

48 *Levante Trade Review*, vol. v/4 (March 1916), 335-8 and Aynizade Hasan Tahsin, "Gümrük Tarifeleri" in *İktisadiyat Mecmuası*, vol. i/1 (Feb. 1916), 3-5.

49 *Tanin*, 4 March 1916 and *İktisadiyat Mecmuası*, vol. i/1 (Feb. 1916), 3-5.

Just as the abrogation of the capitulations had aroused the hostility and protest of the western powers, the policy of economic nationalism also led to bitter attacks on the Turks. The government was accused of pursuing a chauvinistic policy which was dangerous for trade and commerce. Hüseyin Cevat Bey, Turkey's ambassador to Scandinavia tried to explain his government's policy:

> "The Turkish people ... (he told the press) is now fighting for its political and commercial independence. We are trying to foster national trade and supporting newly founded Turkish companies. It is not through hatred and malice that we have removed all shop names in foreign languages-we are doing only what all peoples have done before us. We are called chauvinists and rebels. I assure you we have only one object: our commercial and political independence. On this point we are all united. There are no more Young Turks and Old Turks but only Turks, and in war we are all young."[50]

During this period the CUP began to play a more direct and open role in the economy. At the 1916 congress which opened in İstanbul on 28 September the CUP reported the tremendous effort it was making to uplift the Turkish economy in the field of industry and the actual accumulation of capital. Independently of the government the Committee had been raising capital in order to invest in fields which would lead to the development of national resources. So far it had set up three major companies:

1) The Ottoman Joint Stock Company for National Produce (Milli Mahsulat Osmanlı Anonim Şirketi), with a capital of TL 200,000 which was expected to increase to TL 500,000;

2) The Kantarya Joint Stock for Imports (Kantarya İthalat Anonim Şirketi), with capital worth TL 200,000;

3) The Baker's Company (Ekmekçiler Şirketi), with a capital of TL 100,000.

---

50 Interview with *Politiken* (Copenhagen n.d.) quoted in *Vossische Zeitung*, 28 February 1916. See also H. Stuemer, *Two War Years in Constantinople* (London 1917), 165-8.

The CUP saw this as the most effective way to create a national economy and considered it a part of its mission to continue to raise capital in large amounts in order to set up more companies. It only intended to provide the initial capital to found the enterprises, which, once they became going concerns would plough back capital for other enterprises.[51]

The creation of commercial companies –and to a much lesser extent indutrial ones– was the most important step taken by the Unionists to create a Turkish bourgeoisie. Since the beginning of the war, wrote *Revue de Turquie* (Lausanne) in September 1918, some eighty joint-stock companies had been founded in the Ottoman Empire. Many of them had large capital outlays and nearly all were Ottoman, i.e. Turkish and Muslim. For the first time, foreign companies were having to compete on equal terms. The article then lists 72 companies, ranging from the Ottoman National Bank (Osmanlı İtibarı Milli Bankası) with a capital of four million Turkish liras to the Syrian Agricultural Company with a capital of TL 16,000. It is also significant that these commercial organisations were not restricted only to İstanbul and the cities. They were to be found in many Anatolian towns; a few examples will suffice:

The Ottoman Loan Bank of Akşehir, capital TL 50,000;

The National Bank of Aydın, capital TL 50,000;

The National Bank of Karaman, capital TL 20,000;

The Islamic Commercial Bank of Adapazarı, capital TL 100,000; in the Republic the head office of this bank was moved to Ankara where it became the Türk Ticaret Bankası A.Ş.[52]

The Agricultural Bank of Manisa, capital TL 150,000;

The Commercial Development Company of İzmit, capital TL 5,000;

---

51 See the Turkish press, especially *Tanin* for 29 September to 14 October 1916, even though the congress ended on 5 October, and *İktisadiyat Mecmuası*, vol. i/30 (19 October 1916), 1-2, the article "İttihad ve Terakki Fırkası'nın İktisadi Faaliyeti".

52 Gündüz Ökçün, "1900-1930 Yılları Arasında Anonim Şirket Olarak Kurulan Bankalar" in Osman Okyar (ed.), *Türkiye İktisat Tarihi Semineri* (Ankara 1975), 436-7.

The General Commercial Company of Konya, capital TL 5,000;

The National Commercial Company of Konya, capital TL 5,000;

The National Commercial Company of Kastamonu, capital TL 15,000;

The National Turkish Import - Export Company of İzmir, capital TL 400,000;

The Star Commerce Company of Uşak, capital TL 10,000;

The Commercial Company of Karaman, capital TL 200,000;

Company for the Manufacture of Iron and Wood Materials at Adapazarı, capital TL 34,000;

The Exploitation Company of Konya, capital TL 100,000;

Company of Steam Bakeries and Oilworks at Manisa, capital TL 60,000;

The Textile Company of Konya, capital TL 10,000;

National Weaving Company of Ankara, capital TL 50,000;

Company for the Manufacture of Woolen and Cotton Goods at Ankara, capital TL 60,000;

National Commercial and Industrial Company of Eskişehir, capital TL 50,000;

The Improvement and Building Company of İzmir, capital TL 300,000;

The Fig Cooperative Company of Aydın, capital TL 10,000.[53]

This is of necessity only a partial list and a great deal of research will have to be done into the local sources before we can have a more complete picture of economic and social activity during these years. But even this partial picture, or rather sketchy outline, shows us that

---

53 Ziya Şakir in *Son Posta*, 28 and 29 Nov. 1934 mentions the following companies: Konya Köylü Bankası; Manisa Bağcılar Bankası; Tütüncüler Bankası of İzmir, İzmir Teşkilât Şirketi (set up by Celâl Bayar); Dokumacılar Şirketi of Bursa; and *İktisadiyat Mecmuası*, i/35 (7 Dec. 1916, p. 8) give the only company in Eastern Anatolia: Erzurum Milli Ticaret Şirketi; see also Ökçün in n. 52.

54 *İktisadiyat Mecmuası*, i/13 (25 May 1916) and i/16 (15 June 1916).

most of the commercial-industrial activity was concentrated in İstanbul and the western provinces, with some activity in central Anatolia, and hardly any activity in the east, much of which was threatened by Russian troops. However, judging by the fact that this regional disparity did not change over the next half a century, this sketch is not so inaccurate, despite the lack of detail.

There were even some companies set up in the Arab provinces of the Ottoman Empire, for example the Commercial Bank of Palestine in Jerusalem (capital TL 25,000); the Syrian Agricultural Company of Damascus (capital TL 16,000); the Cooperative Commercial Society of the Hejaz Railway (capital TL 5,000); the Tobacco Joint-Stock Company of Lazakiye (capital TL 15,000); and the New Joint-Stock Company of Beirut (capital TL 20,000).[54] In 1916, Azmi Bey, the Governor of Beirut set up a big factory for the weaving of oriental carpets, and brought in Armenian experts from Konya. He set up a similar enterprise in Zor.[55]

Since even an incipient Muslim enterpreneurial class hardly existed when the Young Turks carried out their revolution, the initiative for almost any commercial or industrial enterprise came mainly from the bureaucracy of the CUP. In most cases this initiative was exercised in collaboration with either local merchants, traders, and artisans wherever they could be found, or local notables, who the Unionists hoped would eventually acquire a taste for business and enterprise. In 1911, for example, we are told that Nazım Paşa, the Vali of Baghdad, who treated foreign diplomatic agents, especially if they were British, as interlopers, adopted a commercial policy calculated to do harm to British interests, especially the Lynch Company. At the same time he encouraged and helped the son of Abdulrezzak al-Khedeiri, a wealthy merchant, to organize a new Company.[56] In Trabzon, Vali Bekir Sami started projects to improve the provincial capital and other towns of the province. He wanted to develop civic

---

55 *Revue de Turquie*, no. 3 (July 1917), 88.
56 *The Near East*, June 7, 1911. The vali was the provincial governor.

pride amongst the citizens and persuade them to cooperate to improve the conditions of their cities. Under his auspices various problems were discussed by leading merchants and prominent citizens. A committee of twelve, representing all the different religious communities and composed chiefly of businessmen was elected, with Bekir Sami Bey as president and the Greek archbishop as vice-president. "More ambitious work (noted the reporter) may be undertaken as the people become more awakened to the needs of the towns and as they learn the benefits of the cooperation for the public good, a sentiment which is sadly lacking in oriental towns."[57] In Beirut, Vali Azmi Bey was also very active in the field of economic development and *İktisadiyat Mecmuası* often discussed his accomplishment over the years.[58]

It is evident from our sources that the government was the prime mover in the field of economic activity. But we ought to remember that after 1913 the CUP's influence became dominant, forcing the government to give priority to economics. It is no accident that all the valis mentioned above – except Nazım Paşa – were Unionists. But the CUP as an organization also became directly involved in the task of creating a national economy, both in the capital but more importantly in the provinces. It would seem that most of the companies –small and large– which were set up in the towns of Anatolia were set up under the initiative of the local CUP club. The Cooperative Ottoman Joint-Stock Company of the Tobacco Growers of İzmit and Düzce is one such example. It was set up at the local club with a capital of TL 100,000 divided into 20,000 shares of TL 5 each. One of the founders of the company was Hafız Rüştü, deputy for İzmit. In Afyonkarahisar, the capitalists and personalities of the *sanjak* met on 21 October 1917

---

57 Isaac Montesanto's report from Trabzon 21 June 1911 in *Levante Trade Review*, vol. i/1 (June 1911), p. 94.

58 See vol. i/ nos. 20 and 21 (13 and 27 July 1916), p. 4 and 4 respectively and vol. ii/56 (24 May 1917), 3-4. In Syria, Valis Cemal Paşa and Tahsin Bey were also engaged in economic activity, *Ibid.*, vol. ii/67 (8 Nov. 1917), p. 4 and so was Vali Rahmi Bey in İzmir; see *Ibid.*, vol. ii/61 and 65 (2 August and 27 September 1917), p. 4 and 4 respectively. See also İçişleri Bakanlığı, *Meşhur Valiler*, ed. Hayri Orhun and others (Ankara 1969).

at the local CUP club. In the presence of a Besim Bey, secretary of the Afyon CUP, and Salim and Ağaoğlu Ahmed Beys, both deputies for Karahisar, they decided to found an industrial firm with capital worth TL 50,000. The members present immediately subscribed TL 200,000.[59] In Manisa, Mustafa Fevzi, the Unionist deputy, took the initiative to found a Viticultural Bank (Bağcılık Bankası) with a capital of TL 150,000, half of which was immediately snapped up by the local growers.[60] Almost every Anatolian town of any size had a trading company, and it would seem that in most cases the local branch of the CUP was responsible for setting up these enterprises. But research at the provincial level will have to be carried out before such a thesis can be firmly established.

Who were the people who derived most benefit from this policy of creating a national economy and a "national" bourgeosie? Essentially, it was all those who had money to invest in commercial and industrial ventures. This category included those who were already engaged in some kind of commercial activity; they were now able to operate under government patronage. But men of the old regime, who had lost political power following the Young Turk revolution, also took advantage of the situation. These old paşa's had accumulated considerable fortunes under the old regime and this wealth had not been confiscated by the Unionists. It was only natural that they should seek an outlet for their idle capital. Some like İzzet Paşa, former Chamberlain to Sultan Abdülhamid, and Gazi Muhtar Paşa considered setting up a group in collaboration with two other wealthy men in order to exploit the oil fields of Iraq."[61] This endeavor proved too ambitious and did not bear fruit. But other ventures did. The Ottoman Joint-Stock Company for General Transport *(Nakliyat-ı*

---

59 "Karahisar'da Osmanlı Anonim Sanayi Şirketi", *İktisadiyat Mecmuası*, vol. ii/67 (8 March 1917), 8, and *Revue de Turquie*, no. 4 (August 1917), p. 123.

60 *Revue de Turquie*, no. 3 (July 1917), p. 89.

61 Marling to Grey, no. 155 telegraphic-confidential, Constantinople, 10 March 1914, F.O. 371/2120/10784. See also the Anglo-Persian Oil Company's despactches to the Foreign Office in F.O. 371/2120/10880 and 10920.

Umumiye Osmanlı Anonim Şirketi) founded by seven former provincial governors is an example of a successful commercial enterprise. The aim of this organisation was the efficient transportation of goods by land and sea, within the country and abroad, and the establishment of bus, automobile services in İstanbul as well as the construction of workshops for building and repairing such vehicles. Later, the company planned to organize an internal transport service and open agencies at railway stations and ports.[62]

Since so much depended on patronage, members of the CUP and all those for whom the Committee could provide patronage were bound to exploit their opportunities. As we saw earlier, prominent Unionists took advantage of their position in order to make small fortunes and this trend continued throughout the war years. The most notorious examples of this kind of activity were men like Kara Kemal, Emanuel Karasu, Bedri Bey and Topal İsmail Hakkı Paşa, to mention only a few. Karasu is said to have amassed a fortune estimated at TL 2 million; "all honestly made out of my commission on purchase" as controller of food supplies, he told *The Times* correspondent (See his obituary in *The Times* [London] 8 June 1934).

The CUP even tried to draw the minor bureaucrats into commercial activity by setting up an organisation for officials known as the *Memur'in Şirketi*. It was founded in İstanbul with capital of TL 50,000 divided into shares of TL 5 each. The aim of this organisation was to utilise the limited resources of these people for their benefit and to provide them with moderately priced goods which had become difficult to come by during the war. This company also set up workshops in Anatolia to make cheese, oil, wood, carbon, *et cetera* and assist in the development of agriculture. Similar firms (noted *İktisadiyat Mecmuası*) had been set up in Beirut and İzmir and it was hoped that more would follow in other towns.[63] The aim of these organisations

---

62 *Osmanischer Lloyd*, 11 March 1916. See also Stuerner, *Two War Years*, 170 ff.
63 "Memurin Şirketi" in *İktisadiyat Mecmuası*, vol. i/24 (31 August 1916), pp. 4-6.

was not simply to mobilise the capital of this social group, but more important, to ease its suffering during times of acute shortage and rising prices caused by wartime profiteering.

In the provinces, the groups that derived most benefit from the Unionist policy of encouraging the creation of a national economy were the local merchants, artisans and notables *(eşraf)*. The latter, in particular, because they held large resources of idle capital were glad to avail themselves of the opportunity of investing their money in profitable enterprises. Once again much research will be needed before we will have a full and accurate picture. But there is ample evidence to hint a the significance of their role. The Erzurum National Trade Company, with its headquarters in Ankara, was founded by Hacı Ahmedzade Necib and included other notables like Mühürdarzade Hafız Ethem, Arapzade Ziya, Gümrükçüzade Münib and Gözübüyükzade Sadrettin.[64] The Ottoman Tobacco Company of Lazakiye was founded by Hacı Kasım Efendi, while the Import-Export Company of İzmir was founded by Hansazade Bekir and Balcızade Hakkı with capital of TL 100,000. In Beirut, a number of notables from Lebenon set up a company with capital worth TL 20,000 and shares of TL 250 each.[65]

The agricultural policy of the CUP, which deserves to be treated separately and at greater length, was also designed to reinforce the goals of *étatism*. Turkish agriculture had been commercialised and integrated to a large extent into the world market. This tendency received a sharp stimulus during this period, especially during the war, and the Unionists accelerated this trend by consolidating the power of the landowners. By doing so they hoped to make agriculture more efficient and more productive for the market. Thus they never attempted to end sharecropping *(ortakçılık)* by distributing land to landless labourers or to peasants with insufficient land. On the contrary, an attempt was made to end small farming and consolidate land holdings

---

64 *İktisadiyat Mecmuası*, vol. i/35 (7 December 1916), p. 8.
65 *Ibid.*, vol. i/13 (25 May 1916), p. 4 and 9; and vol. ii/65 (27 September 1917), p. 4.

under big landlords. This seems a strange policy in view of the fact that there was no pressure on the land; in fact there was a great shortage of labour on account of the constant needs of the army for cannon-fodder. This policy was prompted by political expediency, for the landowners were the allies of the CUP in the countryside and the Unionists did not conceive of undermining their power.

The Unionists intended to improve agriculture and increase productivity by purely technical means. The government invested large sums in irrigation projects and afforestation. It imported farm machinery and placed it at the disposal of the landowners, along with other implements and seeds. German experts were called in to help modernize agriculture and 150 Turkish students were sent to Germany to learn new farming techniques. In 1916, the Assembly passed a law establishing the Agricultural Bank to provide credit and technical information to farmers and overcome and obstacle in the way of agrarian improvement.[66] To help the landowner, compulsory labour was introduced at the outbreak of war and peasants were coerced into working on the farms.

This policy had the desired effect of raising productivity despite the shortage of farm labour. Where irrigation was introduced or improved, the crop yields doubled and this proved to be most significant for the overall economic situation and Turkey's survival in the war.[67]

Perhaps the greatest incentive for the landlord to increase productivity was the high prices he could obtain for his produce. Prices had been increasing steadily due to the extra-ordinary demand created by the world war. But the Unionist made it even more profitable for the famers by preventing the German and Austro-Hungarian Purchasing Companies from buying directly from the producer. It was for this purpose that many of the local companies were set up. They

---

66 Tekin Alp, "Ziraat Bankası", *İktisadiyat Mecmuası*, vol. i/9-10 (27 April and 9 May 1916).
67 *İktisadiyat Mecmuası* of 5 April cited in *Revue de Turquie*, no. 2 (June 1917), 60-61 and *İktisadiyat Mecmuası*, vol. ii/3 (July 1917), 82-3.

bought the produce from the farmer and sold it to one of the new export companies which in turn sold to the German and Austro-Hungarian Purchasing Companies at monopoly prices. In this way the Germans were forced to pay higher prices and this money circulated in more Turkish hands.[68] The most important result of this policy was to integrate the countryside into the growing national economy, inducing the farmers to produce for the market.

Such was the economic policy of the Young Turks. They, acting through the government and the organisation of the CUP, played a vital role in the attempt to create a national capitalist economy. It is not easy to evaluate their performance because they were in power for a very short time: ten years in all and only five if we consider the years after 1913 when their most radical wing, the CUP, took over the government. Yet their economic policy must be judged a success if only because it enabled the ramshackle empire with a pre-capitalist, and a partially feudal economy to wage a long war against the most advanced powers in the world. But how successful was their policy in terms of the goals they had set for themselves, namely to create a bourgeoisie and to lay the foundations of a national economy?

On both counts the social and economic policy of the Young Turks must be judged a success, especially in view of the very short time they had available to them. As late as August 1917 Yusuf Akçura had issued the warning that "If the Turks fail to produce among themselves a bourgeois class by profiting from European capitalism, the chances of survival of a Turkish society composed only of peasants and officials will be very slim."[69] but by the end of that year both Turkish and foreign observers began to note the emergence of a national economy –in which the Turkish element was dominant– and a new class, the Turkish bourgeoisie. Tekin Alp, in an article entitled "the Phase of Capitalism is Beginning", wrote of an emerging capital-

---

68 See Trumpener, *Germany and the Ottoman Empire* (Princeton 1968), 317 ff and Frank Weber, *Eagles on the Crescent* (Ithaca 1970), 187 ff.

69 In *Türk Yurdu* no. 140, August 12, 1333 (1917) quoted in Berkes, *Secularism*, p. 426.

ist régime "which would now continue to develop", but also warned the government that "this state of affairs could not fail to provoke the conflict between capital and labour in our country" unless timely measures were taken.[70] *İkdam* also commented on the emergence of the new class which engaged in commerce and industry, encouraged by the guarantees of great profits.[71] The Balkans correspondent of the *Nieuwe Rotterdamsche Courant* announced that "A new spirit has come over the Turkish merchant. His proverbially slow eastern methods have given place to quick decision and rapid action. He has imbibed a taste for making money quickly; in short, he has become a wide-awake modern businessman. Besides there has come a remarkable awakening of national pride. The Turk wanted to do everything himself now, and he is especially bent on cutting off the Armenians and the Greeks.

> "The companies and business houses, purely Turkish all of them, are springing up daily, and the Government has seen fit to grant many of them privileges that virtually place the foreigner out of competition."
>
> ...
>
> ...
>
> "Meanwhile, the Turks are very busy pushing their own industries, especially those that are capable of turning out simple articless of everyday use which they are determined to make for themselves. Number of handicraft and industrial schools have sprung up all over the country, and hundreds of Turkish youths have been sent abroad to pick up experience in the trades and industries which they will ultimately conduct in their own country."[72] The

---

70 "Kapitalizm Devresi Başlıyor", *İktisadiyat Mecmuası*, ii/67 (8 Nov. 1917), pp. 1-2. Later *İkdam* issued a similar warning about the potential for class struggle and this was quoted by *Revue de Turquie*, no. 9 (March 1918), p. 337.

71 "Yeni Bir Tabaka", *İkdam*, 13 January 1918; see also "Bolşevikler ve Müslümanlar - Hükümeti Muvakkatinin Müslümanlara Beyannamesi", *İkdam*, 15 January 1918 in which the theme of a Muslim bourgeoisie is again discussed.

72 *Nieuwe Rotterdamsche Courant* (n.d.) reported by Associated Press and published in Department of State, Weekly Report on Matters Relating to Near Eastern Affairs, 21 Feb. 1918, p. 1.

> Weekly Report of July 18, 1918 issued by the State Department
> noted that "Turkish nationalism is also rampant in the economic
> sphere. The plundering of Armenians and Greeks, the inflation of
> paper currency, and the attraction of new money into the country
> through purchases made by the Central Powers has momentarily
> placed capital in Turkish hands. There is a fever of company pro-
> moting by Turks, especially in the towns of Anatolia, and much
> complacent talk of a new national Turkish bourgeoisie."[73]

For more convincing evidence of the existence of this new class
was its role in Turkey. There was a tremendous public outcry against
the profiteering of the bourgeoisie yet the governments of the day did
little to arrest this anti-social activity. The bourgeoisie, still weak and
unsure of itself, was in a position to influence public opinion through
the press and manipulate state and government through the CUP. To
manipulate the State via the party was only logical since the bourgeoisie was the child of the mono-party state. It was unlikely that the
CUP would commit infanticide by taking serious measures against the
activities of the bourgeoisie and stifling its own creation.

Nevertheless, the public outcry against the profiteers, the notorious "merchants of 1332" (1916), forced the government to pass
laws which were not enforced and set up commissions which tempo-
rized in typical bureaucratic fashion. However, the very policy of creating a new class which was behaving so irresponsibly came into question and was debated in the press. In 1917, a commission was set up
to formulate a policy for post-war Turkey since the war was expected
to be waged to a favourable conclusion. In its conclusions the commission was divided. One group argued in favour of a purely statist
economy, abandoning reliance on individual initiative and the bourgeoisie. This group argued that in the domain of economics the individual never thought in terms of the general good but only in terms of
his own maximum profit. In an abnormal situation as the one in

---

[73] Department of State, Weekly Report, no. 24, 18 July 1918, p. 2.

wartime and one which would continue to exist after the war, such behaviour on the part of the bourgeoisie would lead to chaos, and speculation would accentuate class differences and conflict. The answer was to establish a statist economy which would presumably be run by the bureaucracy, so as to avoid problems of class conflict.

In view of Turkey's wartime experience, the opponents of this line of argument had little to say except to argue that the statist economy was only a "sort of socialism". That argument was expected to be sufficient to make statism anathema to all Turks. Others, like Tekin Alp, continued to argue the definition of *étatism* which the Unionists had been applying. Under *étatism*, not only did the State not supplant the private sector, it sought to obtain the maximum possible profits for it. The State would intervene not so as to replace the individual but rather to show him the way, to allow him to function in conditions most favourable for the national economy. The model for Turkey, Tekin Alp argued, should be Germany's wartime economy where the State's functions were supervision and control.[74]

This definition of *étatism* which accepted and guaranteed the existence of the bourgeoisie triumphed in 1918 suggesting that however weak and immature the new bourgeoisie may have been, it was influential enough to defend itself and promote its interests. Thereafter the bourgeoisie, still not the dominant political factor, was a factor to be reckoned with in any political debate. The definition of *étatism* formulated during this period was also accepted by the Republican State, though it was not fully applied until the multi-party period after 1945, marking the political triumph of the Turkish bourgeoisie.

---

74   Tekin Alp, "Harbden Sulha İntikal İktisadiyatı - Devlet İktisadiyatı", *İktisadiyat Mecmuası*, vol. ii/62 and 64 (16 August and 14 Sept. 1917), pp. 1-3.

The Agrarian Policy
of the Young Turks 1908-1918

The Young Turk revolution of July 1908 aroused great hopes in town and country as revolutions, or radical changes of régime are apt to do. In both cases these hopes were largely disappointed as the governments of the new régime did little to satisfy the expectations of the urban poor or the peasantry. Not that the peasants were particularly demanding, judging by their complaints to Ahmed Şerif, a journalist who toured Anatolia during 1909-1910. He does not even mention any signs of peasant militancy, except indirectly when he relates incidents of banditry which were quite widespread in Anatolia during this period.[1] A year after the restoration of the Constitution, nothing seemed to have changed for the better. The reply of an old peasant, responding to Ahmed Şerif's questions as to how the State treated the peasantry, and whether they were happy with the newly restored liberty, deserves to be quoted at length as an illustration of the prevailing situation in the countryside:

---

[1] Ahmed Şerif, *Anadolu'da Tanin*, 1977, pp. 25-6, 156, 217 et 321. Originally published as articles in *Tanin*, an İstanbul daily, these articles were collected and published in 1910. Çetin Börekçi's 1977 edition is more complete as some articles were left out of the first edition.

Liberty [he said] was a word we only began to hear recently. But from what we have heard, and from some activities, we understand that it is something worthwhile... But we thought that everything could be rectified; taxes would be collected justly and peacefully [i.e. without coercion]; murderers and thieves in the village would be reformed; our children who go to military service would not be kept hungry and naked for years, but would be discharged in time; officials would not do things as they pleased and everything would be changed. But so far nothing has happened. In the past some things used to even function better; today everything is in a mess. If we go to a government office we do not know who is in charge... The government still does not look into our problems... Several people hold the deed for a particular field and we are not sure whether the ground we till belongs to us or not. Because of that there are fights everyday and sometimes people are killed. We go to the state office and the court but we cannot explain our problem. They only think of collecting taxes when they are due... We work all year round and we pay our taxes annually; if we don't they take them by force, even selling our pots and bedding. Thus we are always in debt. During the past few years there have been many peasants in the village who have not had seed to sow. Since there is no help from anywhere else we have to buy seed from the *ağa* at either 100-125 *kuruş* per *kile* or return him three *kile* for one. Those *ağas* became a menace; they can have the peasant beaten by their toughs, have him jailed, or sometimes have him intimidated by the intervention of the state. In this way they collect their debt from those who cannot pay. As a matter of fact the Agricultural Bank is giving loans but that does not help us. That money runs out before it reaches our village.[2]

The passage, one of many in which Ahmed Şerif desribes the problem of the peasantry as well as its expectations, reflects the situa-

---

2   *Ibid.*, pp. 46,7. Earlier, on p. 25, Ahmed Şerif commented: "What the peasant cannot understand is that even though he has been hearing a great many promises during the past year, he has not seen them kept, not even those which would have been easy to carry out. He wants to see the venal and corrupt official removed: he wants to know that there is no need to quake any longer with fear before the gendarmes whom he feeds free of charge, and provides food for his beasts. He wants to see those things change which seem unimportant to us but are very important to him."

tion in September 1909. But there was no change for the better during the rest of the decade, or indeed even in the generation that followed. In fact, the foundations of Republican rural policy may be said to have been firmly laid by the Young Turks.[3] Not that they intended to maintain the status quo in the countryside and pursue a conservative agrarian policy,[4] on the contrary, it was generally agreed that:

> according to the rural policy of the day, it was vital to save the peasant from the feudal lords *(derebeys)* and their successors, the *ağa*s and the notables *(eşraf)*.

Nor was all the talk against feudalism *(derebeylik)* mere political rhetoric, the Unionist *vali* of Aleppo Hüseyin Kâzım issued a proclamation to the people of the province in which

> he used strong language about the notables and the *ağa*s announced that an end would be put to their oppression. There was a reaction to this proclamation from all sides. Because the İstanbul paper *Avvam* printed this proclamation, it received letters of congratulations from many of its readers in Anatolia and Rumelia.[5]

Despite such threats by prominent Unionists, the CUP as a body never seems to have envisioned changing the status quo in the countryside by ending the social, economic, and political domination of the landlords. Şanda has a point when he argues that the only way the Ottoman state could continue to pay its foreign debts and balance its budgets was by retaining the tithe, described by Namık Kemal as a curse on the peasantry. Moreover, exploitation of the peasantry had become the principal source of capital accumulation, especially, as we

---

3 The term 'Young Turks' describes all factions opposed to Abdülhamid's autocracy, while 'Unionists' refers only to members of the Committee of Union and Progress (CUP), who were also Young Turks.

4 Hüseyin Avni Şanda, *Reaya ve Köylü*, 1970 ed., p. 10. See also İsmail Hüsrev [Tokin], *Türkiye Köy İktisadiyatı*, 1934, pp. 154-72, 176ff. for a description and analysis of *derebeylik* in the late Ottoman Empire and the early Republic.

5 *Avvam*, 23 oct. 1910, cited by Şanda, *Reaya*, p. 10.

shall see, after the start of the war in 1914 when the demand for farm produce increased very sharply.[6] However, apart from these practical reasons, there were also structural reasons which hampered an active policy against landed interests.

During the course of the nineteenth century, as the Ottoman economy was progressively penetrated by European enterprise, land was the last bastion to be threatened. The Porte stubbornly refused to allow foreigners to own land under the privileges of the capitulations because "... if Europeans were to come among us in that way, and to hold estates, [said a bureaucrat of the Sublime Porte to Charles MacFarlane] they would soon drive us out of the country."[7] Meanwhile all Tanzimat legislation relating to land, especially the Land Code of 1858, seemed to be designed to strengthen the power of the landowning notables by legitimizing their holdings. At about the same time – in 1857 and 1864 – the laws on the reorganization of the municipalities and the province gave these notables representation on the various councils and they therefore emerged as communal leaders. The proclamation of the constitution in 1876 and the parliament that was elected the following year increased their political power for they could now actively lobby for their interests. The same was true after 1908 but they could now go a step further and organize themselves in political parties. Despite their political inexperience, the Unionists rec- ognized the reality of the situation and abandoned all attempts – even the talk of eradicating feudalism. Before going any further, let us examine briefly how this controversial term may be used fruitfully to understand an important aspect of the late Ottoman Empire.[8]

6   *Ibid.*, p. 12-13, of course production fell dramatically, increasing prices even further.
7   Charles MacFarlane, *Turkey and Its Destiny*, 1850, vol. ii, pp. 171-7 quoted by Ali Tosun Arıcanlı, *The Role of the State in the Social and Economic Transformation of the Ottoman Empire 1807-1918*, unpublished Ph. D. Harvard University 1976, p. 111. See also Nasim Sousa, *The Capitulatory Régime of Turkey*, 1933.
8   Arıcanlı, "Tha State", chapter 1 and sections iii-v of ch. 3; Kemal Karpat, *An Inquiry into the Social Foundations of Nationalism in the Ottoman Empire*, 1973, p. 98; idem, "The Ottoman Parliament of 1877 and Its Social Significance", *Association Internationale d'Études de Sud-Est Européen*, 1969.

If we consider feudalism as a system of government then we must conclude that there was no feudalism in the Ottoman Empire after the abolition of the *timar* system. Thereafter the state was too centralized and bureaucratized to need personal ties, or to share power with the army. But if we are more generous with our criteria of feudalism and feudal society and include the question of the social organization of production, the forms that landed property took, or the methods of extracting surplus in our discussion, then elements of feudalism lived well into twentieth-century Turkey.[9] In nineteenth-century Turkey there were two seemingly contradictory tendencies to be observed. On the one hand there was the transformation from overlordship based on traditional *timar* rights to the landlord's claim based on private ownership, in fact if not in theory. Claim to ownership became increasingly important as land values increased with improved communications and commercialized agriculture. With the formation of the Agricultural Bank in 1888 land was used as collateral against loans, and that implied ownership as a peasant proprietor or landlord could hardly mortgage his "feudal privileges" and claims. On the other hand, the landlord continued to exercise his traditional powers based on his right to demand service from his peasants, both in the form of labour and a share of his produce. The landlord's economic superiority gave him a social and political control over his peasants that went beyond his economic resources. He extracted services and surplus, if need be by illegal means and intimidation, using hired retainers or his links with the local state apparatus the *vali* or *kaymakam*, the judge or tax collector.[10] This factor of coercion – common to feudalism in general – needs to be stressed, as well as the extra-market character of domination which prevailed in the social relationship. Thus, to repeat, the principal method of extracting surplus from the peasant continued to be labour – rent or *corvée (angarya)* as against

---

9   Hüsrev, *Köy*, pp. 154-73 and 176; Şanda, *Reaya*, pp. 40-41.

10   Ahmed Şerif, *Tanin*, passim; Ahmed Emin, *Turkey in the World War*, 1930, p. 80; Behice Boran, *Toplumsal Yapı Araştırmaları*, 1945, p. 40 and passim.

post-feudal wage labour. It is not that wage labour did not exist, it did in certain regions. But in such regions there was a shortage of labour and the prevailing high wages encouraged the landlord to continue using forced labour. Thus while land was rapidly taking the form of a commodity, labour was not.

The elements of feudalism are to be found in the relationship between lord and peasant at one level, and between lord and state at another. Political authority continued to be personel and decentralized even after the bureaucratisation of the Tanzimat reforms. While the power of the state was acknowledged by the lord it was not allowed to prevail in the local relationship for the notables exercised "seignorial jurisdiction" i.e. de facto judicial and sometimes administrative authority over the peasants. In such circumstances state authority did not go beyond the payment of taxes by the notables. Thus a relatively small group of people monopolized local power and they alone enjoyed political rights, especially under the constitution. To the peasant the existence of the state became virtually irrelevant even though he continued to pin great hopes on it as his saviour. Another reason why feudal relations continued to prevail into the twentieth century was the insecurity in the countryside during the long period of decline marked by rebellions, wars and banditry. The peasants met their need for protection by organizing their villages close together and seeking the patronage of local Beys. A sociologist reporting the findings of her fieldwork in the Manisa region in 1941, concluded that "Essentially, insecurity and the need for protection are prominent features of a feudal-type society, and the stories about the founding of the villages of Kepenekli and Sarı Çam reflect these elements explicitly."[11]

İstanbul recognized reality by accepting the status quo, and a precarious social peace and stability continued to prevail in the countryside. Attempts to modify these feudal relationships tended to produce sharp reactions from both lord and peasant, dangerous to the

---

11   B. Boran, p. 61.

régime in the capital. The Unionists – like the Kemalist after them – understood the situation too well to attempt a "bourgeois revolution" by destroying the power of the anti-reformist landlords. Instead they compromised with them by giving them control over parliament, effectively tying their own hands and making legislation threatening to landed interests impossible. In return they were able to carry out some institutional reforms, thus modernizing the state structure.

After the restoration of the constitution, there was, nonetheless, apprehension and expectation in the countryside; apprehension among the landlords who feared a radical agrarian policy threatening to their position, and expectations from the oppressed peasantry which believed, naively as it turned out, that the new régime would introduce changes beneficial to their lives. In their first flush of glory and while they were at their most radical, the Unionists did propose measures intended to lighten the burden of the peasant. The land question was discussed at the 1908 Unionist congress in Salonica, and the Committee decided to ask the government to prepare conditions for distributing land to peasants provided that ownership of land legally held and protected by lawful possession was not violated; to facilitate this by providing loans at minimum interest; to reduce the tithe by half as a sound basis for taxation and to introduce this wherever possible. Later on a cadasteral system would be introduced gradually. For the rest the CUP promised to encourage the development of agriculture in every way possible, especially by establishing agricultural schools throughout the empire in order to teach modern methods.[12]

This was Unionist land policy at its most radical. Never again would they officially propose land distribution or cheap loans for the peasantry. Not that there was pressure on land, there was not.[13] But

---

12 T. Z. Tunaya, *Türkiye'de Siyasi Partiler, 1859-1952, pp. 206-10.*
13 Orhan Erinç, "Toprak Politika ve İnsanlar", *Cumhuriyet*, 17 April 1971 gives the following breakdown for landownership in 1913: One per cent of the population, including feudal lords (*derebey tip ağalar*) occupied 39 per cent of the land; 87 per cent, including small and middle families, occupied 35 per cent of the land; 4 per cent, including large landowners *(toprak*

land distribution which enabled the peasantry to subsist independently of the landlords would have deprived the latter of forced labour. Ironically, that might have forced them to mechanize to compensate for expensive labour, thereby unwittingly modernizing agriculture. But as with landlords everywhere they preferred the old ways which required hardly any investment to a new system which would have needed considerable capital investment and also challenged their traditional domination.

The experiences of the first year of the constitution also made the Unionists cautious about reform. Austria-Hungary's annexation of Bosnia and Herzegovina, Bulgaria's declaration of independence, the Cretan question, and the generally unsympathetic attitude of Europe towards the CUP weakened their position. Domestically, the Unonists were confronted with the opposition of both the conservatives and the liberals which culminated in the reactionary rebellion of April 1909.[14] As a result of all these setbacks, the Unionists reconsidered their already moderate agrarian policy and took the path of least resistance. They adopted the Tanzimat policy of strengthening the hold of the landlords through laws which further extended their control over the land. At the same time they encouraged the farmers to use modern methods and increase productivity for both home consumption and export. This policy was reflected in the decisions of the CUP congresses held before 1913 when Unionists were not in power but only influential behind the scene, and in 1913 after they had seized power. In 1909 Unionist delegates, having dropped all talk of land distribu-

---

ağaları) occupied 26 per cent of the land. 8 per cent were landless. A. D. Novichev, *Ekonomika Turtsii v period mirovoi voin* (The Economy of Turkey during the World War), 1935, 8, writes: "The *métayage* system was all powerful in the Turkish village. Of all the cultivable land 65 per cent belonged to the big and average-scale landowner, while 35 per cent of this land consisted of farmsteads in possession of 95 per cent of the peasants'." A German, writing in 1916, noted that only about three-eights of the cultivable soil was in use and the density of population was 11.5 per square kilometre compared to Germany's 120. He complained that the Turks were not permitting Germans to farm in Turkey. See Dr Kurt Zander's article in *Schwabischer Merkure*, 2 May 1916, in War Office, *Dail Review of the Foreign Press*, 12 May 1916 (hereafter *DRFP*).

14 For the politics of these years, see Feroz Ahmad, *The Young Turks*, 1969.

tion, agreed to encourage scientific agriculture by founding agricultural schools, and to eliminate all obstacles that stood in the way of
agricultural, commercial, and industrial progress. They promised to
give greater importance to agriculture, and to pass legislation to facilitate ownership and the right to transfer land.[15] Nevertheless, once in
power the Unionists again showed some concern for the welfare of the
peasantry. They again spoke of halving the tithe "if the condition of
the state treasury permits", as well as reforming its collection along
cadastral lines. They proposed reducing the tax on farm animals and
reforming its collection, and announced that a law would be promulgated which would regulate the relations between the farmer and
reapers, those hired by the month, and sharecroppers.[16] But these
remained paper schemes and with the outbreak of war the following
year the condition of the Turkish peasantry deteriorated dramatically.

Despite wavering Unionist policy, there was one change
brought about by the 1908 Revolution that had a marked impact on
all aspects of Ottoman life, including agriculture: the transformation
in the character of the state and its ideology. The Hamidian state had
been narrowly based, narrow in outlook, and concerned primarily
about the interests of the dynasty. Its response to interests such as
those of the landlords was pragmatic and manipulative, largely
designed to co-opt. them. The state made no concerted effort to give
direction and leadership to this class by guiding it towards progressive
agriculture. If there was a tendency towards commercialization it
resulted from the empire's absorption into the world capitalist market
and existed mainly in regions close to ports or railways. The state did
little to accelerate this process and without an active parliament the
landlords, even if so inclined, were unable to act as a class on their
own behalf.

All that changed in 1908. Not only did the constitution permit
the various interest groups – economic and ethnic – to express their

---

15 Tunaya, *Partiler*, p. 211-12.
16 *Ibid.*, p. 216.

views in parliament and have the government act on their behalf, but the CUP went even further and adopted a statist policy of creating a class, the bourgeoisie, where none existed.[17] Having abandoned the idea of carrying out a structural change in the countryside, the Unionists set about the task of hastening the process of commercialized agriculture. The state, too, was most receptive to the needs and demands of the landlords, who often found the provincial governors or Unionist members of parliament taking the lead in initiating modern farming methods, hoping that the local farmers would take note and follow. That, in short, became the agrarian policy of the Young Turks. But they found so much resistence to their schemes, that they came to regard agriculture as secondary, giving priority to commerce and industry in their endeavour to construct a modern national economy.

The behaviour of the farmers, far from being irrational and tradition bound, was based on their experience of competing in the world market against the agricultural produce of North America and nearer home, Russia and Rumania. With the advent of steamships foreign grain could be transported more economically to İstanbul than grain from the interior. The Porte could have protected Ottoman agriculture by raising tariffs but the capitulations did not permit that. Thus in the period after 1860 Ottoman agriculture declined, the farmers calculating that investments to modernize the methods of cultivation just were not worthwhile. "In the early 1880's [writes Engin Akarlı] the Ottomans were concerned about increasing exports, but by the mid-1890's they would be pleased if only domestic production could compete against imported crops."[18] By the end of the nineteenth century, even while the trend in the world market was changing in favour of

---

17 Feroz Ahmad, "Vanguard of a Nascent Bourgeoisie: the Social and Economic Policy of the Young Turks 1908-1918", in Osman Okyar and Halil İnalcık (eds.), *Social and Economic History of Turkey (1071-1920)*, 1980, pp. 329-50.

18 Engin Akarlı, "Economic Problems of Abdülhamid's Reign (1876-1909)", paper presented at the Conference on Economy, Society, and Polity in the Magreb and Turkey, İstanbul, May 1975, p. 26.

Turkish grain, the area under cultivation remained stagnant, except for tobacco whose production continued to increase.[19] The Ottoman farmer refused to take any initiative or risk while he was unable to rely on a state too weak to resist foreign manipulation. He preferred to obtain his income from rent, living as an absentee landlord in the town and letting his bailiff *(subaşı)* deal with the tenants who were usually share-croppers. Lucy Garnett, writing around 1904, noted:

> The way in which an absentee proprietor spends his time when on an occasional visit to his estate naturally depends upon his pecuniary means and personal tastes... His duties as landlord are confined to regulating accounts with his agent, hearing and deciding cases between the functionary and the tenants, giving instructions for future farming operations, and, lastly, realizing the profits. As to improving the soil, introducing modern and labour-saving machinery, building model cottages, and otherwise ameliorating the moral and material conditions of his tenants – these are things that do not enter into the philosophy of a Turkish landed proprietor.[20]

Such landlords, comfortable in their way of life, were unwilling to abandon it unless the state could guarantee a better future. Initially therefore they looked with alarm and suspicion at the schemes of the Young Turks and offered active opposition to them. But their opposition was not ostensibly caused by Unionist radicalism, which was their real fear, but rationalized by their social snobbery towards the CUP leadership. Consul Samson, reporting on the situation in Edirne in June 1910 wrote:

> The view of the chief Turkish landowners, which I have gathered from conversations with certain of the more prominant amongst

---

19 *Ibid.*, p. 29; information based on Parvus, *Türkiye'nin Can Damarı*, 1914, p. 154-64. See also A. D. Novichev's essay translated in Charles Issawi (ed.), *The Economic History of the Middle East 1800-1914*, 1966, p. 66.

20 Lucy Garnett, *Turkish Life in Town and Country*, 1904, pp. 107-8. Her model is obviously the idealized enlightened English landlord.

them, is that the men at present responsible for the direction of affairs are unfitted for the task which they have undertaken.

Holders of these views contend that the higher officials of a country should possess at least one of two qualifications – either that of belonging by birth to a governing class, or the possession of exceptional administrative capacity. The party at present in power, it is stated, have no claims to it from either point of view. The Adrianople Beys reserve a special measure of scorn for the Minister of the Interior [Talât Bey, Paşa and grand vezir in 1917], whom they know as an official in the Telegraph Department here, and of whose qualifications they hold a very poor opinion.[21]

Another consul, writing from Diyarbakır, reported that local opposition was based on the protection of vested interests. In an earlier dispatch he had informed his ambassador about reforms being carried out in the province. Following up this despatch he wrote:

> ... It is evident that a small but powerful class is daily becoming more and more enraged against what they consider as an attack upon their special privileges. These malcontents are the eshreffs of the town, and certain other tribal beys and aghas, who naturally look with loathing upon the democratic and, to their own interests, hostile intentions of the vali and the other reformers. Upto now they have, perforce, held their peace, but disturbances in the town fomented, it is generally admitted, by the eshreffs, have lately become more frequent."

Acting Vice-Consul Rawlins then described how the *eşraf* undermined the position of an active reformer:

> ... One of the most energtic amongsts the local reformers is a certain Behjet Efendi, a captain in, but virtually commandant of, the gen-

---

21 Consul Samson to Lowther, Adrianople, 30 June 1910 in Lowther to Grey, no. 446, Constantinople, 4 July 1910, F.O. 371/999/24852. On the notables of Ayancık near Sinop, the Şükrüoğulları who were former *ayan* dating back to at least Mahmut II's reign see Rıza Nur, *Hayat ve Hatıratım*, i. 1967, pp. 255-8. Such families were to be found throughout Rumelia and Anatolia.

darmerie force of the vilayet. This man has brought down the anger of the eshreffs by his systematic patrolling of the neighbouring villages, and his fearless attacks upon, and intervention in, all cases of oppression and corruption. Under his leadership the gendarmerie has made good progress, and, instead of being as formerly a disorderly and corrupt body, it is rapidly becoming a well-trained force and an active agent for the preservation of law and order. All this is not at all to the liking of many of the local notables, who are beginning to understand that they must keep their places and cannot rule in the town and villages as heretofore. On the evening of the 10th instant matters came to a head when a large band of roughs, well known to be under the orders of some of the eshreffs, broke into some cafés and started a series of disturbances. Upon hearing of this, Behçet Efendi set out immediately for the scene of disorder, which appears was what the roughs wanted, and on his arrival was surrounded and severely beaten and mauled. Threats were also openly uttered by the roughts that the vali himself would shortly be treated in the same way if the "reforms" were persisted in. All this has made some stir in the town, and it is worthy of remark as being further evidence of the hostility of certain classes of the population to the methods of the new régime and the system of reforms...[22]

The landlords operated on two fronts: locally where they had economic and political power they obstructed reform; and in parliament where they used their majority to either halt measures directed against them, or to introduce measures designed to further their interests. An example of the latter was a proposal by İsmail Sıtkı Bey, deputy for the grape-growing province of Aydın, to remove the tax on spirits. In his speech of 23 June 1909 he argued that this tax was the ruin of wine-growng districts and its removal would help discourage the rise of a new industry in harmless spirits. It was also necessary to take measures to prevent the import of foreign alcohols. As compensation for the loss of revenue by the state, the wine growers, he said, were even willing to pay a tithe on wines of up to 12 per cent. Finance

22 Acting Vice-Consul Rawlins to Lowther, Diyarbekir, 12 Jan. 1910, in Lowther to Grey, no. 45, Constantinople, 30 Jan. 1910, F.O. 371/1002/4225.

Minister Mehmed Cavid, one of the first Unionists in the cabinet, was sympathetic but observed that the suppression of the tax on spirits was impossible as it had been inserted in the Decree of Muharrem of 1881. That was an international engagement guaranteed by the capitulations and therefore inviolable. Moreover, its revenues were assigned to service the public debt and that too made it an international concern.[23]

This example merely shows how foreign privileges had firmly tied the hands of the reformers and one may assume that this realization demoralized the progressive farmer, curbing his desire to modernise and innovate. Given the limitations imposed upon them by internal and external factors, the Young Turks could only hope to encourage agriculture by providing aid and incentives to the farmers. They wanted to create a market for rural goods by constructing a substantial network of roads and railways. Cavid's Salonica speech of 11 August 1910 sums up some of the aspirations of the reformers. He promised that 30,000 kilometres of roads would be constructed in the next five years not only suitable for pedestrians, horses, and wagons but also for motor traffic. That would be a great service for the rural population for in many provinces the cultivator was not able to transport his goods to market and was obliged to sell them locally at derisory prices; he sometimes even had to burn them. The construction of railways would also be accelerated; not only would existing projects, namely the Baghdad Railway, be completed, but new ones, opening up Anatolia and the Arab provinces, would be initiated. Turkey would have a further 9,000 kilometres of railways in addition to the 6,000 it already had.[24] But, as the correspondent of the *Deutsche Levante*

---

23 Enclosure of proceedings in parliament in Lowther to Grey, no. 624, Therapia 4 Aug. 1909, F.O. 371/761/29787.

24 *La Turquie* and *Tanin*, 12 Aug. 1910. The public works contracts were being parcelled to the Great Powers and E. G. Mears has noted that the parcelling out of special privileges to foreign nationals hindered the possibility of a unified transportation system and at the same time turned trade from its natural routes. After all, foreign concessionaries were more concerned with the commercial privileges which the railway concessions carried rather than the railway itself. See Mears, *Modern Turkey*, 1924, pp. 202 and 207.

Zeitung pointed out, roads and railways would now be built on an economic and not on a strategic basis as in the past.[25]

If communications were going to create a new integrated market and demand, production would have to be stepped up to meet the challenge. The Young Turks intended to do that through ambitious irrigations projects in Anatolia and Iraq. The surveys to irrigate the plains of Konya and Cilicia were being carried out by the Deutsche Bank with the aim of irrigating 123,767 and 1,237,970 acres respectively. The irrigation of the Cilician plain would, it was thought, turn the country around Adana into another Egypt.[26] All these measures tended to increase land values with the result that the landlords were even more anxious to establish claim to lands which belonged to the peasantry. But the reformers seemed unconcerned about these injustices to the peasantry which they viewed as the price that had to be paid for modern agriculture, a price Europe, whose example they wished to emulate, had already extracted from her own peasants.

Side by side with these longer term schemes, the Porte also encouraged the farmer to mechanize. In some regions like western Anatolia and Adana, mechanization had already become a necessity on account of scarce and therefore expensive labour which could undermine production. In 1910, for example, there was an excellent harvest in the province of İzmir but a large portion of the crops was ruined because of a lack of labour at harvest time.[27] Mechanization was the answer and the state encouraged that by exempting farm machinery from import duties. It also appointed an official who directed an industrial exhibition which travelled throughout the province in 1910. A

---

25 Cited in *Levante Trade Review* (hereafter *LTR*) I/iii, Dec. 1911, pp. 252-6.
26 *LTR*, I/1, June 1911, 59-61. A later issue noted: "These irrigation improvements will greatly favor the raising of cotton and sugar cane. The Cilician plain is also traversed by the Baghdad Railway. There is also a railroad connecting Adana and Mersina. However it is intended also to render the Saihun and Jihan navigable. The rivers of Cilicia lend themselves to the generation of electric power, and the Turkish Government expects to develop an intense industrial life in that region." *LTR*, vi/i, June 1916, p. 46.
27 *LTR*, I6/i, June 1911, pp. 59-61.

correspondent of the British monthly *The Near East* (20 Sept. 1911), vitally interested in the import of his country's machinery into the empire, noted that while farm machines were not in general use in Anatolia, the demand for ploughs, harvesters, and other farm tools was growing. According to his estimates for 1910 there were already 4,000 ploughs, 150 harrows, 50 cultivators, and 100 reapers in use in İzmir province. And among the reasons why many farmers were not mechanizing he listed insecurity of land tenure, the lack of land banks, and a lack of organizations of the peasants. This suggests that the middle peasant, who lacked security, was simply not willing to risk investing money on land he might lose at any time.[28]

Despite all these measures to encourage agriculture, the question of property rights remained fundamental to progress in the countryside. An American observer of the Ottoman economic scene, noted that:

> Throghout the Empire, especially in the rural districts, gold is hoarded in the form of jewelry and money. The present laws regarding real estate, while unduly restricting the mobility of invested capital, make for conservative dealings and solidity of position.
>
> The passing of the proposed "Landed Property Code" by the incoming Parliament, which seems likely, will release wealth now tied up, accelerate industrial and commercial activity, increase land values, and generally contribute to the financial uplift of the country. This act will extend the right of inheritance, regulate the proprietorship (and transfer of land, render the ecclesiastical and

---

28 Some landlords, anxious for more rapid progress and profits soughts foreign collaboration. The correspondent for *The Near East*, 20 Sept. 1911, p. 477, reported: "Several large landowners in Asia Minor have asked me to say that they are prepared to offer good terms for British co-operation in fructifying their estates, which are well adapted for cotton growing and cereals as well as fruits...

"The kind of proposition I have is one that cannot give any profit for a year or two, and possibly three, but which after that time may be expected to return a hundred per cent per annum of the capital expended for irrigation and for planting. Not only money is scarce in the country, but skill and machinery also."

Government property, (vakıf and miri lands) subject to mortgage, and enable corporation. Under present conditions, large areas, especially around the cities and towns, have become the property of pious foundations... Other areas are in effect rendered similarly unavailable, the title being vested in the Government, where it remains. While all such religious and public possession may be held by natives and foreigners alike, they are, in reality, only lease-hold.[29]

The Law of Transfer of Immovable Property was passed in 1913, marking an important step in the direction of establishing private property on land, and securing the confidence of the landed proprietors.[30] The law probably had the effect anticipated by Bie Ravndal and others, but that has yet to be confirmed. There is certainly evidence of capital accumulation in the countryside and that is manifested in the founding of agricultural companies formed to market and process regional produce. The Unionists actively encouraged this trend and on 8 June 1914 we find parliament authorizing the Agricultural Bank to aid the National Bank that was to be opened at Aydın by purchasing shares to the extent of half the proposed capital of TL 50,000.[31] By the end of the year parliament began to debate amendments of the Agricultural Bank law so as to make its capital available not only for agriculture but agricultural industry referring to the processing and packaging of produce such as figs, tobacco, olive oil, etc. Not only would the bank merely participate in such ventures, it would, if necessary, become the major shareholder. That prompted Vartakes Efendi, the deputy for Erzurum, to say that "in that case it

29 Consul General g. Bie Ravndal, "Commercial Review of Turkey", *LTR*, II/i, Sept. 1912, pp. 138-51.
30 Gabriel Baer, "The Evolution of Private Landownership in Egypt and the Fertile Crescent"in Issawi (ed.), *Economic History*, pp. 85-6. For a detailed legal history of the evolution of private property in land in the Ottoman Empire see Halil Cin, *Miri Arazi ve Bu Arazinin Mülk Haline Dönüşümü*, 1969, pp. 148-53, and passim for the period under discussion.
31 Y. S. Atasağun, *Türkiye'de Zirai Borçlanma ve Zirai Kredi Politikası*, 1943, pp. 134-51; *The Orient*, V/24, 17 June 1914, p. 233, and Ahmad, "Nascent Bourgeoisie", p. 342, n. 17 above.

would be the bank that would be doing business and not the people." But the director of the bank was reassuring. He said that "the bank would withdraw completely from the venture after the companies had come into being."[32] Here surely is the early practice of the Kemalist economic philosophy of étatism as defined in the 1930s.

The war years proved most profitable for the new capitalist farmers. High prices were the best incentive to increase production, and prices rose sharply as the demand for country products grew. In another place I have noted that "the Unionists made it even more profitable for the farmers by preventing the German and Austro-Hungarian Purchasing Companies from buying directly from the producer. It was for this reason that many of the local companies were set up. They bought the produce from the farmer and sold it to one of the new export companies which in turn sold to the German and Austro-Hungarian Purchasing Companies at monopoly prices. In this way the Germans were forced to pay important result of this policy was to integrate the countryside into the growing national economy, inducing the farmers to produce for the market."[33] This policy may be said to mark a new phase in the relationship between the state and the landlords, reflecting the growing strength of the latter. In 1838, by signing the free trade treaty with Britain, the Porte liberated the landlords from the monopolistic buying policies of the sultan; in 1916 the landlords were being freed from the virtual buying monopoly of Germany and Austria-Hungary.[34]

---

32 Y. S. Atasağun, *Türkiye Cumhuriyeti Ziraat Bankası 1888-1939*, 1939, pp. 48-55, of Mevzuat İlavesi.

33 Ahmad, "Nascent Bourgeoisie", p. 345, n. 17 above.

34 The farmers were now organized into an association, the *Çiftçiler Derneği*, founded in July 1914 but which became effective only in 1916. Talât became its first honorary president and Minister of Agriculture Ahmed Nesimi its second. Its office holders included high bureaucrats and its members the notables of Anatolia, as well as important Unionists like Kara Kemal. See *İktisadiyat Mecmuası*, I/20, 13 July 1916, p. 3. Tunaya, *Partiler*, p. 205, n. 118, and 458-61, says that an *Osmanlı Çiftçiler Derneği* which began as an agrarian lobby to pressure the state to include agriculture in national policies, converted itself into a political party during the armistice period. On the 1838 Treaty and agriculture see Birinci Köy ve Ziraat Kalkınma Kongresi, *Türk Ziraat Tarihine Bir Bakış*, 1938, pp. 69-74.

The war, however, also had a detrimental effect on agriculture. The acute labour shortage which had made wages relatively high became critical when the Porte declared mobilization in August 1914. To make matters worse, farm animals were requisitioned for military purposes throughout the empire. The impact of both measures was felt in the countryside.[35] The Porte had already seen the impact of war on labour during the Balkan Wars. Therefore before war broke out the army had already schemes to give courses in modern farming to enlisted men, and to release some of them during sowing and harvesting.[36] The government met the war emergency by legalizing forced labour at the outbreak of hostilities and enforced it more rigorously during the war. With the men being killed at the various fronts, women and children were forced to assume the heavy tasks on the home front, both in the factories and in the fields. Tekin Alp, one of the principal Unionist ideologues and propagandists, eulogized the contribution that women made in the economic struggle for survival:

> While the men found themselves at the front struggling heroically for the very survival of the motherland, the women at home struggled equally hard with all their might to provide food for the country and guaranteed its economic future...
>
> The activity of our peasant women is to be seen above all in Konya province. Samih Bey, the vali of Konya, has decided to build a monument to perpetuate the memory of this noble achievement of Turkish women in this historic epoch through which we are passing.[37]

Forced labour, male and female, was the only was to keep land under cultivation. The total area under cultivation had, according to

---

35 Novichev, *Ekonomika Turtsii*, devotes the first chapter to agriculture and provides interesting detail about the impact of mobilization and requisitioning. He wrote: "... the worst losses in livestock were suffered by the animal most used in Turkish agriculture, i.e. the oxen which was almost wiped out." Its population declined by 85.5 per cent between 1913 and 1919. See pp. 18-19.

36 *The Orient*, V/20, May 20, 1914, p. 198.

37 Tekin Alp, "Bu Seneki Mahsulümüz", *İktisadiyat Mecmuası*, I/ii, 22 July 1916, pp. 1-2.

one estimate, declined from 60 million *dönüm* in 1914, to 30 million *dönüm* in 1915, and 24 million in 1916.[38] The Minister of Agriculture, interviewed in the first issue of *İktisadiyat Mecmuası* (Feb. 1916), emphasized the extraordinary circumstances during the war and how military needs prevented expansion. Despite all the aid they had given the farmer the results never came upto their expectations. "Drought, hail storms, floods, locusts, and disease" only aggravated an already terrible situation. Therefore their efforts would have to be redoubled this year. Yet during these critical times the landlords often took over the lands of peasants who failed to return from the front, and there were thousands who did not.[39]

By 1916, however, the food situation had become sufficiently critical for the state to intervene even in the affairs of the landlords. There was now an undeclared war economy in operation, influenced no doubt by the German example, and by the many German officials serving as advisers in the various ministries, with Geheimrat Dr Hahl at the ministry of Commerce and Agriculture. A decree was passed in the summer obliging farmers to work their lands only under state supervision. The goal was to produce more food to feed people rather than the highly profitable cash crops. The state did not forbid these completely, but tried to establish a balance. In return, it supplied the farmer with machines, manure, and met his other needs, including labour. The decree was implemented by a commission chaired by the Minister of Agriculture and by his officials in the provinces; there were severe penalties for non-compliance. The state had no intention of making a profit and would reinvest any surpluses that accrued from these measures for the benefit of the farmer. These reforms were seen by some to have significance far beyond the short run. "By this means

---

38 *Écho de Bulgaria*, 1 March 1917 in War Office, *DRFP*, 17 March 1917. Novichev, *Ekonomika Turtsii*, pp. 19-20 gives similar figures: area under cultivation declined from 64 million *dönüm* in 1913 to 30 million in 1915, and 25 million in 1916. Talât Paşa gave the figure of 40 million *dönüm* in his 1917 Congress speech in Sept. 1917. The increase may be due to a more effective use of forced labour, as well as the reoccupation of Ottoman territories under Russian control.

39 Şevket Süreyya Aydemir, "Toprağın Hikâyesi", *Cumhuriyet*, 29 March 1971.

[commented *Wirtschaftszeitung der Zentralmäche*] one of the greatest drawbacks of Turkish agriculture, 'small farming' as it is called, will be abolished. In Anatolia the land is very much broken up among small owners, hence intensive cultivation is difficult, but it will now be made possible by the nationalization of agriculture and the joint cultivation of the soil."[40]

It is possible to see two basic trends in the land policy of the Young Turks, and specifically that of the Unionists. The first, articulated by intellectuals in the press, emphasized the importance of the small farmer for the empire's future prosperity and survival. The writings of Ahmed Şerif in *Tanin* and Parvus in *Türk Yurdu* circa 1912-13 are representative of this trend. This group wanted to protect the small farmer from the predatory practices of the landlords, and they considered a co-operative movement as a way to guarantee his interests from the usurers, who were often also the landlords. In 1913, the government sent a special commission abroad to study the working of the co-operative system in Rumania, Bulgaria, and Austria-Hungary, which concluded that such a system in the empire would also render a valuable economic service. Such people also wanted the Agricultural Bank to serve the small farmer by providing him with low interest loans, enabling him to stand on his own two feet. Despite their writings, they exercised no discernible influence on their comrades in government who represented the other trend favouring the large landowner, convinced that it was there that the salvation of the empire lay. They were the policy makers and the executives, seemingly unconcerned with the populist ideology propounded by CUP organs. Their aim was to introduce capitalist agriculture into Anatolia as rapidly as possible no matter what the social cost. So once again the 1916 Agriculture Bank law and the decree of 1917 favoured those engaged in mechanized agriculture and agricul-

---

40 6 Oct. 1916 in War Office, *DRFP*, 28 Oct. 1916; see also Gustave Herlt's article in *Weltwirtschaftliches Archiv*, Feb. 1917 in *DRFP*, Economic Survey, i, 27 March 1917.

tural companies with bank credits.[41] The small farmer had to continue to survive as best he could.

This policy was successful in so far as it enabled Turkey to last out the war. Production must have increased substantially even though cultivated acrage declined by a third, if we accept Talât Paşa's figures. *Hilal* reported that production had increased sufficiently to feed the local population and to export great quantities to other regions in need.[42] This must not be understood to mean that everyone was well or even adequately fed; on the contrary the poor in the towns were close to starvation, with occasional bread riots, as by the women of the Fatih district of İstanbul.[43] But high prices had also brought wealth and prosperity to a small class of farmers throughout Anatolia. Dr. Nazım, an important Unionist exaggerated of course when he said that the war had enriched *the population* of Turkey, especially in the region around İzmir. "In nearly all parts of the town one can see traces of our economic revival. The coffee houses which used to line the quayside before the war have made way for shops... The value of money has declined so much that our peasants, who made fortunes through the unwarranted rise in food prices, can pay three liras for a pair of stockings for their daughters."[44] But there is no doubt that a powerful and prosperous agrarian class had indeed emerged, conscious of its interest and capable of fighting for them in the arena of politics. It would show its power during the period of national struggle and the throughout the Republic.

In contrast to the landlord, the position of the peasantry deteriorated throughout the Young Turk period. Not only did successive governments not remove the abuses and burdens the peasants com-

---

41 Atasağun, *Ziraat Bankası*, 202; Tekin Alp, "Ziraat Bankası", *İktisadiyat Mecmuası* I/9-10, 27 April and 5 May 1916.

42 *Hilâl* (n.d.), quoted in *Revue de Turquie* (Lausanne), 4, August 1917, 121.

43 Galip Kemali Söylemezoğlu, *Hariciye Hizmetinde 30 Sene*, 1955, pp. 405, 408-410.

44 *Tanin*, 8 Dec. 1917, pp. 2-3. Despite this prosperity, farmers and tax farmers (tithe collectors) were exempt from the tax on war profits which went into effect on 1 Jan. 1918. See *Hilâl* and *Tanin*, 26 Dec. 1917.

plained of, they added to them. As production became increasingly for the market, – internal and export – the rate of exploitation increased as the farmer kept more of the surplus. Thus Parvus observed even in 1913 that the tithe collected from the peasant was significantly greater than the 'permissible'. Constantly rising land prices, resulting from improved communications and irrigation and therefore profitability, encouraged local notables to expropriate commons or the lands of peasants unable to enforce their claims or rights. For a while peasants benefitted from scarce labour and obtained high wages. But with the outbreak of war they could no longer do so because they were made to provide forced labour.[45]

How did the peasantry respond to this increasing oppression? Their answer was the traditional one: they became outlaws. This is the usual response of peasants whose political horizon is limited and restricted by parochialism, and in our case by ethnic and religious divisions which the notables exploited. For example they manipulated the division between local peasants and Muslim immigrants (refugees) coming from he Balkans. In such circumstances a mass peasant movement was hardly possible and so the peasants became bandits to escape from their oppressive lives. This was especially true after the outbreak of war and Behice Boran writing about the villages in Manisa province, learned that "During the years an age of disorder prevailed in the mountain villages as in the villages of the plains; bandits multiplied." Their ranks were swelled by deserters from the army, and in one case at least they overcame ethnic and religious rivalry by sheltering with Greeks in the Samsun region. The result was that the government decided to deport Greeks as a war measure to better controlled areas.[46] The problem of insecurity in the countryside had

45   Boran, *Toplumsal Yapı*, p. 37; see also p. 32.
46   Elkus to Secretary of State, Constantinople 2 Jan. 1917, in *Foreign Relations of the United States 1917*, Supplement i, pp. 15-16. Novichev, *Ekonomika Turtsii*, pp. 32-4, confirms the Porte's policy of manipulating ethnic and religious differences. He also mentions a pact between Greek and Georgian villagers in the Samsun region. Turkish deserters seeking refuge with Greek bands, a peasant uprising in Feb. 1917 in the Fatsa disttrict which was put down by govern-

become so acute by 1917 that it was one of the reasons for requiring a stronger government than the one headed by Said Halim Paşa. Yet Talât Paşa's policies did nothing to alter the rural situation which continued to get worse. By 1918 the press carried reports of serious outbreaks of brigandage throughout Anatolia, especially in the province of Bursa. Even fairly large provincial towns were insecure and public life was threatened. The government was asked to take prompt action and in July 1918 Talât appointed İsmail Canbulat as his Minister of the Interior, specifically to deal with this problem energetically. But the new minister resigned on 30 September complaining that the government lacked the power to restore order in the countryside. His resignation came in the wake of a second bandit attack on the Bandırma train.[47]

The alienation of the peasantry from the state became a cause of grave concern and the CUP redirected its attention towards the problem. Yusuf Akçura for one considered the peasants "the basic matter of the Turkish nation" as well as the ones who needed and deserved the greatest aid.[48] They were, after all, by far the most numerous groups amongst the Turks and if they were neglected the very existence of the nation would be in doubt. Ideas like these led the CUP to found an association in İzmir to work for the moral and physical improvement of the peasantry. The *Halka Doğru Cemiyeti* would create institutions like librairies and lecture rooms for the education and welfare of the peasants, and a printing press for pamphlets and reasonably priced books.[49] These measures came too late but much of

ment forces, as well as revolts and insurrections. His information, he says, is based on the reports of tsarist secret agents operating in Turkey during the war.

47 Mehmed Cavid, "Meşrutiyet Devrine Ait Cavit Bey'in Hatıraları", *Tanin*, 10 July and 2 Aug. 1945; *Tasvir-i Efkâr* 14 July 1918 and *Tanin* 1-2 July 1918. Throughout July and August 1918 the press reported brigand activity which hampered the harvest as peasants were threatened by marauding bands.

48 Yusuf Akçura, "İktisadi Siyaset Hakkında", *Türk Yurdu*, xii, 1333/1917, p. 3521, quoted by David Thomas, "The Life and Thought of Yusuf Akçura (1876-1935)", unpublished Ph. D., McGill University 1976, p. 149.

49 *Tanin*, 8 and 15 Dec. 1917.

this idealism was carried into the Kemalist movement and its most famous manifestation is Mustafa Kemal's speech describing the peasant as "our master."[50] For a brief moment it seemed as though the Kemalists might carry out the much needed revolution in the countryside but in the end they also adopted the Young Turk policy of reaching a political compromise with the landlords and accepted the status quo in the countryside.

---

50 Text in Kazım Öztürk (ed.), *Cumhurbaşkanlarının T. Büyük Meclisini Açılış Nutukları*, 1969, p. 84-5. The speech was delivered on 1 March 1922.

Unionist Relations With the Greek, Armenian, and Jewish Communities of the Ottoman Empire, 1908-1914*

I n July 1908, all the ethnic and religious communities of the Ottoman Empire greeted the restoration of the Constitution with great enthusiasm. Communal leaders fraternized together and joined in the public demonstrations celebrating the opening of a new era. "At Uskub, Monastir, and Salonica", reported *The Times* (London), "Mussulmans and Christians alike are mingling in the popular rejoicing. At Monastir the Greek Metropolitan harangued the crowd, and afterwards joined with the Musulman Mufti and the Bulgarian priests in mutual embraces..."[1] In Jerusalem, a city held in great reverence by all the religious communities, "a curious mixture of sheikhs, priests, and rabbis delivered speeches denouncing the old regime, and Muslims, Christians, Jews, Samaritans, Turks, and Armenians all fraternized and formed into a procession, preceded by banners with

(*) The author would like to thank the American Research Institute in Turkey for the summer grant (1977) which facilitated research for this paper.

1   *The Times* (London), 27 July 1908 (hereafter cited as *The Times*); Leon Sciaky, *Farewell to Salonica*, New York, 1946, pp. 185-187; P. Risal, *La ville convoitée Salonique*, Paris, 1914, p. 308.

emblems of liberty–the Jews by the Torah covered with gilt embroidery."[2] Beirut, which had been the stage for religious and communal strife only five years previously, staged demonstrations in favor of the Constitution. Muslims and Christians fraternized in the streets and much hope for the future was expressed by all.[3]

The reason for this spontaneous jubilation among the communities is not difficult to discern for it was the principal theme of almost all the public speeches: "For thirty-three years thirty-three million people suffered under the yoke of a cruel sultan and his three hundred lackeys and spies. This cruel régime was overthrown by thirty brave men who raised the flag of liberty. Liberty for everyone; for the Turks and for the Christians. Now we are all brothers; Muslim, Christian, Jew, Turk, Arab, Greek, Bulgarian, we are all citizens of the free Ottoman state."[4]

After the initial outburst of enthusiasm for the constitutional regime, the attitude of the Greek and Armenian leaders was no longer unambiguous; the Jewish community, however, continued to support actively the new regime.

Among the Greeks there were those who hoped to aggrandize the Greek Kingdom at the expense of the Ottoman Empire, and those who hoped to Hellenize it. The former wanted Athens to adopt an aggressive and hostile policy toward the Turks. The latter preferred an alliance between Athens and İstanbul to help preserve the empire which would otherwise be partitioned amongst the Powers and irrevocably lost to Hellenism. To such people "the Young Turks revolution offered a gleam of hope" for if the Young Turks really did try to mod-

---

2 *The Times*, 11 August 1908.
3 *Ibid.*, 14 August 1908; and Lowther to Grey, no. 544 confidential, Therapia 5 September 1908, F.O. 371/546/31555.
4 "Abraam Benaroya'nın Anıları" in George Haupt and Paul Dumont (eds.), *Osmanlı İmparatorluğu'nda Sosyalist Hareketler*, İstanbul, 1977, p. 283. Though Benaroya and others speak of Ottoman brotherhood, that was not one of the promises of the 1908 Revolution. The Unionist slogan was "Liberty *(hürriyet)*, Equality *(müsavat)*, and Justice *(adalet)*", and not "Liberty, Equality, Fraternity"!

ernize the multinational empire, the "[Ottoman] Greek élite would come back into its own, it would run the empire and restore to it many of the characteristics of its Byzantine predecessor. ..."[5] For this reason Dimitrios Rallis, an important Greek politician and statesman was initially enthusiastic about the constitutional regime. After the revolution he visited Salonica and İstanbul "to confer with Greek circles there." But he soon "changed his views: he was all for continuing the Macedonian struggle and even sending bands to Thrace and Asia Minor."[6] Athens's hold over the Ottoman Greeks was overwhelming and they, in turn, identified emotionally and politically with it rather than İstanbul. In their relations with the new regime, their principal concern was to retain the traditional privileges of their community and thus maintain their virtually autonomous existence. The Ottoman Greek community was sufficiently monolithic so that within it nationalism overshadowed class consciousness. In its annual report for 1909-1910, the Socialist Workers' Federation of Salonica noted that after the 1908 revolution "nationalist propaganda amongst the workers suffered a setback within a short time. But this kind of propaganda made gains only amongst the Ottoman Greek workers."[7] Such was he hold of the Orthodox Church and the patriarch over the entire community.

The Armenian community was not monolithic as the Greek and that was reflected in its attitude toward the constitutional régime. It was divided politically between the patriarchate which spoke for the interests of the merchant community of İstanbul and its own tradi-

---

5   Douglas Dakin, *The Unification of Greece 1770-1913*, London, 1972, pp. 176-177. The Unionists were aware that amongst Ottoman Greeks there were two factions: those who wanted the empire to break up so that parts could be annexed by Greece, and those who hope to restore Byzantium, albeit in a new from. They described these factions as *Yunancı* and *Bizanscı*. See Celâl Bayar, *Ben de Yazdım*, İstanbul, 1967, vol. 5, p. 1589 where he quotes from the unpublished memoirs of Eşref Kuşçubaşı.

6   Dakin (cited n. 5), p. 177.

7   See Document 6 in Haupt and Dumont (cited n. 4), pp. 78, 88; and Risal (cited n. 2), pp. 321-322.

tional privileges, and the Dashnak – members of the nationalist Armenian Revolutionary Federation *(Hai Heghapokhakan Dashnaksutiun)*–who represented the aspirations of the rising intelligentsia, the artisans and tradesmen of small-town Anatolia, and the agricultural communities. Unlike the Greeks, the Armenians had no existing state they could identify with. But the growing sense of nationalism among the intelligentsia created a strong desire for autonomy and eventual statehood.

The Ottoman Jewish community, except for the community of Iraq, was predominantly Sefardi. Its ancestors had been the Jews expelled from Spain and Portugal in the late fifteenth and sixteenth centuries, and the community had succeeded in retaining much of its traditional language and culture, though somewhat modified by the new environment. It was totally untouched by political Zionism, the Jewish nationalist movement which began to flourish in Eastern Europe in the last quarter of the nineteenth century. Thus when Zionist propagandist sought support for their movement amongst Ottoman Jews, they found their coreligionist unresponsive. Ottoman Jewry seemed too well integrated to seek a separate destiny. This was due to historical factors. In the nineteenth century as the Ottoman Empire was integrated into the European world system and converted into a semicolony, the Jews – unlike the Greeks and Armenians who actually benefited from it – suffered with the Turks the consequences of that process. For this reason the Jews alone identified with the constitutional movement, and particularly with the Committe of Union and Progress (CUP), for they also stood to gain from Ottoman resurgence and the restoration of complete Ottoman sovereignty.

The initial exuberance of the non-Muslim communities at the fall of Abdülhamid's despotism may be explained by the fact that they assumed that any regime would be an improvement on the old one. If the new regime happened to be liberal and committed to administrative decentralization and private initiative, as promised by Prince

Sabahaddin, so much the better.[8] Kâmil Paşa's grand vezir (August 1908) must have suggested that the liberals, and not the Unionists, were about to come to power. But that was not the case. The CUP emerged as the principal political organization and played the role of guardian of the Constitution. Though it could not assume power directly, it members behaved as though they were the real power behind the throne and they often tried to force the government to implement Unionist policies. Before very long, Greek and Armenian leaders realized that Unionist aspirations were not compatible with their own traditional privileges and long-term interests.

The atmosphere of distrust and confrontation between the two communities and the Unionists arose out of this realization. It must be emphasized, however, that the basis of the antagonism was neither ethnic nor religious; it was rooted in class conflict in so far as the Unionist scheme to transform Ottoman society undermined the position of all privileged classes, regardless of race or religion, and brought the petty bourgeoisie to the helm of affairs. Thus the reactionaries and conservatives, who had been ousted from power, and the upper-class liberal Turks and Muslims, who thought that they ought to inherit it, were as hostile to the Unionists as the Greeks and Armenians. Not surprisingly, all these groups soon reached a tacit understanding against the CUP. But before we discuss the CUP's relations with the three communities, let us briefly examine Unionist aspirations.

The fundamental Unionist aim was to restore full sovereignty to the Ottoman state. Only then would the state be capable of carrying out

---

8   On Prince Sabahaddin pre-1908 ideas concerning decentralizaton and personal initiative see E. E. Ramsaur, *The Young Turks*, Princeton, 1957, passim; and Bernard Lewis, *The Emergence of Modern Turkey*, second edition, London, 1968, pp. 202-204. After he returned to Turkey in September 1908, Sabahaddin revised some of his ideas. The "Prince gave some conferences in which he explained that by decentralization he meant not autonomy of particular geographical areas–e.g., Armenia–but the conferring on the provincial authorities of the existing vilayets of the Empire of wider administrative powers on the lines laid down in Midhat Paşa's Constitution." See Lowther to Grey, no. 621 confidential, Therapia, 28 Sept. 1908, F.O. 371/559/34308.

all its duties and obligations. Without full sovereignty, the empire would remain a semicolony under the hegemony of the Great Powers. They would continue to control its finances through the public debt, maintain the totally dependent character of its economy by regulating its import and export duties, and generally speaking, uphold the *status quo* by their insistence on exercising extra-territorial privileges under the capitulations which made a mockery of Ottoman sovereignty. Thus one of the first acts of the Unionists after the revolution was to attack the capitulations, and that brought them into conflict with the Great Powers.

Non-Muslim communities also enjoyed extensive privileges under the *millet* system, and by the late eighteenth century each community was virtually responsible to its own religious leaders, who acted as intermediaries between the community and the state. As the empire declined, the Great Powers began to adopt the *millet*s as clients, exploiting them to further their own interests in the empire. Thus the Treaty of Küçük Kaynarca of 1774 became the pretext for Russia to establish a protectorate over the Greek *millet*. France claimed a similar right to protect the Catholic subjects of the sultan. By the end of the nineteenth century all the non-Muslim *millet*s, save the Jews, had found a *de facto* protector. The powers sometimes intervened in concert in Ottoman internal affairs so as to prevent one of their number from making unilateral gains. Such was the case during the Greek War of Independence and again during the Eastern Crisis of 1875-1878 which culminated in the Congress of Berlin. At Berlin, Armenian leaders sought Great Power support for reform in the eastern provinces of Anatolia which had the largest concentration of Armenians.[9] Article LXI of the Treaty of Berlin granted that support and thereafter the "Armenian question" was internationalized.

---

9   On the Armenian population, whose details need not concern us here, see S. J. Shaw and E. K. Shaw, *History of the Ottoman Empire and Modern Turkey*, Cambridge, England, 1977, vol. 2, pp. 200-205. The authors conclude that in none of the provinces claimed by Armenian nationalists did they have a majority. Richard Hovannisian, *Armenia on the Road to Independence 1918*, Los Angeles, 1967, pp. 34-37, gives higher figures but agrees with the Shaws' conclusion.

Parallel with this process of Great Power protection of minorities and intervention in Ottoman affairs was the process by which non-Muslims began adopting what amounted to foreign citizenship. Thus Ottoman Greeks tended to become Russian or, after 1830, subjects of Greece, or indeed, subjects of any other power willing to grant protection. Other Christians followed their example, and even some Jews became Italian subjects after 1871. This practice was restricted largely to the commercial community which could then benefit from the capitulations and also serve as an intermediary between the Europeans and Ottoman society. Until January 1869, when the Ottoman citizenship law was introduced, there were good reasons why a merchant might require foreign citizenship for legal and commercial purposes.[10] The 1869 law should have put an end to this practice. But it did not, and non-Muslims continued to adopt foreign citizenship for the privileges it conferred rather than from necessity.

As a result of these nineteenth-century trends, the Turks, of whom the majority were peasants, became the most depressed element in the empire. Except for the minute Turkish ruling class composed of military officers, officials, and land-owners, some of whom now produced for the export market, the vast majority of the Turkish population suffered the consequences of the old regime. This regime lacked the will and the power to regain its sovereignty and assert itself against the encroachments of an aggressive Europe. Unable to increase its revenues by raising customs duties or commercial taxes, the state simply extorted more from the peasantry. The condition of the peasant, wrote Count Ostrorog,

> is very like that of the peasants in seventeenth-century France. ... They also, bending under brazen law, painfully earn the wherewithal to pay taxes and maintain just sufficient strength to pay

---

10 The law is published in George Young, *Corps de droit Ottoman*, Oxford, 1905, vol. 2, pp. 238-240. In fact a *mahmi* (a protected person or protégé) did not actually become a citizen of the protecting power. But the Ottoman authorities had to treat him as though he were. I owe this observation to Professor Sina Akşin of Ankara University.

them. If they fail, then Constantinople is hard pressed for money, the tax gatherers dun them mercilessly, and beat them if need be, like tired horses whom pain alone can goad to climb the steep hill. And if, even then, they cannot pay, their poor property is distrained and everything sold save that which is necessary for the accomplishment of their primary function of tax paying. For they have a secondary function: that of providing fodder for cannon. ... They are weighed down by the heavy burden of almost perpetual obligatory military service.[11]

The condition of the urban petty bourgeoisie, composed of minor officials, school teachers, artisans, and tradesmen, was only a little better than that of the peasants. This class, being more politically conscious than the peasantry, realized the need for a strong sovereign state to deal with all existing problems. They therefore supported the CUP which, after 1908, began to rectify the situation by attacking the privileges of both the foreigners and their non-Muslim clients. The Unionists were convinced that only the end of privilege would enable Muslims to compete on equal terms with their rivals. In their opinion, the *Tanzimat* reforms and the Constitution had already created *de jure* equality. But foreign protection and traditional communal privilege created *de facto* inequality and that had to be changed by the implementation of the laws.

The question of equality had both psychological and socioeconomic dimensions for the minorities. They had always lived outside the mainstream of Ottoman society, isolated and secure within their own communities. Now they were being asked to be Ottomans, sharing the same rights and obligations as all other citizens. For obvious reasons the minorities resisted this policy; as the British ambassador observed "equal rights for all Ottoman subjects–a basis which inspired the Greeks and other national entities within the Empire with a certain

---

11 Count Leon Ostrorog, *The Turkish Problem*, London, 1919, pp. 95-96. That the state exacted more from the peasant during tis period is shown by Shaw and Shaw (cited n. 9), p. 233. Tithes increased from 425.7 million kuruş (1877-1878) to 609.5 million kuruş (1908-1909) while grain export went up from 465 million kuruş (1877-1878) to 753.9 million (1907-1908).

uneasiness, as, by implication, it threatened their old established privileges."[12]

THE UNIONISTS AND THE OTTOMAN GREEK COMMUNITY

In 1908 the Ottoman Greek population was about 2,900,000, of whom about 1,800,000 lived in Anatolia (175,000 in İstanbul) and the rest in Thrace and Macedonia.[13] Ostrorog, who drew vivid sketches of various communities, wrote:

> The Greek is almost as much a townsman as a mariner, banker, trader, lawyer, doctor, he competes with and frequently surpasses the Armenian. At Constantinople the only great native bankers are Greek. Finally, owing to their inclination and gift for the retail sale of spirits and colonial [imported] products, well-neigh every grocer (or *bakkal*) in the Ottoman Empire is a Greek.[14]

Sussnitzki, who gave a more detailed account of the ethnic division of labor, observed that almot every aspect of the economy was dominated by the minorities, especially the Greeks and the Armenians. Yet the Turkish role was not as insignificant as one is often led to believe. The Greeks monopolized coastal trade, and if they engaged in agriculture as in western Anatolia it was to raise cash crops for the local and export markets. Trade and commerce were generally controlled by the two Christian communities to the extent that they were able to establish virtual monopolies, "the Greeks in western Asia Minor and the Armenians in the eastern." Sussnitzki furnishes various reasons for this state of affairs but as a "final cause" puts forward "the protection they enjoyed from foreign powers, whose subjects they

---

12 Lowther to Grey (cited n. 8).
13 Dimitri Pentzopoulos, *The Balkan Exchange of Minorities and its Impact upon Greece*, Thessaloniki, 1962, pp. 29-31; Shaw and Shaw (cited n. 9), pp. 241-242.
14 Ostrorog (cited n. 11), pp. 12-14. See the occupational makeup of İstanbul's population in 1886 in Shaw and Shaw (cited n. 9), p. 244.

sometimes were, thus becoming, thanks to the former Capitulations, exempt from taxation."[15]

The CUP's attitude towards the Greek community, however, was not based on the latter's economic standing in the empire. Initially the Unionists were Ottoman patriots rather than Turkish nationalists; their main concern was to make Ottomanism viable by including rather than excluding the non-Turkish elements. The success of this principle depended on the positive responses of the communities and Greek cooperation would have been of great significance. But the Greek response was negative, and the reason is not difficult to find.

Despite the citizenship law of 1869 there was no attempt to dissolve the *millet* system and create an Ottoman identity. The Greeks continued to live as in the past "organized in separate legal communities of an autonomous nature, discharged all their communal functions themselves, worshipped freely and supported their churches and schools which had kept alive through centuries the national sentiment. ... In this way, the Christian population did not assimilate with Moslem society and, more important, kept its national consciousness."[16] Moreover, the Greeks saw themselves as the people from whom the sultans had seized the empire in earlier times, and now as the empire declined they believed they were the rightful successors, the heirs of Byzantium. This tendency had found encouragement following the creation of the Greek state and the developments of the nineteenth century. Ottoman Greeks were loyal either to Athens or a resurgent Byzantium, two sides of the same coin. Ottoman, and later Turkish, revival was seen as the greatest threat to such aspirations and therefore to be prevented at all cost.

The Unionist-Greek relationship was further complicated by Russia's traditional use of the Greek community to pursue her politi-

---

15 For A. J. Sussnitzki's article published in 1917 see Charles Issawi (ed.), *The Economic History of the Middle East 1800-1914*, Chicago, 1966, pp. 120-121.

16 Pentzopoulos (cited n. 13), p. 33; see also Roderic Davison, *Reform in the Ottoman Empire 1856-1876*, Princeton, 1963, pp. 114-135.

cal and economic goals in the empire. This process was legitimized by the Treaty of 1774 but became effective only after the Russo-Turkish war of 1877-1878 which enabled Russia to use the Turkish war indemnity for poltical and economic ends.[17] By this period a "significant number of residents of the Ottoman Empire held patents conferring Russian citizenship upon them" and some Greek merchants even enjoyed diplomatic status as consular officials. "The [Russian] vice consuls at Bursa and Tekirdağ (Rodosto) were both Greeks. The former had interests in mining and commerce. The latter owned a *çiftlik* (estate) at Lüleburgaz. The consular agents at Aydın and Rethyennon (Crete) were also Greeks. One owned a *çiftlik* and the other was engaged in commerce."[18]

Despite these negative factors, the Unionists were optimistic that representative government would soon remove all elements of disunity and fuse the various communities into a pluralistic Ottoman nation. The Constitution had already bestowed equal rights and obligations. The new Assembly, soon to be elected, was expected to provide unity and cooperation amongst the different ethnic and religious groups. But events soon proved Unionist hopes to be both sanguine and naive.

The Greek Patriarch, Yuvakim (Joāchim Efendi) clearly perceived the threat posed by the new regime to the privileges of his community. He attempted to meet this threat by issuing a proclamation urging the Ottoman government to make concessions that would undercut the program of Ottomanism. He urged the Porte to: guarantee the freedom of person and conscience and accept the traditionally acquired rights of the *millet*s as fundamental principles; confirm ecclesiastical and educational privileges; restore completely the privileges accorded to the Ecumenical Patriarchate and the Greek community *(millet-i Rûm)*

---

17 Michael Milgrim, "The War Indemnity and Russian Commercial Investment Policy in the Ottoman Empire: 1878-1914" in Osman Okyar (ed.), *Türkiye İktisat Tarihi Semineri*, Ankara, 1975, p. 298.

18 *Ibid.*, p. 356, and *passim*.

in the past, as well as privileges that had been violated; permit the various communities of the empire to develop on the basis of their religion, beliefs, traditions, and characteristics; implement a system of military recruitment in which units would be formed on the basis of religious affiliation and be used in the district of recruitment; and enlarge and make independent of İstanbul all existing local councils.[19]

If the Unionists were disappointed by the Patriarch's proclamation they did not express their disappointment publicly. Instead, they sent Fazlı [Tung] to see Yuvakim Efendi to assure him that the CUP did not intend to curtail in any way the special rights and privileges heretofore enjoyed by the patriarchate.[20] The choice of Fazlı Bey was significant since he was a member of Sabahaddin's decentralist group and not a Unionist, and therefore more likely to seem convincing to the Patriarch. Some days later Sabahaddin himself visited Yuvakim Efendi and "reassured him as to the maintenance of the privileges conferred by Mahmut [sic] the Conqueror on the Greek Patriarchate."[21]

However, by September 1908 the Patriarch was more concerned with the outcome of the general election than with Turkish assurances. The advantage seemed to lie with the non-Muslim communities with their long tradition of communal elections. They were already well organized and could therefore expect to elect candidates for out of proportion to the size of their population merely through the process of mobilization and voter turnout. The Turks and Muslims, on the other hand, were totally divided and lacked any such organization or voting tradition. The Unionists attempted to make up this shortcoming by hurriedly founding chapters throughout the empire and by reaching an under-standing with local forces that controlled the votes.

---

19 *Tanin*, 27 and 28 August 1908. *The Times* 528 August 1908) observed that the third demand implied the suppression of the Bulgarian Exarchate as well as Rumanian religious communities which had been Orthodox in the past.

20 *Tanin*, 29 and 30 Augst 1908; see also Lowther to Grey, no. 535 confidential, Therapia 1 Sept. 1908 F.O. 371/546/30971.

21 Lowther to Grey (cited n. 8).

At the polls the patriarch learned that large numbers of his flock were not allowed to vote as they could not establish their Ottoman citizenship. Many were in fact foreign subjects, though the majority had never registered as citizens, or applied for a *tezkere* (identity paper) so as to evade taxation.[22] For the Greeks, these explanations were only a thin disguise for what they denounced as fraud and foul play in the elections, designed to keep down their representation in the Assembly.

There is no doubt that there were irregularities during the elections; it would be surprising had there not been in such an unstable and immature political environment. Initially, only the Greeks felt aggrieved and the patriarch complained to the authorities. Receiving no satisfaction, he decided to complain directly to grand vezir Kâmil Paşa. He obtained no satisfaction there either for Kâmil declared that he saw no evidence of fraud or foul play and that Greek claims must be based on false information. Thereupon Yuvakim Efendi threatened to boycott the elections and to resign unless the Porte took measures to rectify the injustices.[23]

The atmosphere in İstanbul was tense. The Unionists therefore decided to mediate and break the deadlock between the Porte and the patriarch. On 23 October a deputation of two Turks and a Greek visited Yuvakim Efendi and offered him representation in the Assembly proportional to his community's population. The offer was accepted and the Patriarch appointed two representatives to work out the details with the CUP. Responding to public speculation, the Committee denied any connection between its initiative and the deadlock between Kâmil and the Patriarch. Its sole purpose in holding these meetings was to bring about union and harmony between the

---

22 *İkdam*, 4, 5 and 6 November 1908; D. Dakin, *The Greek Struggle in Macedonia 1897-1913*, Salonica, 1966, p. 391, n. 47. Abraham Galanté, *Turcs et Juifs*, İstanbul, 1932, p. 116, writes concerning the activities of an Ottoman official: "Lors des fonctions à Salonique, Joseph Krieger it renter à la sujétion ottomane onze mille Grecs et à Rhôdes ... plus de mille Grecs, qui se reclamaient de sujétion hellène."

23 *Stamboul*, 23 and 24 October 1908.

communities and to assure them all fair and proportional representation in the Assembly.[24]

The Patriarch began to have second thoughts about negotiating with the CUP. The Committee was, after all, only a political body and by dealing with it he was adding to its prestige while undermining his own. He ought to have been dealing with the Porte on a "government to government" level as he had traditionally done instead of coming down to the level of a political party.

At the beginning of November, when discussions with the CUP ran into difficulties, the Patriarch again approached the government. But this time he was received not by the grand vezir but the minister of the interior, İbrahim Hakkı Bey. Yuvakim Efendi repeated his grievances and accused the government of discriminating against his community in the election. To the specific question of the eligibility of the Greek peasants in Epirus, the minister replied that as they were not Ottoman citizens they would not be permitted to vote. However, there would be Greek deputies representing that region. Meanwhile, the government would do its best to correct any injustices that may have taken place.[25]

A few days later, Greek and Armenian leaders agreed to present a common front in the İstanbul election. Their first joint venture was a delegation that went to the Porte to present a list of grievances. The two communities complained that they were not receiving representation appropriate to their numbers, the Greeks claming forty deputies and the Armenians twenty.[26] Hakkı Bey defended the government and said that thus far elections had been conducted in a manner more honest than those in many other states with longer-established constitutional traditions. He accused the delegation of inflating the claims of

---

24 *Tanin*, 24-26 October 1908.

25 *Tanin*, 4 November 1908.

26 *Stamboul*, 11 November 1908. In fact the Greeks had twenty-six and the Armenians fourteen deputies in the 1908 Assembly. See F. Ahmad and D. A. Rustow, "İkinci Meşrutiyet Döneminde Meclisler 1908-1918" in *Güney-Doğu Avrupa Araştırmaları Dergisi*, 4-5 (1976), p. 247.

the two communities totally out of proportion to their populations, and assured them that the authorities had made every effort to respect the rights of the minorities. He concluded the interview by expressing sorrow at the fact that a sense of Ottomanism had not yet replaced the communal identity.[27]

The elections continued to generate controversy, especially in İstanbul where voters were asked to produce identity papers before they could vote. On 21 November the Greeks of Pera protested against this measure and the next day, led by their notables, they demonstrated outside the Sublime Porte. After hearing their griev-ances, Kâmil Paşa pointed out that only the Greek community kept complaining of electoral irregularities. If there were in fact complaints, he asked that they be brought before the Assembly, which could then decide whether or not to invalidate particular elections. The grand vezir's statement appeared to satisfy the notables. But the large crowd of demonstrators became unruly and had to be dispersed by the cav-alry, almost turning the occasion into a riot.[28] Thereafter, the elections were conducted more or less without incident and the new Assembly opened its proceedings on 17 December.

Thus far, the Unionists's relations with the Patriarch could hardly be judged a success. They had failed to persuade him to sup-port the election of Greek deputies like Orfanides Efendi, one of the very few Unionist Greeks, who believed in Ottomanism. On the whole, Greek deputies in the Assembly were pan-Hellenists and their contempt for Ottomanism may be illustrated by Boşo (Boussios) Efendi's remark "I am as Ottoman as the Ottoman Bank!"[29] Few were quite as blunt, but almost all shared this sentiment.

The reasons for the Greek attitude are not far to seek. Unlike the Armenian (and Bulgarian) community whose divisions found

---

27 *Stamboul*, 11 November 1908.

28 *Ibid.*, 22-24 November 1908; Hüseyin Cahit Yalçın, *Siyasal Anılar*, Ankara, 1976, p. 52.

29 The remark may be apocryphal but it catches the spirit of the time; and it is widely quoted. See H. C. Yalçın, "On Yılın Hikâyesi", *Yedi Gün*, vol. 7, no. 176 (July 1936), p. 22.

expression in political parties, the Greek community was politically monolithic, accepting without question the absolute authority of the Orthodox Church and the Patriarch. Even the Greek proletariat and its trade unions accepted the Church's political supremacy, refusing to work within the broad Ottoman socialist movement that emerged in 1908. Implicit in the attitude of the Greek community was its total identification with Athens where the twin flames of irredentism and the *Megali Idea* burned strongly and for whom the Ottoman community was composed of "unredeemed Greeks." That remained true until the "Anatolian adventure" of 1919-1922, and ended only with the exchange of populations.

One of the most important factors that helps to explain the relationship between the Unionists and the patriarchate was the latter's informal electoral alliance with the Ottoman Liberals. Initially the Liberals collaborated with the CUP but they soon learned that they would not be able to dominate their partners. Therefore, in September 1908 they formed a political party, the Liberal Union *(Osmanlı Ahrar Fırkası)*, to oppose the CUP. In contrast to "union and progress" the Liberals proposed "administrative decentralization and personal initiative", and in general espoused the ideas of Prince Sabahaddin, their unofficial, spiritual leader. This program appealed to the Greeks and some Armenian groups, as did the proposal for an economic system that would guarantee the *status quo*, and they supported the party enthusiastically.

On 11 November a Liberal delegation visited the Patriarch to discuss the possibility of cooperation in the election. Yuvakim Efendi agreed to the proposal in principle. But after consulting his notables, he declared that his position obliged him to remain above politics and he therefore could not agree to open cooperation with a political party. However, he continued, he saw no reason why Greek and Liberal deputies should not support each other in the Assembly.[30] The

---

30 *Stamboul*, 12-14 November 1908.

two sides did support each other's electoral lists though that did not help Liberal candidates, not one of whom was elected in İstanbul. In the Assembly the Liberal Union attracted all the anti-Unionist elements, the Muslim Arabs and Albanians as well as the non-Muslim groups. The Greeks in particular supported the Liberals and that marked the end of any further contacts between the Committee and the Patriarchate.

After their abysmal electoral performance against the Unionists, the Liberals, led by Kâmil Paşa, decided to eliminate the Committee's political strength by establishing control over the armed forces where they thought the CUP had its basis of power. In February 1909 Kâmil appointed his nominees as ministers of war and marine. But the Unionists challenged the constitutionality of his appointments in the Assembly and brought about his fall by a vote of no confidence. Kâmil's fall was a severe blow to the Liberals and their supporters and they resolved to destroy the CUP even by the use of extra-legal methods.

In the reactionary anti-Unionist campaign which followed in the wake of Kâmil's fall and culminated in the abortive counterrevolution of 13 April 1909, the Greek press of İstanbul played a prominent role. On 25 March, grand vezir Hilmi Paşa brought this matter before the Assembly. He appealed for a press law that would not allow divisive and subvertsive journalism which poisoned relations between the different ethnic and religious groups. He singled out for mention an article in *Neologos* which he claimed was particularly irresponsible. In the debate that followed Hilmi's statement the activities of *Prodos* were also discussed and criticised. The proposed press law failed to pass because of the anti-Unionist opposition in the Chamber.[31] As a result the Liberal and reactionary press continued its

---

31 *Tanin*, 26 March 1909; enclose of Hilmi Paşa's memorandum in Lowther to Grey, no. 223 confidential, Pera 30 March 1909, F. O. 371/761/12788. On the hostility of the İstanbul Greek press towards *Tanin*, and therefore toward the CUP, see Yalçın (cited n. 28), pp. 52-53.

activities unrestrained until it came into its own during the counter-revolution.

The true character of the "reactionary movement" was soon revealed by the attitude of the Greek press toward it. An outbreak of "Muslim fanaticism" should have struck terror in the hearts of the non-Muslim minorities. This time, however, they had no cause for alarm for the "fanatics" were carefully seeking out the "godless Unionists", and not harming the more Westernized and therefore "more godless Liberals" let alone "infidel" Christians and Europeans. Thee Greek press was full of praise for the anti-Unionists and *Neologos*, in particular, congratulated the rebellious soldiers for the role they had played: "The Army has gained the great prize for patriotism, and April 13, 1909 ought to be henceforth marked with no less splendor than July 24, 1908. The Army was inspired yesterday by its love for the country and by no other sentiment."[32]

Until the counterrevolution the Unionists tried to accomplish their goal of Ottomanism by negotiating with the minorities. The bankruptcy of that method led them to try and achieve it through the Assembly. Therefore, in June 1909 they began to introduce legislation whose aim was to curb the political and cultural autonomy of the minorities, and to give control of these activities–for example, education–to the state, which would then set about creating a common Ottoman culture through the schools.

This policy is sometimes described as "Ottomanization", yet that term does not have the same meaning as "Germanization" or "Magyarization" had for the Slavs in the Austro-Hungarian Empire. Ottoman was a dynastic designation and as such lacked national overtones. In a sense the small upper crust amongst the minorities that served the state had already been "Ottomanized". But that was

---

32 Quoted in Feroz Ahmad, *Young Turks*, Oxford, 1969, p. 43; the text of the *Neologos* article republished in *İkdam*, 15 April 1909, is given in İsmail Hami Danişmend, *31 Mart Vakası*, İstanbul, 1961, pp. 210-221. The most detailed account of the counterrevolution is Sina Akşin, *31 Mart Olayı*, İstanbul, 1970.

accomplished without violating the religious or ethnic identity of the subject. The Unionists wanted to extend this process on a broader scale so as to embrace all subjects of the empire.

As this policy required the teaching of Ottoman Turkish *(Osmanlıca)*–strictly speaking, the language of the Ottomans and not of the Turks, certainly not the peasants–as well as a common history designed to encourage unity rather than particularism, it is also described by its critics as Turcification. Yet in 1909 it was too early to talk of a general awareness of Turkishness even amongst Unionists; such a tendency would become noticeable only around the time of the Balkan Wars. Hüseyin Cahit Yalçın makes the point that the new regime stifled Turkism in order to promote Ottomanism. "The word 'Ottoman' had never been valued so highly as it was after the Constitution, not even during the period of repression [i.e., under Abdülhamid]. ... As soon as the Constitution was restored events forced us to forget that we were Turks. The only word we used was 'Ottoman'."[33] Yet even Unionist implementation of Ottomanism was half-hearted. They wanted to introduce the Ottoman-Arabic script in Albania. But confronted with opposition and rebellion they abandoned this scheme and allowed the Latin script to prevail.[34] After the Balkan Wars the Unionists began to compromise even on the principle of centralization.

The language question was never the crux of the problem though it was certainly exploited as such by the minorities. So far as the school-going population of the minorities was concerned, it read and wrote better Ottoman Turkish than the majority of its Muslim counterpart. That was simply because Christian schools, except for the elite state schools and the newly founded Unionist *Terakki* schools, were far superior to the average Turkish school.

---

33 Yalçın (cited n. 28), p. 39.
34 Stavro Skendi, *The Albanian National Awakening 1878-1912*, Princeton, 1967, 389-390 and *passim*.

Ahmed Şerif, who described the state of Anatolia in this period, was confronted with this fact time and again. For example, in December 1909 he visited two schools in Nallıhan, a small town in Ankara province. The Turkish school consisted of "a tiny, damp, smelly classroom into which twenty pupils belonging to three different levels were crammed together." The teacher was as

old and decrepit as the school itself. ... If you had been with me [he laments to his reader] you would have seen how helpless the children were when the *kaymakam* tested them; you would have wept with me. Some pupils did not even have books. ... Not one understood what he read for he only learned by rote. ... In contrast to the terrible situation of the schools I have described today, the picture we see from comparing them with Armenian schools should provide a model for action and an encouraging shot-in-the-arm *(darbe)*.

I went to a school belonging to our esteemed Armenian citizens in the company of our *kaymakam*. In a long classroom there were fifty pupils. A kind and polite headmaster received us. He told us about the organization and education in his school. His bearing and manner suggested tat he was proud of his living products, namely his pupils. The *kaymakam* asked for four or five young gentlemen and tested them on a variety of subjects like geography, arithmetic, Turkish and Arabic grammar, and the boys gave good answers to all the questions. ...

The truth is that the pupils in this school have a much better education and training than the pupils in other [Turkish] schools, and are even more advanced in their knowledge of Turkish grammar as well as reading and writing.[35]

If Ahmed Şerif had any misgivings about such schools, it was that "the children of this country *[Vatan]* do not learn the names of continents and countries in geography, and certain arithmetical terms

---

35 Ahmed Şerif, *Anadolu'da Tanin*, İstanbul 1325/1909, pp. 137-139; pp. 120-122 in new modern Turkish edition, edited by Çetin Börekçi, Ankara, 1977, hereafter cited as Şerif, 1977. In the Assembly on 3 July 1909, Hasbi Efendi's remarks that Greek schools were superior to Turkish ones drew protests from the ranks of clerical deputies.

in Turkish. I do not find that right because these respected citizens of ours know Turkish as well as we do. If they use Turkish in their classes [to teach other subjects] I believe it will be easier and more profitable."[36]

Throughout his reports, Ahmed Şerif constantly repeats the Unionist conviction that the only formula for union and progress was a common education for all Ottomans. The CUP proposed to do that by passing laws making the minister of education responsible for supervising the curricula of all the schools in the empire. Non-Muslim fears concerning their right to provide spiritual guidance to school children were to be met by including in the law "the guarantee of religious instruction *ab antiquo*." When the new law came before the Assembly on 8 June 1909, the non-Muslim deputies–Greeks, Armenians and Slavs, but not Jews–asked that it be amended to read "the systems of education *ab antiquo* shall be maintained."

The debate that followed showed the wide gulf between the ideas of the Unionists and the non-Muslims. Kozmidi Efendi, Greek deputy for İstanbul, pointed out that each communal school taught subjects peculiar to its community and asked whether Greek students would be forbidden to read Aristotle and Plato under the new law. He asked whether the study of national literature–meaning Greek literature!–would be forbidden, for as the law stood the minister had the right to do so. He agreed that education did tend to unite the country but maintained that each community should be allowed its own program of education. He ended by asking if the law would in fact permit the maintenance of Greek and Armenian schools. Kozmidi's line of argument was supported by Yorgi Huneyos (Salonica), Pançedoref (Monastir), Krikor Zohrab (İstanbul), and Boşo Efendi (Serfice), but only the latter raised the question of traditional and time-honored privileges of the *millet*s that were being threatened by the new law.

---

36 Şerif (cited n. 35), p. 140; Şerif, 1977 (cited n. 35), p. 111.

The question of communal privilege was the fundamental issue in this and other debates, and Cavid Bey (Salonica), who spoke for the CUP, took up the challenge. All the speakers before him, except Boşo Efendi, he said, had not spoken openly and had carefully avoided raising the question of "privileges." He personally failed to understand, now that equality had been established, how people still found it possible to speak of privileges other than those of a purely religious kind. ("It is a matter of national survival", heckled Kozmidi and Zohrab Efendi.) If the inviolability of the educational system were established, how, asked Cavid, would the Ministry of Education be able to make any future observations on the state of affairs contrary to Ottoman unity? In his opinion, the desire to maintain the old system based on communal privileges proved that "Ottoman unity exists only in your words and not in your hearts." He concluded by saying that while primary education would be free in all communities, "we [the state] must have control over the ideas which pervade the schools otherwise it is impossible to have a constitution and Ottoman unity."[37]

Mustafa Rahmi (Unionist deputy for Salonica) responded to the question whether the government intended to prohibit the study of classical Greek literature. He said that that was not the government's intention, and furthermore, classical Greek literature was not the exclusive property of the Greeks but belonged to all humanity.[38] He could have added that the Assembly was privileged to have in its midst Süleyman Bustani (Beirut), the translator of the *Iliad* into Arabic. Finally, Talât Bey (Edirne) said that he failed to understand how, at a time when the Capitulations were about to be abolished, educational privileges could be retained. Soon afterward the minorities' amendment was put to the vote and defeated.

---

37 The account of the debate is from the İstanbul press, 9 June 1909; see also Yalçın (cited n. 28), p. 145 where he quotes an article he wrote in *Tanin*, 13 June 1909. A brief account of these discussions may be read in Lowther to Grey, no. 624, Therapia, 4 August 1909, F.O. 371/761/29787.

38 İstanbul press, 9 June 1909.

The non-Muslims, especially the Greeks, also raised problems about the implementation of the Military Service Law which provided for the conscription of all Ottoman subjects, regardless of race or religion. They welcomed the law in principle but they neither wanted to serve nor pay the military exemption tax. The Patriarch, for example, "insisted on separate companies and barracks for the Christian recruits and safeguards against 'conversion' to Islam."[39] The Unionists, while providing the option to serve in the army, would have preferred the non-Muslims to continue paying the exemption tax for it raised an estimated TL 120,000 *per annum* for the treasury. Moreover, integrating non-Muslims into the armed forces was bound to create problems, especially if the Patriarch's demands were met. Thus the law was passed and the constitutional requirements of equality fulfilled. But the *de facto* situation continued to permit non-Muslims (and Muslims) to buy their way out though many non-Muslims did enroll in the Ottoman army during this period. Finally, on 15 February 1915 the Assembly officially restored the tax on exemption of military service, thus restoring the *status quo ante*.[40]

The debate on the Law of Associations was as controversial as the one on education. The government wanted to place all associations under its supervision and to proscribe political ones whose basis was ethnic, national, or religious. The Unionists claimed that such political bodies encouraged separatism and undermined the unity of the empire. The aim of the law was to prevent that, and its intention was not to subvert the cultural pluralism of Ottoman society. The law would therefore be no obstacle to the formation of cultural and literary societies.

---

39 Dakin (cited n. 22), p. 414, n. 24; Assembly discussions may be followed in the İstanbul press, 10, 16, 21, and 26 June, and 26 June, and 1, 3, and 5 July 1909. The law was finally passed in August. See *Takvim-i Vekayi* 11 August 1909. For the implementation of the law see Annual Report 1910 in Lowther to Grey, no. 103 confidential, Constantinople 14 February 1911, F.O. 371/1245/6167.

40 *The Orient*, vol. 6, no. 9, 3 March 1915, p. 62.

Non-Muslim deputies were not satisfied by such explanations. Vartakes Efendi (Armenian depty for Erzurum) claimed that the object of the law was nothing less than an imposed Ottoman union which could only be obtained, he suggested, by a policy of justice. He warned the government that if the law passed, it would provoke great discontent in certain communities and be an incitement to rebellion. Pançedoref defended the right of all communities to develop separately, each contributing to the general progress of Ottoman state and society according to its own genius. The Turks and Bulgarians, he said, were agricultural, the Greeks and Armenians, commercial peoples. The combination of these different elements constituted the strength of the Ottoman nation. Karolidi Efendi (İzmir) also spoke against the law because, he said, its effect would be contrary to that desired by the government. He concluded with the remarks: "I cannot be a good Ottoman without being a good Greek, I cannot love the Muslims without being a good Christian. We have the 'Great Idea' because we are the descendents of a great people."[41] But it was Haristo Dalçef (Serez) who remarked "that union of different elements would not be brought about by the passing of laws, but by community of interests."[42] That was precisely what was lacking amongst the peoples of the Ottoman Empire.

The interests of the communities were in fundamental conflict, and the Greeks and Armenians had much to lose if the Unionists successfully applied what Sir Gerard so aptly described as "the 'levelling' policy of the Turkish Government."[43] That is what would happen if certain communities were deprived of their privileges, thus losing their advantage over the Turkish petty bourgeoisie, the class whose aspirations the Unionists represented.

---

41 İstanbul press, 20 and 21 July 1909. Karolidi Efendi had been professor of history at Athens University and was the author of the article "Turkey" in the 11th edition of *Encyclopedia Britannica*. After his election, his Ottoman citizenship was questioned in the Assembly.
42 Ahmad (cited n. 32), p. 62.
43 Lowther to Grey, no. 611 confidential, Therapia 29 August 1910, F.O. 371/998/32221.

Moreover, the Unionists deeply resented the division of labor Pançedoref had described in which the vast majority of the Turkish population was made up of a backward and exploited peasantry, while the bulk of the urban population was composed of lower rank officials and soldiers serving a bankrupt state, and tradesmen and artisans who were incapable of competing against the protected minorities and Levantines. They resented the Greco-Armenian economic domination established, they thought, by unfair methods, and the refusal of these communities to participate in Ottoman regeneration. The Unionists were determined to raise the level of their own social class even at the expense of the minorities and the Ottoman ruling class. They would have preferred the collaboration of these groups but counter-revolution had proved that such hopes were a pipe dream.

In late 1909 the Porte began to implement the new laws, particularly the Law for the Prevention of Brigandage and Sedition and the Associations Law. It wanted to disarm the non-Muslim population in Macedonia and close down the political clubs. This brought it into conflict with Greek and Bulgarian bands which soon began to cooperate against the forces of İstanbul. This law and order policy was initiated, not by the CUP, but by Mahmut Şevket Paşa and the generals who assumed power after the counterrevolution. The Unionists understood band warfare too well and knew that such a war was impossible to win.

While they half-heartedly supported repression in Macedonia, the Unionists were more actively engaged in a general boycott of Greek commerce aimed at punishing Athens for supporting the Cretan declaration of *enosis*. But the aim of the boycott was also to raise political and national consciousness amongst the Turks. In time, this factor became more important than the original aim, for the Committee became aware of the need for a "national economy" and a Turkish bourgeoisie.

However, neither the boycott nor anti-Greek militancy proved effective. The boycott did not catch the imagination of the masses as

Crete was too far removed from their consciousness. Therefore, by the second half of 1910 the CUP became more moderate and conciliatory. In its proclamation on the second anniversary of the revolution, the Committee confessed that it had shown excessive zeal during the first two years to bring about a speedy union. It now hoped that the communities would themselves work for gradual unity. As for the flagging boycott, the proclamation noted that "Our people's spirit of moderation is a sign of very great affection; from the moment Greece's interference in Crete seemed to be ending they made the boycott less severe."[44]

In İstanbul, the Liberal opposition, supported by the non-Turkish elements, again began to challenge the CUP. It formed, in November 1911, the *Entente Libérale (Hürriyet ve İtilâf Fırkası)* an anti-Unionist coalition in which Turkish liberals and conservatives, Arabs, Albanians, Greeks and Armenians harnessed their energies in order to defeat the CUP. The party's program appeased the minorities by promising to respect all the privileges that had been granted to them by Imperial *irade*s, *ferman*s, and *berat*s. But Greek support for the Liberals was half-hearted, suggesting a desire to retain freedom of action. Initially they agreed to disband their political clubs and merge with the Liberal party. But that never materialized, and Greek members were never appointed to the central committee though, writes Dr. Rıza Nur, "they continued to help us in our work."[45]

Just prior to the founding of the *Entente Libérale*, the government made important concessions to the Christian communities. The privileges of the religious heads were officially recognized once again and the situation was restored virtually to what it had been in 1908.[46] The Unionists seemed to be back on square one.

---

44 *Tanin*, 27 July 1910; see also Dakin (cited n. 5), p. 178.
45 Rıza Nur, "Hürriyet ve İtilâf Nasıl Doğdu, Nasıl Öldü", in *Cumhuriyet*, 23 October 1946; and Tarık Z. Tunaya, *Türkiye'de Siyasî Partiler 1859-1952*, İstanbul, 1952, pp. 315-344, who gives the founding members.
46 Y. H. Bayur, *Türk İnkılâbı Tarihi*, İstanbul, 1943, vol. 2, part 1, pp. 245-247, where the author quotes from cabinet minutes. No doubt war with Italy forced the Porte to be conciliatory toward the minorities.

During the course of the Turco-Italian war which broke out in September 1911, Italian forces occupied a number of Aegean islands and encouraged pan-Hellenism amongst the Greek inhabitants. When it became clear that the great powers would not insist on the restoration of these islands to Ottoman sovereignty, Athens put forward her claim to them and carried out propaganda in favor of union with Greece. The support for union was quite general among Ottoman Greeks on the islands, but not all were in favor of it. Describing the situation on Castellorizo, Vice-Consul Biliotti wrote:

> Two parties have arisen in the island. One, consisting of the wealthier inhabitants, who have important interests on the [Anatolian] mainland, do not wish any change in their present situation, the other consisting of the very low class, who have nothing to lose and aspire to annexation to Greece. It is said that a great number of the former, fearing the presence of the insurgents [who wanted union], have fled to the mainland.[47]

Was that the prevailing pattern of political attitudes among Ottoman Greeks?

As the Unionists prepared for an early election in the spring of 1912, they too became more accommodating toward the minorities. Hacı Adil's mission to Macedonia in February was designed primarily to placate the Greeks, Bulgarians and Albanians. The CUP still hoped to elect an Assembly with which it could work in harmony. Moreover, intercommunal warfare in Macedonia had assumed such proportions that there was fear of Great Power intervention to restore peace, an eventuality the Unionists desperately wanted to avoid. Hacı Adil's mission was the last attempt to find a peaceful solution. He remained in Macedonia for three and a half months but failed to win over the militant minority organizations.

However, in İstanbul there seems to have been no attempt by

---

47 Vice-Counsul Sir A. Biliotti to Consul-General Barnham, Rhodes, 17 March 1913, in Bilal N. Şimşir, *Ege Sorunu*, İstanbul, 1976, vol. 1, pp. 566-567.

the Unionists to reach an electoral agreement with the Patriarch. The Patriarchate remained politically aloof, seeming not to take the elections seriously this time. The Unionists used violence to win these elections but against the liberal opposition and not the minorities. Without an agreement with the CUP the Greek party did not fare as well as it had in 1908; there were only fifteen Greek deputies in the 1912 Assembly compared to twenty-six in 1908. Relations with the Greek community, though cooling, remained correct, and a Greek continued to serve in the cabinet regardless of its political complexion. This remained true until the end of the First Balkan War, during and after which relations between the two communities deteriorated beyond repair. The policy of appointing Greeks to administrative and diplomatic posts probably also came to an end about that time. We see, for example, Hüseyin Hilmi Paşa replacing Mavroyeni Bey, a member of a prominent Phanariot family, as ambassador to Vienna on 28 October 1912.[48]

The outbreak of the Balkan War on 8 October and the rapid collapse of Turkish armies brought allied troops to the very outskirts of the capital. Greek forces landed at Limni (Lemnos) on 21 October and occupied other offshore islands not held by the Italians. There were grave fears that while the Turks defended İstanbul from the Bulgarians, Greek forces might land on the Aegean coast. Despite that threat, however, no measures were taken against local Greeks, as they would be during the First World War.

The conquest of Ottoman territories by Montenegro, Serbia, Greece, and Bulgaria prompted a migration of Turks and Muslims to Anatolia. The mass migration was caused partly by the ravages of war which simply forced people to abandon their homes in search of

---

48 M. K. İnal, *Osmanlı Devrinde Son Sadrazamlar*, İstanbul, 1940-1953, pp. 1674-1675. Ahmed Şerif writes that in Haçın, today's Saimbeyli, a Greek was traditionally appointed *kaymakam*, and Yorgi Efendi, he heard, opposed and discouraged public collections for the navy fund and was openly hostile to the CUP. With Greek officials, their loyalty to the Ottoman state had become suspect. See Şerif, 1977 (cited n. 35), pp. 269-270.

security. But the major cause was the policy of terror adopted by each of these states to purge conquered territories of alien peoples. In some regions the character of the population was very mixed and in many cases Turks and Muslims constituted the largest single group if not the majority. In such circumstances, they were expelled, or in the case of the *Pomaks*, Muslims who were Bulgarian by race and language, converted by force to Christianity.[49] Only in this way could the conquering state "nationalize" this newly acquired territory or become the majority community. Such methods are said to have a long history in this region, and may be described rather appropriately as "demographic warfare."[50] They could be justified by nationalism and the prerogatives of the nation state, and the Unionists, latecomers to nationalism, soon adopted these methods though never so explicitly as Greece or Bulgaria for they still retained the illusions of empire.

As their former homelands changed hands and acquired a new national character, hundreds of thousands of Turks and Muslims fled from the Balkans to Anatolia. The Turkish press of this period is full of accounts of inhuman treatment to which Muslims were being subjected. Some of these accounts were undoubtedly exaggerated, though many were verified in the European press and by non-Turkish sources. The Greeks, with their missionary zeal for the *Megali Idea*, were most thorough in Hellenizing the conquered lands. Here is how the "de-Turkification" of Salonica took place following the Greek occupation on 9 November 1912:

> L'entrée des Grecs avait changé considérablement l'aspect de la
> ville. Dès les premiers jours, pour éviter les services, tous les habi-

---

49 Carnegie Endowment for International Peace, *Report of the International Commission to Inquire into the Causes and Conduct of the Balkan Wars*, Paris, 1914, pp. 71-78, 148-151, 155-157, 186, 201-202. The Bulgarian Holy Synod conceived of a novel way to convert the Pomaks *en masse*. They were lined up in the fields and a priest went down the line making them take a bite from a pork sausage!

50 The terms is taken from Mark Pinson's unpublished Ph. D. thesis, Harvard 1970, entitled "Demographic Warfare."

natnts non musulmans s'étaient empressés des troquer les fez contre les chapeaux. Militaires, fonctionnaires et rentiers turcs, s'étaient embarqués avec leurs familles pour Constantinople et l'Anatolie. ... La ville s'était déturquisée comme par miracle. Le Turc, langue commune des rues, disparut presque complètement de la circulation. Sur les places, dans les cafés, dans les tramways, encombrés d'officiers et des soldats, on n'entendit plus resonner que le grec châtié des Athéniens. ...[51]

The resettlement of these refugees posed a serious problem for the government, truly Unionist since the *coup d'état* of 23 January 1913. Initially its primary concern was to obtain the most favorable peace terms so as to retain as much territory a possible in eastern Thrace and regain the Aegean Islands, considered vital for the defense of İstanbul. Consequently, it hardly found time for the refugee question. The CUP was totally preoccupied with regaining Edirne from Bulgaria and that was accomplished in July 1913. But by the end of the year the Unionists began to recover from the trauma of the Balkan disaster and began to deal with the urgent problems confronting them.

The Unionists decided that one way to resolve the refugee problem was to implement a *de facto* exchange of population by forcing Greeks (and Bulgarians) to migrate from Anatolia and Thrace. In their view the Balkan states had begun this process–the Bulgarians after they declared their independence in 1908 and the Greeks in October 1912–it was for the Turks to reciprocate. But it was never official policy, for the Porte feared foreign intervention on behalf of the Christians. In fact the government was embarrassed by the activities of the *Teşkilât-ı Mahsusa*, a Unionist organization that dealt with such matters.[52] It is worth noting that the Unionists had been in power too short a time to establish complete control over state and government,

---

51 Risal (cited n. 1), pp. 338-339; Aram Andonyan, *Balkan Harbi Tarihi*, 1975, pp. 400-404. This book was originally published in Armenian (İstanbul, 1912-1913).

52 Bayar (cited n. 5), pp. 1568-1600.

so that initially there were differences over policy between the Committe, the government, and the bureaucracy.

The period of the Balkan Wars also coincided with the growing awareness of Turkish nationalism, a response to the increasing isolation of the Turkish element in the empire. At this point the CUP began to see the commercial boycott as more than an instrument to use against a foreign enemy. The anti-Greek boycott of 1912-13 was used as a weapon against Greek (indeed Christian) economic domination and, at the same time, to promote Muslim enterprise and Muslim entrepreneurs. The boycott went hand in hand with refugee resettlement which was partially accomplished by placing Turks in jobs monopolized by Greeks, as in the case of the railway workers on the French-owned İzmir-Kasaba line.[53]

Throughout 1913 the Porte protested against the Greek persecution of Muslims in Macedonia. In the press there were articles expressing fears that such actions might lead to reprisals against the Greeks of Turkey.[54] Such reprisals began in earnest after January 1914, and Athens and İstanbul protested and made claims and counter claims. By the summer of 1914 the situation had reached an impasse and the two states seemed prepared to negotiate an agreement on the exchange of populations.[55] But war intervened and the project was postponed until 1923.

Despite the hostile climate after the Balkan Wars, the Ottoman Greek community was too powerful and well organized to be disrupted by Unionist pressures. In the 1914 general election, the Committe was again forced to negotiate with the Patriarch and accept his choice of Greek candidates for the Assembly. Far from being demoralized by the general state of affairs, the outcome of the Balkan Wars seemed to strengthen the faith of the Greek leaders in Hellenism and the *Megali*

---

53 *Ibid.*, pp. 1554-1558.
54 See in particular H. C. Yalçın's article published in *Revue Politique International* (n.d.) quoted in *The Orient*, vol. 5, no. 6 (11 February 1914), p. 54.
55 Dakin (cited n. 5), p. 202.

Idea.[56] Their optimism was not totally misplaced for it came very close to fruition in the aborted Treaty of Sevrès.

THE UNIONISTS AND THE ARMENIAN COMMUNITY

Compared to the Greek community, the Ottoman Armenian community was not as politically homogeneous. For one thing, there was no Armenian state to provide a focus of loyalty or a comparable yearning for union. For another, the community was divided between two repressive empires (Ottoman and Russian) and forced to struggle on two fronts, hardly a guarantee of success. Moreover, the Armenians were split into two actions along essentially socio-economic lines: the Dashnak–members of the Armenian Revolutionary Federation *(Hai Heghapokhakan Dashnaksutiun)*–who, like the Unionists, spoke for the Armenian petty bourgeoisie of Anatolia and sought autonomy if not ultimate freedom and statehood; and the Patriarchate which represented the interests of the "clerico-wealthy" commercial community–the *amira* class–of İstanbul and other commercial centers like İzmir. This group had prospered during the second half of the nineteenth century though it had lost some of its political power as a result of constitutional reform within the community.[57] Its goal after the revolution was to regain its hegemony within the community and protect its traditional privileges from the encroachments of the Porte.

Before the revolution the Porte recognized the Patriarch as the official leader of the community; the Dashnak had the status of a proscribed revolutionary party. In July 1908 when the Dashnak became

---

56 According to Pallis, after 1913 "the national idea is no more the creation of a purely Hellenic Greece but the establishment of a large Hellenic state in which many foreign elements would coexist with the Hellenic one, keeping naturally their particular national consciousness under the sovereignty of the Hellenic element and [using] as their connecting link the Greek language–the official language of the state." A. A. Pallis, "Racial Migration in the Balkans during the years 1912-1924", *The Geographical Journal*, vol. 66, no. 4 (October 1925), p. 330, quoted in Pentzopoulos (cited n. 13), p. 28.

57 Louise Nalbandian, *The Armenian Revolutionary Movement*, Berkeley, 1963, and Davison (cited n. 16), pp. 114-135.

legal, the Patriarch tried to establish his authority over this body and bring it under his control. But the Revolutionary Federation, which enjoyed greater support and prestige in the community because of its struggle against the old regime, refused to submit, denouncing the Patriarch and his supporters as "money-worshipers and psuedo-patriots."[58] The attitude of the Dashnaks toward the *amira* class resembled the attitude to the Unionists toward the Liberals; both resented the privileged position of their upper classes.

Relations between the Unionists and the Dashnaks were cordial. According to Cemal Paşa, the aim of Unionist policy with regard to minority organizations was "to form the various revolutionary political committees [Bulgarian, Greek and Armenian] in the country into one 'Political Committee of Ottoman Unity'." None of these groups was willing to dissolve its political organization and merge with the CUP. But the Dashnaks agreed to collaborate with the Committee to support the Constitution. They insisted on maintaining their revolutionary organization and retaining total freedom of action to pursue their program though they were willing to abandon secrecy and to work as a political body.[59] The Committee had no choice but to concede to these demands in order to demonstrate its goodwill. But that paved the way for an electoral agreement so that, apart from the Greco-Armenian protest of 10 November–which was discussed above and for which the Armenian patriarch was responsible–the Dashnak protested neither electoral procedures nor results.

---

58 Sarkis Atamian, *The Armenian Community: The Historical Development of a Social and Ideological Conflict*, New York, 1955, pp. 159-165, where he quotes from *Pazantion*, 9 October 1909 (the Patriarch's paper) and *Azadamard* 13 and 14 October 1909 (the organ of the Dashnak). Atamian also discusses the Hinchaks, the socialist revolutionaries, but they were not significant in Ottoman politics.

59 Djemal Paşa, *Memories of the Turkish Statesman 1913-1919*, London, 1922, pp. 252-253. The Hinchak, he wrote, "absolutely refused to negotiate with us". These may be the same negotiations as the ones reported by *The Times*, 14 September 1908 and which took place in Van "the most important [Armenian] revolutionary centre in Turkey", according to the British consul. See Dickson to Sir Nicholas O'Conor, Van, 2 March 1908, F.O. 371/533.

Despite the working relationship, the aspirations of the Committee and the Dashnak were antithetical. The Committee wanted to bring together all religious and ethnic communities in an Ottoman union while the Dashnak wanted local autonomy or even total independence. But for the moment the CUP showed greater interest in attacking the Patriarch's privileges. That was consistent with its desire to restore full sovereignty to the state. The Unionists imagined that they would win over all malcontents with their reform program which would fulfill the promise of liberty, justice and equality. Meanwhile, the Armenian Patriarch was no less determined than his Greek counterpart to preserve his communal privileges. "We demand", he told an English visitor, "a perpetuation of the privileges now enjoyed by the Armenian community and a complete decentralization of the administration."[60] But Monsignor İzmirlian was no less alarmed by the radicalism in his community, expressed in the policies of the Dashnak. He was

> firmly convinced that the only safe course for Armenians ... lay in working in loyal union with the Turks on the line of prudence and moderation and eschewing all extremist ideas in the war of autonomy. ... He was counseling his flock in this sense and had let it discreetly be understood that he would resign the Patriarchate rather than countenance any advance tendencies on the part of the Henchaq, Droshaq or other Armenian societies. ...[61]

The Patriarch spoke for the Armenian bourgeoisie, whose interests could be satisfied within a cosmopolitan empire so long as it was a dependent part of the European economy. For this class autonomy or independence in eastern Anatolia could mean only isolation and decline and so they opposed the program of the *Dashnaksutiun*. A decade later (in 1919) when the question of independent Armenia was being seriously discussed by European and American statesmen, Sir

---

60 E. J. Dillon, "The Reforming Turk", *Quarterly Review*, 210 (1909), p. 247.
61 Fitzmaurice to Lowther, 54 D, 30 November 1908, F.O. 195/228.

Adam Block whose acquaintance with the Armenian bourgeoisie was quite intimate, observed that "Armenians [who] were chiefly devoted to commerce and trade ... for example, the Armenians of Constantinople, would not go to Armenia, nor would most of those who emigrated to other countries desire to go back to primitive conditions and to real hardship."[62]

Unionist-Dashnak cooperation continued into 1909, the Patriarch being politically isolated by both the CUP and the Porte. A fundamental issue that was a source of constant and bitter friction in some of the eastern provinces was the "agrarian disputes ... between the Armenians, Turks, and Kurds." Its quick and satisfactory resolution might have made all the difference to Turkish-Armenian relations. The Unionists were aware of this and they persuaded Hilmi Paşa–grand vezir from 12 February to 13 April 1909–to send a commission to inquire into the disputes and settle them. But the opposition of deputies from these provinces, representing landlords–the notorious *ağa*s–with strong interests in maintaining the *status quo*, prevented the Commission from going.[63] As though these vested interests were not a sufficiently serious obstacle in the way of Turkish-Armenian relations, the Adana massacres, which were part of the counter-revolution of 13 April 1909, damaged the little goodwill that had been created between the two communities since July 1908.

The relationship between the events in İstanbul and in Adana was an intimate one: both were the doing of reactionaries behind whom stood the anti-Unionist Liberals. In the capital the reactionaries shouted that Islam was in danger; in Adana they claimed that the Armenians were about to rise up and destroy the Muslims. From

---

62 Heck to Secretary of State, Constantinople, 17 January 1919, 867.00/846. Adam Block, a long-time resident of İstanbul, had served as first dragoman at the British embassy, as British representative on, and president of the Ottoman Public Debt Administration, and in 1919 he was also financial adviser to the British high commissioner at İstanbul. Lewis Heck was US commissioner at İstanbul.

63 Djemal (cited n. 59), pp. 254-255.

Turkish accounts it seems that Archbishop Musheg, the leader of the Adana community, played into the hands of the reactionaries by adopting a chauvinistic and provocative attitude toward the Muslim population.[64]

The Unionists feared that these outbreaks of violence in İstanbul and Adana might provoke foreign intervention, and that would mean the end of the new regime and their own organization. Thus Hilmi Paşa failed to take immediate, energetic action against the rebellious soldiers in the capital in case they responded by attacking Christians and foreigners and induced Great Power intervention. For the Liberals foreign intervention was the last card to be played against the CUP if all else failed. They miscalculated in İstanbul and tried to play this card in Adana, but to no avail. In Adana there was also Archbishop Musheg, described by Cemal Paşa as a reformist Hinchak, who may not have abandoned the idea of foreign intervention (as the Dashnak had, at least temporarily) as a means of achieving Armenian aspirations.[65]

Moreover, the pattern of the massacres lends credence to the hypothesis that they were indeed perpetrated to as to provoke intervention. According to Agop Babikyan (deputy for Edirne and member of the parliamentary commission investigating the massacres) trouble in Adana began on the afternoon of 13 April after the arrival of news of the rebellion in İstanbul. Since reactionaries had been actively carrying out propaganda in the Adana region for some time, the outbreak may have been a spontaneous response of pent-up feelings. The actual massacres began on 14 April and ended on the 16th. For the next eight days all was quiet and calm and it seemed that order had been restored. Then on Sunday 25 April, the very day that the Action Army

---

64 *Ibid.*, pp. 255-262; Esat Uras, *Tarihte Ermeniler ve Ermeni Meselesi*, İstanbul, 1976, pp. 551-570; Mehmed Hocaoğlu, *Tarihte Ermeni Mezâlimi ve Ermeniler*, n.p. 1976, pp. 572-573; Abdullah Yaman, *Ermeni Meselesi ve Türkiye*, İstanbul, 1973, p. 122; this book is a reissue of the 1916 government publication.

65 Djemal (cited n. 59), pp. 254-255.

from Macedonia began to occupy the capital, there were fresh outbreaks in the Adana province which lasted until 27 April.[66]

Babikyan concluded that the Adana massacres took place
because the counter-revolutionaries hated the Armenians for their loyalty to the new regime and the Constitution. Therefore they had to
destroy the Armenians if they wanted to destroy the constitutional
order. To do so they exploited the ignorance of the masses and spread
rumors and lies about the Armenians which wounded the most sensitive feelings of the people.[67]

There may be something in Babikyan's line of thought though
it is not a very satisfactory explanation for the massacres. If it were
valid we would expect attacks on the Armenians of İstanbul and the
eastern provinces, but there were none. The provocation of foreign
intervention seems a more valid motive, especially for the massacres of
25-27 April.

The Liberals, the true architects of the counter-revolution,
hoped that the army would acquiesce to the destruction of the CUP
and support a Liberal Union government. Their propaganda that the
events of 13 April had in no way affected the constitutional regime
was designed to achieve that end. The Third Army may have accepted these arguments but it could not allow a military rebellion to go
unpunished. Supported by the Unionists in Salonica it marched on the
capital. The Liberals tried to use the influence of the British embassy
to win over the Third Army but to no avail.[68] Their last resort was to
instigate the second phase of the massacres in Adana on the very day
Mahmut Şevket Paşa began to occupy İstanbul. Foreign ships had

---

66 Babikyan's report was first published in İstanbul in 1919 though it was presented to the
    Assembly a decade earlier. It is quoted by Uras (cited n. 64), p. 559; Djemal (cited n. 59), p. 259
    writes that he had heard a rumor that members of the Muhammadan Union, responsible for the
    reactionary movement in İstanbul, had been active in the Adana region warning the Muslims of
    an impending Armenian uprising. Şerif (cited n. 35), *passim*, also heard that outside elements
    had been very active in the region before and during the massacres.
67 Babikyan quoted by Uras (cited n. 64), pp. 559-560.
68 Ahmad (cited n. 32), pp. 43-45.

already sailed to Mersin from where they could send marines to Adana. But the Great Powers were too divided to be able to agree on a joint intervention. Unilateral intervention was too dangerous in the diplomatic climate of the time.

The events of April struck a grave blow to the prestige of the CUP and constitutional government. Both had been caught off-guard and neither acted decisively in a critical situation. The massacres destroyed whatever sense of confidence the Committee had managed to create among the Christians. On 6 May the government tried to make amends by providing TL 30,000 for the relief of victims in Adana. But that was too little and too late. Some days later (12 May), the Assembly passed a resolution expressing regret for the events at Adana and proposed that a proclamation be addressed to all Anatolian provinces enjoining concord and fraternity on all communities of the population. The following day, the grand vezir announced a special commission to investigate the events at Adana. The Assembly voted to attach two of its own members to the government commission and Şefik Bey (Karesi) and Agop Babikyan (Edirne) were elected for the task.[69] Meanwhile, a martial law tribunal carried out its own investigations and punished–in some cases by hanging–those found guilty of complicity in the massacres. Among those executed there were some local notables who exercised great political influence in the region.[70]

In the Assembly debates on education, military service, and the Associations Law, Armenian deputies joined forces with the Greeks

---

69 "Report of Proceedings of the Ottoman Parliament from April 26 to May 20, 1909" in Lowther to Grey, no. 377 confidential, Pera, 20 May 1909, F.O. 371/761/20292; Akşin (cited n. 32), p. 193. Later, when Cemal Paşha went as governor of Adana, he says TL 200,000 were put at his disposal to compensate victims of the massacres. See Djemal (cited n. 59), p. 261.

70 Djemal (cited n. 59), p. 262. The Armenian community, however, found the sentences inadequate and thought that the culprits had gotten off too lightly. There was also much anger at the fact that Armenians were punished by the tribial and the patriarch resigned in protest, though he probably retracted his resignation. See Lowther to Grey, no. 843 confidential, Therapia, 12 October 1909, F.O. 371/774/38364.

(see above). They also criticised government policy but not quite so vehemently. The Armenian Patriarch protested more sharply than the Dashnak against the infringement of his community's privilege. Later, when the Porte required Armenian schools to submit to government inspection, his subordinate, the bishop of Erzurum, refused to comply. The bishop denounced the measure as a violation of the guaranteed privileges of the Armenian Patriarchate, and as "a first step towards the realization of the chauvinistic policy of the new régime in educational matters. ..."[71] Faced with such determined opposition the government made no attempt to enforce the new law, preferring to wait for better circumstances.

Despite the Patriarch's opposition to the Unionists, the Dashnak continued to cooperate with them. In September 1909 the two bodies signed an agreement "to work together on behalf of progress, the constitution, and unity." They promised to fight against reactionaries and 'to dispel old faulty ideas sown by the previous despotic régime that the Armenians are striving for independence."[72] *Puzantion* (18 September 1909), the organ of the Patriarchate, questioned the sincerity of the agreement. It claimed that this declaration of cooperation was only political expediency on the part of the Dashnak who saw it as a means of survival in the face of the recent Associations Law.[73]

If that was indeed the case, Dashnak strategy paid off for their organization remained intact and their relations with the CUP correct and without open friction. But any agreement concerning Armenian (and Greek) presence in the cabinet was probably reached well before September 1909 as *The Times* (London) of 23 September had report-

---

71 Consul McGregor to Mr. Marling, Erzerum, 6 December 1910 in Marling to Grey, no. 908 confidential, Constantinople, 18 December 1910, F.O. 371/1017/46557.

72 Atamian (cited n. 58), pp. 160,161, quoting *Azadamard*, 19 September 1909. The text of the declaration was published in *Tanin*, 16 September 1909 and is given in Uras (cited n. 64), pp. 576-577. *The Times*, 23 September 1909 also reported an agreement to the effect that the Unionists agreed that there would always be an Armenian in the cabinet.

73 Atamian (cited n. 58), p. 163.

ed. An Armenian and a Greek usually served in cabinets formed after 6 August 1908, occupying such posts as public works, and forests, mines and agriculture. However, Gabriel Efendi Noradungian was minister of foreign affairs during the critical months of the First Balkan War. But he was removed by the Unionists who did not trust a non-Muslim in such a sensitive post. Only in the first Unionist cabinet (23 January-11 June 1913) was there no Greek, the latter being replaced by, first, a Kutzo-Vlach (Batzarya Efendi), and then by a Syrian Protestant, Süleyman Bustani.

Unionist-Dashnak cooperation continued into 1912. Prior to the second general election, the two parties agreed on a common platform as well as the numerical representation for the Armenians, which remained the same as in 1908, namely fourteen deputies. They also agreed that if the Committee fulfilled its electoral pledges, they would sign a second agreement providing for cooperation in the Assembly, for the duration of its term.[74] The life of that Assembly was unduly short because of the military intervention in July 1912. However, when new elections were held in February-March 1914 the CUP and the Armenian Revolutionary Federation again worked together. The Patriarch, on the other hand, presented a memorandum to the minister of justice and demanded proportional representation for his community, about twenty deputies for an estimated population of two million. The minister rejected the demand on the grounds that any matter relating to the rights of the Ottoman nation was outside the competence of the Patriarch. The matter ended there, though İzmirlian Efendi continued to put his case before the public through the columns of the press.[75] All that had no effect on the Unionist-Dashnak agreement and the Armenian community again emerged from the elections with fourteen deputies.[76]

---

74 *The Times*, 1 March 1912.
75 *Tanin*, 19 November 1913 and *Stamboul*, 31 October, 15 and 19 November, and 9, 12, 13, and 15 December 1913.
76 Ahmad and Rustow (cited n. 26), p. 247.

Throughout this brief period before 1912, Unionist-Dashnak relations were viable because the Unionists recognized that the Armenians of Anatolia had genuine grievances which needed to be satisfied and which could be achieved with reforms. As for the *amira* class, linked as it was with the world of the capitulations and traditional privileges, the Unionists resented its total lack of Ottoman patriotism. But they also hoped to win it over with a generous dose of economic incentives and by integration into the new bourgeoisie.

Unionist desire to ameliorate the situation in the eastern provinces was not mere altruism. Article LXI of the Treaty of Berlin (1878) which promised reform for these provinces, was theoretically still in effect and could be called upon to justify Great Power intervention while there was no reform. The Porte disliked this article as limiting Ottoman sovereignty but it made no attempt to repudiate it. The Unionists wanted to neutralize it by carrying out the necessary reforms. Their first attempt in February 1909 to send a commission had been failed by the opposition of local landlords. In February 1912 the Said Paşa government reopened the question and allotted TL 100,000 for the settlement of Armeno-Kurdish land disputes. Armenians who had been dispossessed of their land illegally were to be reinstated, and Kurdish squatters thus removed were to be given financial compensation. Moreover, the powers of the local governments of Bitlis and Erzurum were extended so as to enable them to carry out reform.[77]

A year later, after the disasters of the Tripoli and the Balkan Wars, the Unionists began to compromise on administrative centralization. They recognized that what remained of the empire could only be maintained by a policy of stringent reform and decentralization. Professor Hovannisian suggests that "the Ottoman Government, excluded from the preliminary negotiations [of the Great Powers], attempted to counter the Russian project [for reform in eastern

---

[77] *The Times*, 14 February 1912.

Anatolia] by declaring general reform measures for the entire Empire."[78] But Russian proposals were put forward only in June-July 1913 whereas, according to the British ambassador, a committee had already convened in İstanbul, by January 1913 at the latest, "to consider reforms in the administration of Asiatic Turkey on decentralizing lines."[79] A new law on provincial administration was promulgated on 26 March 1913 and went into effect two days later. It increased local autonomy in administrative and financial matters, increased and defined the powers of the governor, and allowed for general provincial councils to be elected by voters of the second degree, namely by local notables and landlords.[80]

The Unionists were inclined to resolve the "Armenian question" through reform. Did Russian pressure promote this endeavor? Quite the contrary, the CUP became suspicious of Petrograd's motives and intentions, and with good reason. Hovannisian writes that by 1912 Russian policy toward Ottoman Armenians had changed: "There were important reasons in 1912 for satisfying the Armenians. By reviving the Armenian question in Turkey, the Tsar would not only regain the loyalty of his Armenian subjects but also would strike a blow against possible anarchy in Transcaucasia. ..." In order to protect her sphere of influence in the northern Persian provinces "and to plan for future expansion, Russia needed a loyal Transcaucasia and a peaceful Turkish Armenia. Moreover, St. Petersburg feared German economic penetration" in this region and reasoned that "Russia-supervised reforms" would be sufficient to keep the Germans out. Given these motives, Tsar Nicholas and his advisors "were therefore prepared, after fifteen years of silence, to resurrect the Armenian question."[81]

---

78 Hovannisian (cited n. 9), pp. 33-34.
79 Lowther to Grey, no. 104 confidential, Constantinople, 7 February 1913, F.O. 371/788/7281. *The Times*, 22 April 1913, wrote that the Porte had turned toward decentralization since the beginning of 1912.
80 Rommily to Secretary of State, Constantinople, 29 April 1913, no. 480, 867.00/53; Shaw and Shaw (cited n. 9), p. 306.
81 Hovannisian (cited n. 9), p. 31.

Armenian leaders, encouraged by Ottoman defeats in the Balkans and the success of Balkan nationalities in achieving their indepedence, judged the time ripe for achieving their own liberation. As in the past (in 1828-1929 and 1877-1878) they appealed to Russia for active support against the Porte. In Turkish eyes they became the instruments of Russian policy.

Russian reforms proposals, submitted to the other Powers, included the main provisions proposed by local Armenian leaders. They soon became a bone of contention between the Triple Entente and the Triple Alliance, supported by the former and obstructed by the latter. The Porte was kept out of the preliminary talks and confronted with a virtual *faith accompli* only after the Powers had reached agreement. However, "Turkish interests" were safeguarded by the German ambassador at İstanbul as Berlin refused to leave the field entirely to Russia. After protracted discussions, the Russians were forced to compromise on the final agreement which, though sanctioned by all six Powers, was signed by only Russia and the Ottoman Empire on 8 February 1914.[82]

For the Unionists, with their experience of Macedonian reform and its consequences, this agreement seemed like a prelude to a Russian protectorate over eastern Anatolia, with eventual Armenian independence. That is precisely how the Russians viewed it.[83] So great was the CUP's fear of Russian occupation that it considered the Şeyh Said Molla Selim rebellion in Bitlis as the pretext for such a move; another Adana massacre but this time on Russia's back door.[84]

---

82 *Ibid.*, pp. 32-34 and Djemal (cited n. 59), pp. 272-274. The Unionists would have preferred an agreement with Britain to reform the eastern provinces and Cemal Paşa said so to Sir Henry Wilson, who was in İstanbul in October 1913. See Sir Charles Calwell, *Field-Marshal Sir Henry Wilson*, New York, 1927, vol. 1, p. 128ff. Ostrorog (cited n. 11), p. xi, confirms this, but thwarting Russia did not suit Britain's interests in Europe and the world. See Feroz Ahmad, "Great Britain's Relations with the Young Turks 1908-1914", *Middle Eastern Studies*, 2 (1966).

83 Djemal (cited n. 59), pp. 274-275, quoting from Russian documents. The growing importance that Russia attached to eastern Anatolia may be seen in its decision to establish consulates at Diyarbakır, Sivas, Harput, and Mosul. See *The Orient*, vol. 5, no. 28 (15 July 1914), p. 279.

84 Bayur (cited n. 46), vol. 2, part 3, pp. 188-189.

Signs of Kurdish unrest in the Bitlis region were visible by March 1914. As a precaution government troops began patrolling the city streets under a 6 PM curfew on 14 March. On the 31st, the Kurds of the region rose in rebellion and Bitlis prepared for an attack. Two days later, the Kurds in the city rioted but government forces crushed the riot and captured most of the leaders. Şeyh Said Molla managed to escape and took refuge in the Russian consulate! The other leaders were tried and eleven were hanged, and their bodies were prominently displayed in the city as a warning to other rebels. Şeyh Said, sentenced to death *in absentia*, remained in the Russian consulate until November when Turkey entered the First World War. With the closing of the consulate he was captured, along with a companion, and both were hanged. According to an official dispatch, his last words were: "The Russians will wreak vengeance on you for me."[85]

Tanin's reaction to the uprising, especially its sense of panic, reflected the Committee's attitude. There was fear that this incident would lead to foreign intervention and the loss of the eastern provinces. That is why the government was urged to act quickly and decisively. "Surely", lamented *Tanin*, "the [the Kurds] must be ignorant of the seriousness of the step they are taking or of the intentions they have, when they attack Bitlis. They naturally can have no idea how serious and how injurious to their own interests and to those of their compatriots is this step of theirs. We cannot believe there are brothers of ours ready to let loose in Anatolia forces such as have just resulted in the loss of Macedonia. ..."[86]

The Porte acted decisively and one-hundred and fifty people are said to have been killed in putting down the rebellion. Troops were called in from Van and Muş and arms were distributed to the Armenians so that they could defend themselves and fight the rebels. This measure had a good effect on the Armenian community, restor-

---

[85] The account is based on reports in *The Orient*, vol. 5, nos. 14, 15, 16 (8, 15, and 22 April 1914 respectively), and vol. 5, no. 51 (23 December 1914), p. 463.

[86] *Tanin*, n.d., quoted in *ibid.*, vol. 5, no. 14 (8 April 1914), p. 131.

ing some badly needed confidence in the government. An Armenian paper congratulated the government on its policy during the uprising, commenting that "for us Armenians there is another fact still more significant and satisfactory, and that is that the Government has complete confidence in the Armenians. In fact, arms were distributed to the Armenians in Bitlis that they might defend the city against the reactionaries. ..."[87]

By April 1914 the two foreign inspectors-general (a Dutchman and a Norwegian) had been selected to supervise reform in the eastern provinces. On 13 July the Assembly voted that budget to meet the salaries and expenses of their staffs. It seemed as though all obstacles to reform had been removed and that it was a matter of time before Armenian grievances were removed. But the outbreak of war in Europe opened a new and more tragic chapter in Turkish-Armenian relations.

THE UNIONISTS AND THE OTTOMAN
JEWISH COMMUNITY

Anyone who studies the revolution of 1908 on the basis of British Foreign office reports, the dispatches of the İstanbul correspondent of *The Times* (London), or the conservative press of he Ottoman capital, is likely to be struck by the outsanding role of the Jews in the CUP movement. All these sources misunderstood the true character of the movement and therefore misrepresented it as a Jewish-Freemason conspiracy manipulated by the Jews for their own ends. The British ambassador spoke of the CUP as the "Jew Committee of Union and Progress", and of the "combination of self-seeking spurious freemasons and Jews that represent the Committee of Union and Progress."[88]

---

87 *The Orient*, vol. 5, no. 4 (8 April 1914), p. 131.
88 Elie Kedourie, "Young Turk, Freemasons and Jews", *Middle Eastern Studies* 7 (1971); B. Lewis (cited n. 8), p. 211, n. 41. See also a dispatch on Freemasonry from Lowther to Grey (1910) in F.O. 371/1010/20761 and a dispatch on Zionism (internal, i.e. in the Ottoman Empire) written in February 1911 and given in F.O. 371/1244. Such views were not unique to the British but were held by conservative circles throughout Europe. Father Herman Gruber, a clerical adviser

Philip Graves of *The Times*, who probably received much of his information from British embassy sources, repeated this theme. The indigenous conservative press, in some cases owned by Greeks, also sought the scapegoat for Unionist policies in the Jews and so-called crypto-Jews (the *Dönme*) of Salonica, thereby implying that Unionist policies could not but be harmful to the Islamic community.

Those who saw the Jewish connection in the CUP–though it was never international–were not totally wrong, however. They were mistaken in their explanation, in seeing the CUP as a front for Jewish aims and aspirations as though the Turks were mere dupes of such ambition. Ottoman Jews did play an important part in the Unionist movement before and after 1908, but never as the force capable of manipulating the movement for their own ends. Historical circumstances united the destinies of Jews and Turks and, as a result, the two elements ended up cooperating within the CUP. In fact, such was the unity of interest that the Jewish community's support for the committee was virtually unconditional.

Scholars such as Goitein and Chouraqui claim that the destiny of the Middle Eastern Jewish community was linked intimately with that of the Muslims, virtually from the rise of Islam.[89] Abraham Galanté holds the same views for Ottoman Jewry and his historical periodization for Ottoman Jewish history fits closely the history of the Ottoman Turks. The period from 1453 to 1602 for both was one of greatness and glory. 1602 to 1856 was a long period of decline, and from 1856 to 1908 one of revival. Finally, the years after 1908 were years of reassertion and resurgence.[90]

---

to Archduke Ferdinand of Austria-Hungary, wrote a treatise in three volumes on "the role of Freemasons in contemporary revolutionary movements since 1776." He "claimed that the revolution in Brazil in 1889, the uprising in Cuba in 1899, the revolution of the Young Turks in 1908, and the revolution in Portugal in 1910 were all organized by Freemasonry." See Vladmir Dedijer, *The Road to Sarajevo*, New York, 1966, p. 113 and *passim*.

89 André Chouraqui, *Letter to an Arab Friend*, Amherst, 1972, and S. D. Goitein, *Jews and Arabs*, New York, 1955.

90 Abraham Galanté, *Rôle économique des Juifs d'Istanbul*, İstanbul, 1942, p. 4ff.

The centuries of decline for the Jews were centuries of Greek and Armenian revival when the two Christian *millet*s began to replace the Jews in many economic and administrative functions. Ottoman Christian communities benefited and developed as European merchant capital penetrated the Ottoman economy, and thrived in the shadow of the Capitulations. By the second half of the eighteenth century, the interests of these communities began to diverge from those of the Turks (and the Jews). Their prosperity and power now depended on the continuing weakness of the Ottoman state whose very revival posed the most deadly threat.

Ottoman Jews are sometimes described in the same terms as the Greeks and Armenians, as members of a comprador bourgeoisie that enjoyed foreign protection, and in some cases foreign citizenship. This may have been true for individuals, but the description did not fit the outlook of the community as a whole. Those Jews who adopted foreign citizenship became Italian subjects, and Italy was a latecomer among the Great Powers, as was Germany, but without the latter's potential. Therefore its political and economic standing in the empire was very limited, and in order to break the monopoly of the dominant powers, England and France, Italy was often willing to renegotiate the Capitulations in return for some advantage over its rivals. The Jews could hardly play a comprador role on behalf of Italy and there is no evidence that they did. On the contrary, they suffered social and economic decline as part of the same process that affected the Turkish community; thus the common interest in the revival of the Ottoman state.

Apart from the economic motive, there was another more potent reason which drew Jews politically to the Turks: the fear as to the future of their community if Ottoman lands were lost to Greece or Bulgaria. This fear applied to the Jews of Macedonia and western Anatolia, and not to those of Iraq. But it united the entire community in its allegiance to the CUP, for Ottoman rule was the best protection against Christian anti-Semitism. Traditionally, Christian communities had persecuted Jews in the empire and the Ottoman state had guaranteed that justice prevailed. Fear of such persecution motivated the steady Jewish migration to territory ruled by the Porte as the Ottoman frontier receded during the nineteenth century. It was particularly true after the Balkan Wars.[91]

After the revolution we do not find any declarations of principle or agreements of cooperation between the CUP and the Jewish community as we do with the other communities. After all, Ottoman Jews had neither political nor national aspirations separate from those of the Committee and therefore no separate political organization to pursue them. While the Zionist movement had an office in İstanbul, it found virtually no support amongst local Jews. In fact, the Zionists were hard put to find a Jewish deputy who would put forward the case for Zionism before the Assembly. Finally, Vlahof Efendi, the Socialist deputy for Salonica, agreed to speak on their behalf.[92]

Amongst the minorities, only the Jewish community identified totally with the CUP. It alone provided a front line leader, in the person of <u>Emanuel Karasu</u>, for the collective leadership of the party. He was never a member of the Central Committee or a minister, yet he was an important figure in the movement both before and after the revolution. For those who viewed the Committee as a front for a Jewish-Freemason conspiracy, he was the evil genius. He was elected deputy for Salonica in 1908 and served also in the 1912 and 1914 Assemblies along with three other Jewish deputies.[93]

---

91 *Idem., Histoire des Juifs d'Anatolie*, İstanbul, 1937, vol. 1, p. 161ff.

92 "Vlahof Efendi'nin Anıları" in Haupt and Dumont (cited n. 4), pp. 257-262. In Palestine there were not enough Ottoman Jews to elect a representative to the Assembly; see Walter Laqueur, *A History of Zionism*, New York, 1976, p. 222, though Iraq sent a Jewish deputy to İstanbul. S. Landshut, *Jewish Communities in the Muslim Countries of the Middle East*, London, 1950, p. 45, wrote: "there never has been any feeling of solidarity with the poltical aspirations of Zionism." The same was true of Salonica, see Ben Gurion, *Ben Gurion Looks Back*, New York, 1970, pp. 43-46; and even Egypt, see Jacob Landau, *Jews in Nineteenth Century Egypt*, 1969, p. 275.

93 Ahmad and Rustow (cited n. 26), p. 267. Karasu was a lawyer by profession. Before the revolution, as grand master of the 'Macedonia Risorta' Lodge, he provided a cover for Unionist

There was a general revival in the fortunes of the Jewish community under the new regime. The merchants, long depressed on account of Greco-Armenian economic domination, benefited from the policy of anti-Greek boycotts which went into effect in 1909 and continued intermittently thereafter. It is important to note that this policy was selective. The first boycott of 1908 was against Austrian goods. In 1909 Greek goods and shops were boycotted because of the Cretan question, and during and after the Balkan Wars the boycott was extended to Christian commerce generally. *The Orient*, a publication of the Bible House in İstanbul, emphasized this fact and noted that "the trouble does not extend to Hebrew shops."[94]

The Unionists also encouraged Turks and Jews to challenge the economic hegemony of the Christians, and these two groups became an important feature of the indigenous bourgeoisie the CUP wanted to create. By 1912 Unionists were discussing the possibility of establishing a "national economy", a concept they derived from the German political economist Friedrich List. Prominent amongst the promoters of this concept was Moise Cohen, a Jew from Salonica who settled in İstanbul in 1912. He also tried to popularize the idea of Jews identifying themselves primarily as Turks, as Turkish Jews, and he himself adopted the Turkish name Tekin Alp, under which he wrote and is generally known. Judging by his writings, his contribution to the development of the nationalist ideology, especially in the economic field, is considerable though it has yet to be evaluted.[95]

---

clandestine activities, and acted as a courier. After 1908, he belonged to the 'Jacobin' wing of the CUP and was close to Talât. During the war he was appointed a food controller and is said to have amassed a fortune. In 1919 he migrated to Italy and this suggests that he may have been an Italian subject.

94 *The Orient*, vol. 5, no. 11 (18 March 1914), p. 105.

95 Moise Cohen was born in Salonica (date unknown) and settled in İstanbul in 1912 after Salonica was lost to Greece. He then adopted the name Tekin Alp and wrote in *Yeni Mecmua* and *İktisadiyat Mecmuası*, which he also edited during 1915-1917. Through his writing he helped to popularize the idea of a national economy and the need for a Turkish bourgeoisie. In 1915 his *Türkismus und Pantürkismus* was published in Weimar and it explained Turkish nationalism to the CUP's German allies. After the war, Tekin Alp supported the nationalists, and in 1935 wrote *Kemalizm* (*Le Kemalisme*, Paris, 1937), an important contribution to the artic-

So far what we have said applies to the Jewish communities of Macedonia and western Anatolia where their principal rivals were the Greeks. The province of Iraq, especially the city of Baghdad, was also a major center of Jewish life. The community witnessed a revival in the second half of the nineteenth century as Baghdad and Basra became important points in the developing trade with Asia. The "Jews gradually acquired an important share in the country's foreign trade, until they displaced Muslims, Christians, and even European merchants, including the British who settled in Iraq. The latter found it difficult to compete with local Jewish merchants, and local Muslims were compelled to take Jewish partners. ..."[96]

Does Jewish preponderance in Iraq explain Unionist reluctance to permit the takeover of the Hamidiye Steamboat Company by the English Lynch Company? It was undoubtedly an important factor, for the merger would have strengthened England's economic position in Iraq—hence the opposition of deputies from that region, and especially the Unionist writer and deputy for Baghdad, İsmail Hakkı Babanzâde, "who cherished a sincere, if unfounded, belief that the scheme of amalgamation covered an ingenious design on the part of Great Britain to effect the economic conquest of Iraq."[97]

In Baghdad there were violent demonstrations against the granting of the navigational monopoly on the Tigris and Euphrates to a foreign company. The situation became sufficiently serious for the Porte to consider martial law for both Baghdad and Basra. After long debate in the Assembly, the cabinet was given a vote of confidence and

---

ulation of the nationalist ideology. In the multiparty period after 1945, he supported the Demokrat Parti, especially its promotion of a *laissez-faire* economy. See Galanté (cited n. 22), p. 127, and idem. (cited n. 90), pp. 58-64. Despite Tekin Alp's significance, he is not given a place in Hilmi Ziya Ülken, *Türkiye'de Çağdaş Düşünce Tarihi*, Konya, 1966.

96 Hayyim Cohen, *The Jews of the Middle East 1860-1972*, New York, 1973, p. 90, where he seems to follow Phebe Marr, "Yasin al-Hashimi: The Rise and Fall of a Nationalist", unpublished Ph. D. dissertation Harvard University 1966, p. 30; and Landshut (cited n. 92), p. 42.

97 *The Times*, 11 December 1909. Sasson Efendi, Jewish deputy for Baghdad, had been director of the Ottoman Steamer Company (Hamidiye) and was said to be opposed to the merger. See Lowther to Grey, no. 510 confidential, Therapia 1 July 1909. F.O. 371/778/25436.

therefore the authority to grant the concession to Lynch. In practice, however, this authority was annulled when the grand vezir resigned on 28 December 1909, for his successor claimed that he was no longer bound by the vote.[98]

Until 1914 the coincidence of interest between the CUP and the Jews of Iraq remained strong. But with the outbreak of war, and especially after the British occupation of Basra in November, the Jews rallied to Britain. Many left for Basra to evade military service, and after the war the Iraqi community welcomed the British mandate.[99] The Anatolian Jewish community, on the other hand, remained loyal to the Ottoman ideal throughout the war.

As we would expect, Jewish deputies did not oppose the policy of Ottomanization when various laws were discussed in the Assembly, laws bitterly opposed by Christian deputies. The Jews had no vested interest in the old order and a great deal to gain from the new one.

It is true that there were never any Jewish cabinet ministers. But there was never any question of satisfying the *amour-propre* of the community by making token appointments and the Jews never made an issue of it. Unionist Jews did, however, occupy important positions as undersecretaries and technocrats in key ministries where their role in policymaking was probably more significant than that of the minister. Emanuel Salem prepared the new laws to be introduced in the Assembly; Ezechiel Sasoon (deputy for Baghdad), formerly undersecretary at the Ministry of Agriculture was moved to Commerce; Nissim Russo served as *chef du cabinet privé* at the Ministry of Finance, while Vitali Stroumsa was a member of the Supreme Council for Financial Reform. Samuel Israel occupied the most sensitive post of chief of the political section of the capital's police; he was with Enver Paşa when the latter carried out the coup on 23 January 1913![100]

---

98 Ahmad (cited n. 32), p. 67.
99 Landshut (cited n. 92), p. 43.
100 Galanté (cited n. 90), pp. 51-52; *idem.* (cited n. 22), pp. 116-117, 123-124; Tunaya (cited n. 457, p. 412.

If Ottoman Jews benefited from the Unionist alliance, they also suffered the consequences. In October 1908 reactionaries demonstrating against the new regime attacked Jews in Baghdad for supporting the CUP.[101] During and after the Balkan Wars Jews in Macedonia and Thrace suffered persecution along with the Muslims and also migrated to Anatolia.[102] So great was the concern of Ottoman Jews for the future of the empire during these wars, that those residing in southern Africa joined local Indian Muslims to raise money for the Ottoman army.[103] In the spring of 1913, when there was a threat of a Greek landing in Anatolia, the Unionist government armed not only the peasantry but also the Jews of the region, demonstrating its total confidence in the community.[104] This mutual sense of trust guided the relations between Turks and Jews until the end of the empire and into the republic.

---

101 Yusuf Ghanima, *Nuzhat al-mushtāq fî tarîkh yahud al-Irāq*, Baghdad, 1924, p. 180, cited in Cohen (cited n. 96), p. 24. Note the striking contrasts to the reactionaries' attitude toward non-Muslims who were not Unionists.

102 Galanté (cited n. 22), pp. 41-47; idem. (Avram Galanti), *Türkler ve Yahudiler*, İstanbul, 1947, pp. 25, 42-46.

103 *Ibid.*, p. 64 and 67-68 respectively.

104 Acting Vice-Consul Harris to Sir G. Lowther, Dardanelles, 26 March 1913, and Lowther to Grey, Constantinople, 9 April 1913 with reports from the Dardanelles and İzmir, in Şimşir (cited n. 47), pp. 574-575 and 591-594.

Great Britain's Relations with the Young Turks, 1908-1914

The Young Turk Revolution of 1908 was a turning point in Great Britain's relations with the Ottoman Empire. The revolution destroyed the anti-British regime of Abdülhamid and the Palace, and replaced it with a constitutional regime which sought encouragement and inspiration from Britain. German influence at Constantinople, totally dependent on the good-will and patronage of Abdülhamid, also declined. The first manifestation of this decline was the dismissal of the pro-German grand vezir Ferid Paşa on July 22, 1908, on the very day he received the German order of the 'Black Eagle.'[1] Hereafter the door was wide open for the expansion of British influence in the Ottoman Empire.

But in July 1908, Britain's relations with the Young Turks were inhibited by the political developments which had taken place in Europe during the last quarter of the nineteenth century, and which had resulted in the Anglo-Russian Entente of 1907. As a consequence

---

1 Mr. G. H. Fitzmaurice to Mr. Tyrrell, Nos. 210, 211, Constantinople, 25 August, 1908 and 11 January, 1909 respectively, in G. P. Gooch & H. Temperley (Eds.), *British Documents on the Origins of the War*, 1898-1914, London, 1928, v, 270-2 (Hereafter cited as B.D....).

of this 'diplomatic revolution', the Foreign Office was forced to modify its traditional policy towards the Porte. This policy, with its dogma of the integrity of the Ottoman Empire, had originated as a countermeasure against Russian expansion towards Constantinople and the Straits.[2] In 1908 the F.O. found itself in an anomalous situation: having to practice its traditional policy with the traditional enemy now a friend.[3]

The Foreign Office received the revolution with great sympathy and pleasure. Though the long term implications of the constitutional movement were far from clear, one of its immediate results was to relieve Britain and Russia from the responsibility of reform in Macedonia, 'so long a nightmare' at the Foreign Office.[4] Macedonia was an explosive issue in the politics of Europe. Any Anglo-Russian scheme to force reform upon the Sultan would offend Muslim feeling in Egypt and India.[5] The revolution saved Britain from this impasse. But potentially it held the possibility of a greater threat to Britain's position in both Egypt and India. A successful constitutional movement was bound to have an effect on 'Young Egyptians' and the freedom movement in India. No one was better aware of this than the Foreign Secretary, Sir Edward Grey. On July 31, 1908 he wrote:

---

2   On British policy towards the Ottoman Empire prior to 1908 see: C. Webster, *The Foreign policy of Palmerston*, 1830-1841, London, 1951, ii, 270; H. Temperley, 'British policy towards parliamentary Rule and Constitutionalism in Turkey, 1830-1914', *Cambridge Historical Journal*, 1932-4, iv, 156-91; W. N. Medlicott, 'Lord Salisbury and Turkey', *History*, October, 1927, xii, 244-7, and 'Gladstone and the Turks', *History*, July, 1928, xiii, 136,7.

3   Sir Edward Grey's Minute, in Sir G. Lowther to Sir E. Grey, No. 218, Telegraphic-Confidential, Constantinople, 7 August, 1908, F.O. 371/545/27371, Public Record Office, London. Grey commented: 'The difficult point will be Russia – we cannot revert to the old policy of Lord Beaconsfield; we have now to be pro-Turkish without giving rise to any suspicion that we are anti-Russian.' Also T. P. Conwell-Evans, *Foreign Policy from a Back Bench*, 1904-1917, Lonon, 1932, 23; L. S. Stavrianos, 'The Balkan Committee', *The Quen's Quarterly*, Autumn, 1941, xlviii, 260.

4   Sir Charles Hardinge to Sir Francis Bertie, Foreign Office, 30 July, 1908, The Bertie papers, Public Record Office, London, F.O. 800/172; and Grey to Barclay, No. 134, Tel/Confid, Foreign Office, 27 July 1908, F.o. 371/545.

5   Conwell-Evans, n. 3, 10-15.

'If Turkey really establishes a Constitution and keeps it on its feet, and becomes strong herself, the consequences will reach further than any of us can yet foresee. The effect in Egypt will be tremendous, and will make itself felt in India. Hitherto whenever we have had Mahometan subjects, we have been able to tell them that the subjects in the countries ruled by the head of their religion were under a despotism which was not a benevolent one; while our Mahometan subjects were under a despotism which was benevolent... but if Turkey now establishes a Parliament and improves her government, the demand for a constitution in Egypt will gain great force, and our power of resisting the demand will be very much diminished. If, when there is a Turkish Constitution in good working order and things are going well in Turkey, we are engaged in suppressing by force and shooting a rising in Egypt of people who demand a Constitution too, the position will be very awkward. It would never do for us to get into conflict on the subject of Egypt, not with the Turkish Government, but the feelings of the Turkish people.'[6]

Immediately after the revoluton Grey adopted a policy of conciliation towards the new regime with the intention of winning it over to Great Britain. He made it clear to the Young Turks that Britain's quarrel in the past had been, 'not with the Turkish people but with the government of creatures' against whom the Turks themselves had finally protested.[7] He said he would give sympathy and encouragement to the new regime on the condition that it 'does well', and promised not to embarrass it by any British demands. In conclusion he added: '... just as we used all our influence, when Turkish Gov(ern)men)t was bad, to press reform from outside, so now if reforms are being developed from inside we shall use all our influence to prevent their being interfered with from outside.'[8]

---

6   Grey to Lowther, Private, London, 31 July, 1908, The Grey Papers, F.O. 800/78; Hardinge to Bertie, n. 4; and Eldon Gorst's Note: Egypt and Turkey, 19 August, 1908, in the Lowther Papers, 1908-13, F.O. 800/185A (Turkey).
7   Grey to Lowther, Private, London, 31 July, 1908, F.O. 800/78.
8   Same to Same, Private, Fallodon, 23 August, 1908, B. D. No. 208, v, 266.

To Sir Gerard Lowther, the new British Ambassador at the Porte, he wrote: 'Meanwhile, as regards Turkey herself, our course is clear; we must be ready to help the better elements, to wait upon events, and give sympathy and encouragement when required to the reform movement.'[9]

Grey's policy, than, was one of caution and non-interference in the intrigues and politics at the Sublime Porte. He did not intend to create any vested interests in any Ottoman government, or to acquire the position of 'most favoured nation' for Great Britain at Constantinople, as Germany had done. He was content to give moral support and encouragement to 'the better elements' in the reform movement, and to have a government in power not hostile to His Majesty's Government. Grey hoped to have the best of both worlds; he wanted to win over the Young Turks to Britain's side without asuming any responsibility or arousing the suspicions and jealousies of the other Powers jockeying for position at Constantinople.

Britain's sympathetic policy soon paid handsome dividends. The new regime became distinctly pro-British and tended to be guided by advice from the Foreign Office and the British Embassy at Constantinople. This was partly a reaction to Abdülhamid's pro-German policy, and partly because the revolution had been constitutional in character and therefore looked to Britain, 'the mother of parliaments' for guidance and inspiration. As an expression of this Anglophile sentiment Kâmil Paşa was made grand vezir.[10] but the real reasons for the pro-British proclivities of the Young Turks are to be found in the character of their movement.

Subsequent events of the 1908 Revolution have distorted the real origins of the Young Turk movement and created certain myths about the period as a whole. The exploits of Enver Paşa have been projected back in time, and this has exaggerated the role of the mili-

---

9 Same to Same, n. 7.
10 Fitzmaurice to Tyrrell, n. 1.

tary (always assumed to be monolithic and pro-German) in the revolution. As a result, the part that civilians played in the revolution and the constitutional period has been minimised.

The Young Turks of 1908 were the idealogical heirs of the Young Ottomans of the late nineteenth century. Like their predecessors, they were Liberals in the tradition of nineteenth century Europe and took their inspiration from France and England. The leaders of both movements were civilians, and if soldiers played any role in these movements it was one of action and not policy making.[11]

It is true that the revolution was triggered off by a rebellion of junion officers of the Third Army in Macedonia. But it was the civilians in the Committee of Union and Progress (C.U.P.), a revolutionary society in Macedonia, who exploited the rebellion and brought it to fruition. The constitutional regime, up to 1914 at least, was always dominated by the civilian element. It was the civilians (like Talât, Nazım, Cavid, and Hüseyin Cahit for the C.U.P., and İsmail Kemal, Prince Sabahaddin, and Ali Kemal for the Opposition) who formulated the policy for the Young Turks. The junior officers (Enver, Niyazi, Eyüp Sabri and Sadık Bey, to mention only a few of the prominent ones) assumed political importance only during times of crisis, such a the counter-revolution of April 13, 1909, the movement of the 'Saviour Officers' of July, 1912, and the coup d'état of January 23, 1913.[12] As for the senior officers, (Mahmut Şevket Paşa, Mahmut Muhtar Paşa, İzzet Paşa...) it is a misnomer to call them Young Turks because this term has political implications. The higher echelons of the Ottoman Army were by and large apolitical. If the senior officers co-operated with the Unionists, it was because they too wanted to save the Empire. The Unionists 'co-operated' with them because they had

---

11 For a penetrating study of the development of the political ideas of the Young Ottomans up to 1876 see Şerif Mardin, *The Genesis of Young Ottoman Thought*, Princeton, 1962; For those of the Young Turks see Şerif mardin, *Jön Türklerin Siyasî Fikirleri*, Ankara, 1964.
12 Bernard Lewis, *Emergence of Modern Turkey*, London, 1962, 211-20.

the power. The officers were always suspect; idealogically both were-poles apart.[13]

The revolution of 1908 was inspired by the idea of saving the Ottoman Empire. The Young Turks, and the Young Ottomans before them hoped to achieve this by reforming the Empire and turning it into a modern constitutional state. This intention had been stated on earlier occasions, notably in 1839, 1856, and 1876. But little had been done to translate intent into action.

By 1908 the situation had changed both in the Empire and in the rest of the world. Within the Empire the threat of secession by the non-Turkish elements was growing day by day, bringing with it the menace of foreign intervention. In Macedonia where this threat was strongest, there emerged a new social group. This group was created as a result of the military and educational reforms carried out by Abdülhamid during the 1880's and 90's. Unlike its predecessors the Young Ottomans, very few members of this new group were bureaucrats of the Porte. Most of them were teachers and lecturers in the newly established schools and colleges, or junior officers educated there. Therefore this group, which as yet did not have any vested interests, did not see reform as a means of preserving its position as an elite. This group saw constitutionalism and reform as a means of saving the state and bringing it in line with the modern world.

Since the social and economic base of this group was much broader, it was much less committed to traditional values. Once in power it was therefore much less accommodating in its relations with traditional elements and institutions. It could therefore accept more readily the necessity of cultural and social change as an essential part of the process of modernisation. Externally, Japan's success in trans-

---

13 Mehmet Cavit Bey's Memoirs concerning the Constitutional Period, *Tanin*, 16 January, 1944. On Mahmut Şevket Paşa's resignation in June, 1912, Cavit Bey wrote: 'They consider him to be the greatest supporter and benefactor of Young Turk power! They do no know what enmity there is [between Şevket Paşa and the Young Turks]. Alas, all history is written in this manner.'

forming herself into a modern power, and her acceptance in the club of Great Powers, was perhaps the most important factor in raising Turkish hopes in modernisation. So much so that some Unionists saw 'Turkey (as) the Japan of the Near East.'[14]

The determination of the Young Turks to modernise the Ottoman Empire was reflected in the political programme of Kâmil Paşa and other successive grand vezir.[15] The traditional Millet system, being incompatible with the concept of modern state, since it permitted each religious community to have its own law, was sentenced to death. Henceforth all Ottomans, regardless of their ethnic origins or religious beliefs, were granted the same rights and duties. Extra-territorial rights (capitulations) enjoyed by foreigners in the Empire were also inconsistent with the idea of one law for all and were dully attacked. But the Young Turks were practical men. They realised that the political and socio-economic reforms they envisaged could not be achieved in a short span of time. And nowhere did they show more maturity and patience than in their relations with the foreign Powers.

The Young Turks were determined to redeem their Empire from European control. This, however, did not make them into rabid anti-Europeans. Between Young Turkey and Europe there existed a kind of love-hate relationship. Though the Young Turks resented European power and control, they realised the need for capital investment from Europe in order to create and sustain a modern economic structure, and the necessity for European specialists in order to re-organise the decaying administration of the Empire. They were willing to use both European capital and know-how so long as it did not entail the loss of

---

14 Ahmed Rıza and Nazım Bey's interview with Sir Edward Grey and Sir Charles Hardinge, Grey to Lowther, Private, London, 13 November, 1908, F.O. 800/184A.

15 Kâmil Paşa's programme is *Sabah*, No. 6786, 16 August, 1908. Translation of programme in Lowther to Grey, No. 494, Confid. Therapia, 18 August, 1908, F.O. 371/546/29298; Hilmi Paşa's programme in *Tanin*, No. 261, 25 May, 1909; Hakkı Paşa's programme in *Yeni Tanin*, No. 33, 26 January, 1910; Said Paşa's in *Tanin*, No. 124, 19 October, 1911.

political freedom.[16] If, paradoxically, they encouraged Britain to play a more active role, it was because she was the Great Power with the weakest foothold in the Empire. Germany had acquired a strong political position in Constantinople on account of Abdülhamid's patronage and retained it because of the valuable concession for the Baghdad Railway. France had a vast financial stake in the Empire and exercised considerable political control through the Ottoman Bank, a French concern.[17] By encouraging Britain to compete against France and Germany for new concessions, the Young Turks hoped to break the monopoly of the latter Powers, and to acquire greater independence for the Ottoman Government.

On July 12, 1908, while the revolution in Macedonia was taking place, an emissary of the C.U.P. visited the British Vice-Consul in Monastir. He asked Mr. Heathcote what H.M.G.'s attitude would be if a constitutional regime were established locally, and 'laid great stress on the desire of his party to return to the traditional policy of friendship with Great Britain, and, in this connection he said, that no enquiries were to be addressed to the Consulates of the other Powers here.'[18] The reception accorded to the new British Ambassador on his arrival in Constantinople made it quite clear where the Young Turks placed their hopes. Their policy towards Egypt (and Cyrus), about which the British had been most apprehensive, was conciliatory. Lowther noted that 'there have been no murmurs and lamentations over Cyprus and Egypt, and the general view has been that Egypt has

16 In 1908 the Porte used M. Laurent (France) as adviser to the Finance Ministry, Mr. Crawford (England) to reorganise the Customs, Sir W. Willcocks (England) in the Ministry of Public Works, Admiral Gamble (England) to reorganise the Ottoman navy, and General Von der Goltz (Germany) to reorganise the army. Annual Report, 1908, in Lowther to Grey, No. 105, Confid., Pera, 17 February, 1909, F.O. 371/768/7053.
17 'French Interests in the Near East', i and ii, *The Times*, London, 17 and 24 June, 1910. For the role of the Ottoman bank in Turkish politics, see *Tanin*, No. 727, 9 September, 1910, and *The Times* 19, 23 and 24, September, 1910.
18 Heatcote to Barclay, Monastir, 13 July, 1908, enclosure in Barclay to Grey, No. 400, Confid., 20 July, 1908. F.O. 371/544/25649.

under British rule, as well as Cyprus, been blessed by a good government such as is looked for here under the new regime.'[19] When Young Egyptians arrived in Constantinople seeking support for their movement,

'... they met with no encouragement. They were told that they were not suffering from corrupt administration; since they had been under British tutelage their resources had not been squandered or their people oppressed, they had enjoyed civil liberties, and had been raised to the condition of prosperity and security unknown before. The emissaries, not only met with no encouragement, but were practically forbidden to vent their ideas here.'[20]

British prestige stood very high in the months that followed the re-establishment of the constitution. It was further enhanced in October, 1908, by Bulgaria's declaration of independence, and Austria-Hungary's annexation of Bosnia and Herzegovina. The Young Turks were most indignant at Europe's behaviour towards the new regime. Feeling against Austria-Hungary and her ally Germany ran high. There was even some suspicion as to the Russian role in the declaration of Bulgarian independence. Only Great Britain's reputation remained untarnished.

On October 5, Grey informed the Turkish Ambassador that Britain would not recognise the actions of Bulgaria and Austria-Hungary until she knew the opinions of the other signatories of the Treaty of Berlin, especially Turkey.[21] He advised the Porte against war, and promised to give all possible support to Turkey's claim for compensation.[22] Britain's policy throughout the crisis was to localise the issues and, as far as possible, to support Turkey. Grey was opposed to the idea of a conference of signatories because he thought it might lead to a discussion of other outstanding problems notably the question of

---

19 Annual Report, 1908, n. 16, 10.
20 *Ibid.*, 7-8.
21 Grey to Lowther, No. 284, Confid., Foreign Office, 5 October, 1908, F.O. 371/551/34595.
22 *Ibid.*

the Straits. Rather than benefit the Porte, it would make the situation worse. Every power would demand compensation from the Turks and 'it is not easy to see what compensation could be given to France, Germany, and England.'[23]

In Constantinople there was a deep sense of frustration and impotence. The Young Turks felt let down and isolated. Some of this frustration found an outlet in the boycott organised against Austria-Hungary. Apart from this, the Turkish reaction is notable only for its moderation possibly brought about by the fear of reaction against the new regime. The *Tanin* even suggested that this had been Austria's motive in striking a blow against the constitution; to assist reaction in order to bring down the new regime. It therefore advised moderation and restraint.[24] At this point it was difficult to envisage any other line of action.

In this mood and atmosphere, Ahmed Rıza and Nazım Bey, two prominent Unionists went to see Sir Edward Grey and Sir Charles Hardinge. They proposed that Great Britain make an alliance with Turkey, as France would certainly follow.[25] Grey writes:

'I told them that our habit was to keep our hands free, though we made ententes and friendships. It was true that we had an alliance with Japan, but it was limited to certain distant questions in the Far East.

They replied that Turkey was the Japan of the Near East, and that we already had the cyprus Convention with Turkey, which was still in force.

I said that they had our entire sympathy in the good work they were doing in Turkey itself; we wished them well, and we would help them in their internal affairs by lending them men to organise customs, Police, and so forth, if they wished them.'[26]

---

23 Grey to Bertie, No. 477, Confid, Foreign Office, 5 October, 1908, F.O. 371/551/34775.
24 *Tanin*, No. 69, 8 October, 1908.
25 Grey to Lowther, Private, London, 13 November, 1908, F.O. 800/185A.
26 *Ibid.*

Throughout this period Great Britain's relations with the Young Turks were carried out at two different levels; on the one hand at the Foreign Office, where the policy was actually formulated in the context of British foreign policy as a whole; on the other hand there was the British Embassy at Constantinople whose function it was to execute as closely as possible the policy of the home Government. The Embassy also interpreted prevailing public opinion and explained to its Government the arguments and motives of the Porte. Whereas the policy was formulated in an atmosphere carefully weighed and analysed, it was executed in an atmosphere of almost total subjectivity where personalities and prejudices played a major part.

The revolution radically changed the status of the British Embassy at Constantinople. The Young Turks were trying to curb the powers that foreign embassies enjoyed in the internal affairs of the Empire. Consequently, they created difficulties in settling minor questions which the dragomans had been able to settle with ease in the past. Rıfat Paşa, when he became Foreign Minister, refused to receive dragomans and would discuss matters only with the Ambassadors. The Embassy naturally found this change in their situation and 'the froth and arrogance of the Young Turks... very distasteful and irritating...'[27]

Lowther himself found the changes taking place after the revolution a little hard to stomach. He was no newcomer to the Ottoman Empire, having served under Sir William White as head of the Chancery.[28] Soon after his arrival he commented:

---

27 Sir Telford Waugh, *Turkey Yesterday, To-day and Tomorrow*, London, 1930, 131; for a discussion of the role of the British dragomans at their height in nineteenth century Ottoman Empire, see Allan Cunningham, 'Dragomania: The Dragomans of the British Embassy in Turkey', *St. Antony's Papers*, No. 11, *Middle Eastern Affairs*, No. 2, 81-100. On the decline in the powers of the dragomans see Sir Andrew Ryan, *The Last of the Dragomans*, London, 1951, Passim, and Noel Buxton, 'Young Turkey After Two Years', *The Nineteenth Century*, lxix, 1911, 427.

28 Waugh, n. 27, 21.

'The astonishing changes which I found taking place on my arrival here were difficult to realize for one who had known the country previously... But I was at once struck with the impression that the 'Ottoman League of Progress and Union' lacked responsible leaders of position.'[29]

Lowther has been described by one of his subordinates as 'a rich man and very much a grand seigneur... apt to look down on upstarts (Unionists) playing at statesmanship.'[30] It is not surprising therefore, that he preferred to deal with the 'old Turks', particularly Kâmil Paşa, the 'Grand Old Man of Turkey', and a symbol of the Turkey Lowther had known twenty years earlier. While Kâmil was in charge, the Embassy's attitude towards the C.U.P. was one of tolerance. When the Committee challenged Kâmil's position, the Embassy became critical and hostile.

The Committee knew how valuable Kâmil was for maintaining good relations with Great Britain. In September they assured Lowther that in spite of Kâmil's great age they intended to maintain him in power.[31] But having destroyed the despotism of the Palace, the Unionists were determined not to compromise the revolution by permitting Kâmil to transfer this despotism to the Porte.

Kâmil Paşa, a pillar of the Porte, bitterly resented what he considered was interference by a body with no legal standing in the government. To Lowther he complained of Ahmed Rıza and Nazım Bey's mission to European capitals where they spoke as if they represented the Ottoman Government.[32] When the Committee entrusted Kâmil with the duty of entertaining the Balkan Committee, without even consulting him, he was offended and insulted.[33] He was determined to

---

29 Lowther to Grey, Therapia, 4 August, 1908, B.D. v, 264.
30 Ryan, n. 27, 71. For Kâmil Pasa's opinion of Lowther see *Bulletin of the School of Oriental and African Studies*, xxiii, 1960, 147.
31 Talât and Bahaeddin Şakir's interview with Lowther; see Lowther to Grey, No. 541, Confid, Therapia, 2 September, 1908, F.O. 371/559/31787.
32 Lowther to Grey, No. 855, Confid., Pera, 13 December, 1908, F.O. 371/546/43987.
33 *Ibid.*

become independent by ending the Committe's influence in Turkish politics. He thought he could do so once parliament was convened because he felt sure that the Unionists would not be able to command a majority in the Chamber.[34]

The Unionists, alarmed by Kâmil's self-confidence, tried to restrain him by attacking him and his policies in their press. But, apart from a few extremists, the C.U.P. as a whole, had no desire to bring down Kâmil Paşa. That is why they gave him an overwhelming vote of confidence on January 13, 1909, after a debate on foreign affairs.[35] Kâmil and the Liberal opposition saw the vote as their triumph and a rebuff for the Committee. With the Chamber behind them and negotiations with Bulgaria and Austria-Hungary in progress, they considered the moment opportune to appoint their own Ministers of War and Marine, and seize the initiative from the Unionists.[36]

On February 10, Kâmil appointed Nazım Paşa Minister of War in place of Ali Rıza Paşa. Vice-Admiral Hüseyin Hüsnü Paşa replaced Arif Paşa as Minister of Marine. The Committee rose to the occasion. Kâmil's action was denounced as a coup d'état, an encroachment on the rights of Parliament, and a violation of constitutional principles.[37] Meanwhile four ministers resigned from the cabinet protesting that they would not work with a President who made such important changes without consulting his colleagues.[38] The Chamber assembled on Saturday, February 13, to interpellate Kâmil on the ministerial changes. Kâmil was summoned but refused to come, using persuasion and threats to have the interpellation postponed. But the Chamber was

---

34 Lowther to Grey, No. 415, Confid., Constantinople, 12 December, 1908, F.O. 371/557/43443.

35 *The Levante Herald*, 15 January, 1909; Same to Same, No. 40, Confid., Pera, 19 January, 1909, F.O. 371/760/3127; Sir Adam Block to Hardinge, Constantinople, 13 January, 1909, F.O. 371/762/2419.

36 İsmail Kemal, *The Memoirs of İsmail Kemal Bey*, London, 1920, 324.

37 Lowther to Grey, No. 102, Confid., Pera, 15 February, 1909, F.O. 371/760/7050; A.F. Türkgeldi, *Görüp İşittiklerim*, Ankara, 1951, 18-9, Ali Cevat, *İkinci Meşrutiyet'in İlanı ve Otuzbir Mart Hâdisesi*, Ankara, 1960, 35-6.

38 Türkgeldi, n. 37, 20, İsmail Kemal, n. 36, 324.

in no mood to delay, and without hearing Kâmil's explanation, the deputies passed a vote of no confidence in Kâmil by 198 votes to 8.[39]

The C.U.P. knew that Kâmil's fall would have an adverse effect on their relations with Britain. Wishing to avoid this, they sent a deputation to Lowther. They explained that they had opposed Kâmil for unconstitutional acts, and promised to withhold their support from any ministry which might succeed him unless it pursued his policy of friendship for England.[40] Hüseyin Hilmi Paşa, who succeeded Kâmil as grand vezir, personally told Lowther that his policy towards England would be the same as that of his predecessors, and that he would still count on the support and advice of H.M.G.[41] but Lowther had already made up his mind about the Unionists and was therefore not in the least re-assured by these conciliatory protestations.[42]

Lowther's despatches reveal that his attitude towards the C.U.P. had already changed in December 1908 about the time of the Unionist press attacks on Kâmil. He described these attacks as being made under the influence of the German Embassy, hoping thereby to influence the Foreign Office into changing its policy of benevolent neutrality towards the Committee to one of hostility.[43] But at the Foreign Office they remained unconvinced about German influence on the Committee.[44] In later despatches Lowther found the Unionists were getting chauvinistic, and suggested that they be restrained by making it clear to them that 'those who have money to lend will not do so unless the Government is in the hands of men experience on whom some reliance can be placed.'[45] After Kâmil's fall Lowther's attitude towards the Committee crystallised into one of open sympathy and

---

39 Lowther to Grey, n. 37, Türkgeldi, 20-1.
40 Some to Some, No. 51, Tel/Confid., Constantinople, 14 February, 1909, F.O. 371/760/5984; Hüseyin Cahit, "Kabinenin Sükûtu ve İngiltere", *Tanin*, No. 190, 15 February, 1909.
41 Same to Same, No. 53, Tel/Confid, Constantinople, 15 February, 1909, F.O. 371/760/6275.
42 Same to Same, n. 40.
43 Same to Same, n. 34.
44 Hardinge's Minute in *Ibid*.
45 Same to Same, Private, Constantinople, 29 December, 1908, F.O. 800/78.

possibly connivance with the Opposition in order to bring down the C.U.P. From February until the counter-revolution on April 13, 'the British Embassy... paid court to İsmail Kemal and the Committee's enemies.'[46] It was only they who had access to Lowther. They assured him that 80% of the population were opposed to the Committee, and that they 'look to England to help them rid themselves of this new despotism of men who, ... have not even the traditions of the Sultanate or the Caliphate...'[47]

What role the British Embassy played in bringing about the counter-revolution is difficult to ascertain. Foreign Office sources have very little to say on this. Contemporary Turkish sources are also inarticulate. But this may mean two things; firstly that the Embassy did not in fact play any role at all; or secondly, that the Embassy took great pains to cover up its tracks. However, from Halide Edip who witnessed these events, we learn that Derviş Vahdeti, one of the chief architects of the revolt 'was thought to be a paid emissary of the British Embassy, a tool of Mr. Fitzmaurice.'[48] If this is true, it explains how the *Volkan*, the reactionary newspaper Vahdeti edited, could be distributed free in Constantinople on the eve of the counter-revolution. It is said that the Palace financed Vahdeti. But Ali Cevat, first secretary to Abülhamid, writes that though a request for financial aid was made, the Palace turned it down.[49]

Hüseyin Cahit Yalçın, who was a prominent Unionist, Deputy for Constantinople and editor of the *Tanin*, writes how Fitzmaurice worked to undermine the position of the C.U.P. and the revolution. He describes Fitzmaurice as 'a hypocrite who played the most ill-omened role during the period of the Constitution.'[50] P. P. Graves,

---

46 Francis McCullagh, 'The Broad Road', *The Evening Leader*, 3 February, 1910. McCullagh was a journalist who observed these events in Constantinople. His other works are: 'The Constantinople Mutiny of April 13' in *The Fortnightly Review*, 86 1909 58-69 and *The Fall of Abd-ul-Hamid*, London, 1910.

47 Lowther to Grey, No. 151, Confid., Pera, 3 March, 1909, F.O. 371/761/8914.

48 Halide Edib, *Memoirs*, London 1926, 278.

49 Ali Cevat, n. 37, 45-6.

50 H. C. Yalçın, '1908 İnkılabı İnkılabçı Değildi', *Yakın Tarihimiz*, Ankara, 1962, ii, 179.

Constantinople correspondent of *The Times*, reports that Fitzmaurice's visits to Yıldız during the mutiny gave rise to a whispering campaign against the British. But he points out that Fitzmaurice went to Yıldız only 'with the proper object of discovering what the Guard troops were likely to do and whether the Sultan was taking a hand in the trouble...'[51]

The Foreign Office had their own doubts about Fitzmaurice's activities and wrote to Lowther in this vein. Hardinge asked Lowther whether his first dragoman kept him well informed, and told him 'to impress upon Fitzmaurice, who naturally is regarded by the Turks as your 'alter-ego', and who is, as we know an impressionable Irishman, that he should adopt a sympathetic attitude towards the Young Turks...'[52] Three and a half years later Fitzmaurice denied ever having intrigued against the C.U.P. or having supported Kâmil Paşa.[53]

We do know that the *Levante Herald*, a local paper financed by the British played an active role against the C.U.P. prior to the revolution of 13 April. Sir Adam Block who had been a first dragoman of the Embassy, and was the President of the Public Debt in 1909, wrote to Hardinge expressing this view. He even suggested that the Embassy buy out the paper and run it.[54] – So much for the Embassy's part in bringing about the counter-revolution.

In 1913 they were again involved in incidents of doubtful character concerning Kâmil Paşa's arrival in Constantinople some days before the assassination of Mahmut Şevket Paşa,[55] Cemal Paşa, the military commander of the capital, in his memoirs describes Fitzmaurice as 'the embodiment of the devil who was the real master-

---

51 P. P. Graves, *Briton & Turk*, London 1941, 136.
52 Hardinge to Lowther Private, 1 May and 29 June, 1909, F.O. 800/185A.
53 Fitzmaurice to Tyrrell, Constantinople, 18 December, 1912, F.O. 800/79.
54 Block to Hardinge, Private, Constantinople, 12 May, 1909, F.O. 800/184, Hardinge Papers, Public Record Office, London.
55 Lord Kitchener to Lowther, Telegraphic, 7 April, 1913; Lowther to Kitchener, Pera, 8 April, 1913; Kitchener to Lowther, Cairo, 22 April, 1913; Lowther to Kitchener, Telegraphic, Pera, 22 April, 1913 in F.O. 371/2452/1574.

mind behind Mahmut Şevket Paşa's assassination...'[56] Once in Constantinople Kâmil was virtually under the protection of the British Embassy. When Cemal Paşa tried to have the ex-grand vezir extradited, Fitzmaurice successfully intervened on Kâmil's behalf.[57] It seems that the Unionists could do nothing about Fitzmaurice's interference in their politics while Lowther remained ambassador. But after Şevket Paşa's assassination, and the arrival of Sir Louis Mallet as the new British ambassador, the Unionists requested him to have Fitzmaurice and Major Tyrrell, the military attaché, sent home for their role in the assasination plot. This request wa promptly carried out.[58]

The counter-revolution broke out on the night of 12-13 April, 1909. Throughout the revolt the sympathy and support of the British Embassy were always with the Liberals. At the request of İsmail Kemal, leader of the Liberal Union (Ahrar Fırkası), Lowther instructed his consuls in Macedonia 'to assure the population that the Constitution was not compromised' by the revolt. It was hoped thereby to prevent the Third Army from intervening.[59] This measure failed to have the desired effect and the capital was invested by the 'Action Army' (Hareket Ordusu) from Macedonia. Lowther was then asked to send Mr. Fitzmaurice, the first dragoman of the British Embassy, to accompany a deputation which was going to negotiate with the investing army. The Liberals calculated that evidence of British support would strengthen their bargaining position.[60] Once again the object was not achieved and the 'Action Army' remained unmoved.

Lowther's motive for supporting the Opposition seems to have been to bring back Kâmil Paşa to the grand vezir. On the evening of

---

56 Cemal Paşa, *Hâtıralar*, İstanbul 1959, 43. This line is omitted in the English translation, *Djemal Paşa, Memoires of a Turkish Statesman, 1913-1919*, London 1922, 30.

57 *Ibid* (both), 43 and 30-1 respectively.

58 *Ibid* (both), 112 and 100 respectively. This translation once again omits the sentence about their role in the plot.

59 İsmail Kemal, n. 36, 343, Lowther to Grey, No. 287, Confid., Constantinople, 20 April, 1909, F.O. 371/771/15783.

60 Same to Same, No. 129, Tel/Confid., Constantinople, 17 April, 1909, F.O. 371/770/14474.

April 13 he informed Grey that Kâmil had been re-appointed grand vezir, with Nazım Paşa as War Minister and Said Paşa as Foreign Minister.[61] Lowther was obviously misinformed though this is possibly what the Liberals had planned and expected to happen. The new grand vezir, Tevfik Paşa, was appointed after 8.5 p.m., and it was only after the announcement of the appointments of the new ministers, that the mutinous troops dispersed. Lowther consoled himself by thinking that Tevfik had been appointed because he was more 'colourless' and presumably because 'the Sultan could not at once call for Kamil having so recently commended the Committee...'[62] He still hoped that Kâmil would be recalled once the Liberals were firmly in the saddle. Perhaps he would have been had the counter-revolution not been so completely crushed.

Grey's policy towards Turkey was one of benevolent neutrality. Throughout the period 1908-1914 he was naturally more deeply involved in the European situation, and, was therefore pro-Turkish to the extent of not arousing the jealousies and suspicions of the other powers. That is why an Anglo-Turkish alliance was always out of the question. He sympathised with the Young Turks without differentiating between their various factions. His principle was to support 'any Turkish government which pursues these objects (constitutional government and reform) honestly and with a single eye to public interest.'[63] To him it was almost a matter of indifference as to whether it was the Unionists or the Liberals in power.

Lowther's despatches had made the Foreign Office aware that their Ambassador was interpreting their policy too freely, and perhaps even going beyond instructions. On February 6, 1909, a week before Kâmil's fall, Hardinge aired the F.O.'s suspicions. He wrote:

---

61 Same to Same, No. 108, Tel/Confid., Constantinople, 13 April, 1909, 8.5 p.m., F.O. 371/770/13942.

62 Lowther to Hardinge, Constantinople, 14 April, 1909, F.O. 800/184.

63 Grey to Lowther, No. 242, Confid., Foreign Office, 15 April, 1909, F.O. 371/775/15783.

'Unfortunately you do not give us any indication in your telegrams of the language which you used to the Turks, and we are consequently very much in the dark and have to provide you – often unnecessarily, I imagine – with arguments to substantiate our views, and to press our policy... I think it will be better in your own interest if you tell us what you say to the Turks and how they take it... I think that you do not do yourself justice by suppressing the line of argument you take with the grand vezir.'[64]

Regarding Kâmil's fall the Foreign Office was not very happy but they nevertheless took it calmly. They knew that no change, short of the restoration of the Palace regime, would be detrimental to Britain. Therefore Lowther was advised 'not to show in any way that our feelings have changed towards the new regime, and not to do anything which might be interpreted in that sense.'[65]

The counter-revolution did not create a stir at the Foreign Office, and Grey consistent with his policy, recognised the de facto government of Tevfik Paşa on condition that it pursue constitutional government and reform.[66] A fortnight later, after the revolt had been crushed Grey was now more convinced than ever that in Turkey the Unionists were the people to back. To Lowther he wrote:

'I think that during the last three or four months we have let ourselves slide too much into a critical attitude towards the Committee and the Young Turks... but they have shown there is real stuff in them, and we must be less critical and more sympathetic.

'I put these views before you, because it seems to me important that we should be on the side on which there is hope for Turkey, and should concentrate our influence on the advice which is really important.'[67]

---

64 Hardinge to Lowther, Private, 6 February, 1909, F.O. 800/185A.
65 Same to Same, Private, Foreign Office, 23 February, 1909, P.O. 800/185A, also 23 March, 1909.
66 Grey to Lowther, n. 53.
67 Same to same, Private, 30 April, 1909, F.O. 800/78.

The F.O. was aware that if the British Embassy's attitude towards the Committee remained unsympathetic, the Unionists would turn away from Britain and lean on another power. Britain would lose her splendid position on the Bosphorus.[68] This fear haunted the Foreign Office for six years, and on August 2, 1914, it was realised by the signing of the alliance between Germany and Turkey.

Paradoxically Britain's position at Constantinople was not undermined by her Embassy's anti-Unionist attitude. This was largely because the counter-revolution had changed the political situation in the Empire by introducing a new factor in Turkish politics, namely the senior officer. The army, through the junior officers, had already played a major role in bringing about the 1908 Revolution. But the senior officers had, by and large, remained aloof from the revolutionary circles, and some had even sided with the Sultan. The outbreak of 1909 however revealed the civilians' incapacity to maintain law and order. Worse still however, from the point of view of the army, military discipline was allowed to deteriorate, resulting in the mutiny of the Constantinople garrison.

Mahmut Şevket Paşa, Commander of the Third Army Corps, had led the 'Action Army' in order to restore order in the capital and to re-establish the constitution. But once the revolt had been crushed, his actions made it abundantly clear that he intended the Empire to have a tutelary constitutional regime, with the army as its guardians. Martial law, imposed on the capital in May and prolonged until March, 1911, would achieve this by placing the soldier above the politician.[69]

The civilians resented bitterly te intrusion of the army in government. But neither the Porte nor the Committee was able to challenge Şevket Paşa's supreme position. The Committee had suffered a great setback during the counter-revolution. Şevket Paşa had strength-

---

68 Hardinge to Lowther, Private, Foreign Office, 1 May, 1909, F.O. 800/185A.
69 Lowther to Grey, No. 654, Confid., Therapia, 11 August, 1909, F.O. 371/779/30767.

ened his own position by becoming Inspector-General of the first three army corps, an office specially designed to make him independent of the War Minister and the Cabinet. In May, 1909, he was regarded as virtually a dictator.[70] The C.U.P. realised that the army's position could be undermined by attacks on Germany. The senior officers by tradition and training looked to Germany for support and sympathy. Therefore attacks on Germany would be indirect attacks on them. The converse of this manœuvre was friendship with Germany's rival, Great Britain. Consequently, in 1909 political expediency forced the Young Turks to turn to Britain, and the Triple Entente.

In July, 1909 an Ottoman Parliamentary Deputation visited Paris and London.[71] In the same month the Unionists approached Kâmil Paşa offering to bring him back to power if he agreed to include some of their members in his cabinet.[72] They attacked Germany for obstructing in parliament the scheme to fuse the Ottoman Navigation Company, the Hamidieh, with an English concern, the Lynch Company.[73] Mahmut Şevket and the German General, Von der Goltz, were accusedof trying to overthrow the C.U.P. to set up a military dictatorship devoted to German interests.[74] In December, the debate in parliament on the fusion scheme came to be regarded as a trial of strength between British and German influence. When Hilmi Paşa, who supported fusion, was given a vote of confidence, it seemed as if British influence had triumphed.[75]

These pro-British manifestations, however, were somewhat illusory. Not that the Young Turks were insincere in their Anglophile atti-

---

70 Conyers Surtees to Lowther, No. 39, Confid., Pera, 14 May, 1909, F.O. 371/776/19410, H. Z. Uşaklıgil, *Saray ve Ötesi*, İstanbul, 1940, i, 42-5.

71 Lowther to Grey, No. 510, Confid. Therapia, 1 July, 1909, F.O. 371/778/25436. Also the *Times*, 2, 7, 8, 15, 16, 19, 20, July, 1909.

72 Same to Same, Private, Constantinople, 20 July, 1908, F.O. 800/78.

73 *Jeune Turc*, 12 December, 1909, enclosure in Marling to Grey, No. 967, Very Confidential, Constantinople, 14 December, 1909, F.O. 371/781/46061, and Hüseyin Cahit, 'Almanlar ve Osmanlılar', *Tanin*, No. 464, 17 December, 1909.

74 *Jeune Turch, Ibid.*

75 *Times*, 11, 13, 14, December, 1909.

tude. But the issue of Britain's position in the Persian Gulf and Iraq stood in the way of good relations.[76] The Young Turks could not ignore Iraq as they had ignored Egypt. Unlike Egypt, Iraq sent deputies to Constantinople. These men, wary of British penetration, acted as a powerful lobby in parliament against concessions being granted to British concerns.[77] While the Young Turks had supported Hilmi Paşa over the Lynch affair, they could not flout Arab opinion by actually granting the concession to a British firm. This is probably why Hilmi Paşa resigned on December 28, two weeks after receiving an overwhelming vote of confidence in the Chamber.[78]

His successor would not be bound by his decision, and Hakkı Paşa, not only reversed his predecessor's decision concerning the Lynch concession, but he went even further and refused to grant other concessions earmarked for British enterprise in Iraq.[79]

Britain's relations with the Young Turks remained cool throughout Hakkı Paşa's grand vezir. One cause of this cool relationship was Iraq.[80] Another was Britain's support for France in the 1910 loan negotiations with the Porte in which France clearly wished 'to break Djavid Bey' and establish a control over Turkish finances. After protracted negotations in Paris, London, and Berlin, the loan was finally floated in Germany.[81] But Britain once again showed how she

---

76 The term Iraq is used in preference to Mesopotamia. Originally the term Mesopotamia was used for only the northern part of present day Iraq. In the nineteenth and early twentieth centuries the term Mesopotamia was used for both lower and upper Iraq.

77 Ryan, n. 27, 76-7; *Stamboul*, 22 December, 1909 and Folio No. 1236 in series F.O. 371 (1911). For the role of the Arab lobby in the Turkish parliament, see Neville Maudel, "Turks, Arabs and Jewish Immigration into Palestine, 1882-1914', *St. Antony's Papers*, No. 17, Middle Eastern Affairs, No. 4, 92ff.

78 *The Levante Herald*, 29 December, 1909.

79 Grey to Lowther, No. 37, Tel/Confid., Foreign Office, 17 February, 1910, F.O. 371/1004/5693.

80 Memorandum of interview with Hakkı Paşa, grand vezir, on 29 December, 1910. Enclosure in Sir H. Babington Smih to Sir A. Nicolson, Constantinople, 30 December, 1910, F.O. 371/1240/636.

81 Block to Hardinge, Constantinople, 21 September, 1910, f.O. 371/994/38775; Cavid Bey to Mr. Buxton, Conwell-Evans, n. 3, 30-1.

was willing to sacrifice Turkey in order to maintain a strong Triple Entente.

The Turko-Italian War of September, 1911, placed Britain in a strong position at Constantinople. The anticipation of war had forced the Young Turks to woo Britain. Hüseyin Cahit had urged the Ottoman press to refrain from appealing to Pan-Islamic sentiments or from raising the Egyptian question. He had concluded that 'Young Turkey and the C.U.P. have had no connection with the internal affairs of Egypt or its internal organisation... it would therefore be a grave error to raise the question of Egypt and disturb our friendly relations with Britain.'[82] Once again the Young Turks found themselves isolated. The policy of neutrality had proved a failure and they realised the need for an ally. Germany could not possibly help Turkey since Italy was her ally. The only course was to reach an understanding with a Triple Entente.[83]

Said Paşa, who succeeded Hakkı Paşa on September 29, 1911, addressed a communique to Great Britain, appealing for British intervention in the war.[84] A month later he proposed a formal alliance with either Britain alone, or with the Triple Entente. The only condition he laid down was that Britain should intervene and induce Italy to accept an arrangement on the basis of recognition of the sovereign rights of the Sultan over Tripoli.[85]

An alliance with Britain was not forthcoming. Mr. Ryan had already informed Kâmil that Turkey should not look for support to England.[86] Grey had also assured Parliament that Britain's only con-

---

82 Hüseyin Cahit, 'İttihad-ı İslâm ve Matbuat Osmaniye', *Tanin*, No. 1100, 23 September, 1911. The Turks never claimed their rights to send troops through Egypt or the right to call upon their suzerain, the Khedive, to furnish troops for the Ottoman Army. This would have embarrassed Britain. Sir Thomas Barclay, *The Turko-Italian War and its Problems*, London, 1912, 90-3.

83 Hüseyin Cahit, 'İttifak ve İttifaklar Karşısında Türkiye', *Tanin*, No. 1103, 28 September, 1911, and W. Langer, 'Russia, The Straits Question, and the Origins of the Balkan League', *Political Science Quarterly*, 1928, xliii, 359.

84 Grand vezir to Tewfik Paşa, 30 September, 1911, F.O. 371/1252/38346.

85 Turkish Minister of Foreign Affairs to Foreign Office, 31 October, 1911, F.O. 371/1263/48554.

86 Lowther to Grey, No. 236, Tel/Confid., Therapia, 4 October, 1911, F.O. 371/1252/39009.

cern with the conflict was her treaty right, i.e. the capitulations in the area.[87] At this moment Grey could not possibly sign an alliance with Turkey; that might bring the war to Europe. Grey did not, however, reject the idea of an alliance completely. He told the Turkish Ambassador that the time was inopportune to discuss an alliance since Britain had already declared her neutrality. But once relations between Turkey and Italy were pacific, he expressed his readiness 'to discuss and examine with the Imperial Ottoman Government the measures which might be adopted for establishing on firm and durable basis a thoroughly good understanding between the Ottoman Empire and this country.'[88] In spite of Britain's aloofness, her prestige at Constantinople remained high, and the Young Turk press continued to call for a closer understanding with Britain.[89]

The war struck a critical blow at the Committee's position in the country. Hakkı Paşa was forced to resign and in the months that followed, the Committee's influence continued to decline, and by January, 1912, it had reached rock bottom. Only by a constitutional manœuvre did the Unionists retain power for a few months longer. In January they had parliament dissolved and 'in April held a general election so well prepared and conducted that, out of a total of 275, only six opposition members managed to slip through into the Chamber.'[90] Meanwhile strong opposition to the Committee was fomenting and it emerged in May-June, 1912, calling itsel the 'Saviour Officers' (Halaskâr Zabitan). This group succeeded in ousting the C.U.P. from power. Şevket Paşa's resignation was followed by that of Said Paşa, and on July 21, Gazi Ahmed Muhtar Paşa was asked to form a cabinet.[91]

The war with Italy dragged on for the best part of 1912 and peace was made in October 17, only when the Balkan allies attacked.

---

87 Barclay, n. 72, 41.
88 Memorandum by Sir Edward Grey, Foreign Office, 2 November, 1911, B. D. ix, Part i, 780.
89 Lowther to Grey, No. 533, Confid., Constantinople, 24 June, 1912, F.O. 371/1495/27721.
90 Lewis, n. 12, 218.
91 *Ibid.*, 218-9.

Italy retained Tripoli, but allowed the Porte to save face by permitting the Sultan-Caliph to retain his right to appoint the Qadi of Tripoli. His representative to Tripoli was also permitted to act as the religious liaison between the Caliph and his Libyan followers.[92]

Having made peace with Italy, the Porte prepared to deal with the critical situation in the Balkans. In order to assume a diplomatic offensive, the Anglophile Kâmil Paşa was brought back on October 29. On November 7 Kâmil wrote a letter to Grey reminding him that England 'ruled a hundred million Muslims strongly attached by religion to the Caliphate.' He recalled how England had helped the Ottoman Empire during the Crimean War against Russia, and asked if Britain could now induce Russia, her ally, to prevent the war whose aim was to weaken Turkey. He concluded:

> 'If Turkey abandons a pro-English policy in order to follow the policy another power, it will only bring her loss and harm. On the other hand, the stronger and more powerful Turkey is, the more England will benefit; whereas the weaker Turkey is, the more England will suffer in those interests of hers on which it is not necessary to enlarge.'[93]

Neither the change of regime in Turkey nor Kâmil's sentimental reminescing made an impression on Grey. He had no intention of becoming involved in the Balkan conflagration on behalf of Turkey. His main preoccupation was to prevent it becoming a European affair. On September 20, he had instructed his Chargé d'Affaire at Constantinople to reject the Russian Ambassador's proposal to work for the accession of Kâmil to office. He refused to 'take responsibility that such active interference... would entail.'[94] Grey made it known to the Porte that none of the Powers would intervene to save Adrianople,

---

92 Article 2 of Turko-Italian Peace Treaty of 1912 in Karl Strupp, *Ausgewählte Diplomatische Aktenstücke zur Orientalischen Frage*, Gotha, 1916, 256ff.

93 Kâmil Paşa to Sir Edward Grey, 7 November, 1912, F.O. 800/79.

94 Grey to Marling, Foreign Office, 21 September, 1912, B. D. ix, Part i, 701.

just as no one had intervened to save anything else. The idea of territorial integrity was now a dead letter, and the Porte would do better to give Adrianople to the Bulgars, let it lose other things that were not already lost.[95]

However practical and realistic Grey's advice may have been, no cabinet in Turkey could take it with impunity. The Balkan crisis was totally different from all other previous crises. Bulgaria's declaration of independence and Austria-Hungary's annexation of Bosnia and Herzegovina had been issues of prestige. The Porte had exercised only a nominal sovereignty in both these places, and the same was the case with Egypt. The Tripoli war was fought partially because of the pressure of the Arab lobby in Parliament, and partially because the Young Turks felt the need to show some concern over their Arab provinces. But even in January, 1911, they had already admitted to themselves that Ottoman sovereignty in Tripoli was illusory, and since the Porte could not defend Tripoli directly, it would 'fall of its own weight like over-ripe fruit.'[96]

The Balkan Wars were fought over land which had for centuries provided the life blood of the Ottoman Empire. Constantinople and the very existence of the Empire were threatened and no territory could be conceded without a struggle. The very raison d'être of the revolution was at stake. No Turkish cabinet could surrender Adrianople to the Bulgars, and the fear that Kâmil was about to do so had led the Unionists to carry out a coup d'état on January 23, 1913. Adrianople did finally capitulate to a Serbo-Bulgarian army on March 26. But when the allies began bickering over the spoils of war, the Young Turks exploited the situation and recaptured the town and retained it as a part of the now truncated Ottoman Empire.

The diplomacy of the Balkan wars had convinced the Young Turks that Europe would no longer intervene to maintain the integri-

---

95 Grey to Lowhter, No. 11, Confid., Foreign Office, 8 January, 1912, F.O. 371/1757/1337 and Same to Same, 17 January, 1913, B. D. ix, Part ii, 417.
96 *Tanin*, No. 856, 21 January, 1911.

ty of the Empire if the Turks could not do so themselves. The initial reaction of the Young Turks was to call for self-reliance and to give up expecting European help.[97] Therefore immediately after the war military reforms were carried out designed to make the army better equipped for modern war. The Young Turks also realised that the survival of what remained of the Empire would be impossible without the support of a Great Power. The danger of isolation was only too evident, especially to the Young Turks who had seen their country threatened with partition for the past fifty years. Once more they angled for an English alliance. Britain had hardly been favourably disposed towards them, but then neither had any other Power. In an alliance, Britain with her navy still offered the best returns.

Tevfik Paşa reopened the subject of an Anglo-Turkish alliance in June, 1913. He reminded Sir Edward of Turkey's proposal of October, 1911, and of Sir Edward's readiness to discuss it once relations between Turkey and Italy were pacific.[98] Once more Britain turned down Turkey's proposal, and Sir Louis Mallet's memorandum made clear what Britain's attitude was towards the Young Turks:

> 'I assume that it is to the interpretation of Great Britain that the integrity of what remains of the Turkish Empire be maintained – a division of the Asiatic provinces into spheres of interest would not benefit us, but would seriously affect the balance of power on the Mediterranean, our position in Egypt, in the Persian Gulf, to say nothing of India, and might bring about a European war.
>
> 'All the Powers, until quite recently, have been unanimous in this view. The suggestion thrown out by Prince Lichnowsky to you [Grey] for partition into spheres of interest and Herr von Gwinner's remark to sir H. B. Smith are indications of a kind which cannot be ignored and which require careful consideration on our part, although it is not clear how far they are seriously intended or whether His Highness spoke on instructions...'

---

97 Babanzade İsmail Hakkı, 'Harp ve Diplomasi', *Tanin*, No. 1478, 22 October, 1912.
98 Draft of Grey's reply to Tevfik Paşa, Secret and not printed, 2 July, 1913, F.O. 371/1826/27117, kept with 28098.

Mallet then went on to say that the proposal from the Turkish ambassador must be considered in the light of the earlier poposal of 1911, and that:

'The same reasons no longer exist for deferring a decision, which so far, at any rate, an alliance with Great Britain is concerned cannot fail, I think, to be in the negative. If other Powers with confessed ambitions in the Near East did not exist or were not strong enough to make their voices heard, there would be something very attractive in undertaking the regeneration of the Turkish Empire – which we have been practically invited to do – in devoting ourselves to the reform of the administration, the improvement of the condition of the people and the commercial development of a great and rich country. In a short time there is little doubt that British Administration would convert a decaying Power into a strong ally, who owing to her gographical position would be a source of strength to us. But this is not within practical politics and if Turkey is to be reformed it will have to be with the assistance of all the Great Powers.

'An alliance with Turkey would in present circumstances unite Europe against us and be a source of weakness and danger to ourselves and Turkey. The second part of the Turkish proposal – namely that which relates to the inclusion of Turkey in the Triple Entente is a question on which His Majesty's Government will, I imagine, wish to know the views of the French and Russian Governments. To a certain extent the criticism which is applicable to an alliance with Great Britain alone is also applicable to the inclusion of Turkey in the Triple Entente. Such a policy might arouse the jealousy of Germany, Austria, and Italy and altho' Turkey, having lost nearly all her European and outlying African prossession is perhaps now not so vulnerable to the Triple Alliance, it is doubtful whether Germany would not regard an event of this nature as almost in the nature of a challenge from the Triple Entente to the Triple Alliance. Subject to a discussion with France and Russia, I should be disinclined to encourage Turkey to lean exclusively upon the Triple Entente. I do not however think that we can be satisfied with a purely negative attitude which might throw Turkey into the arms of the Triple Alliance who would conceivably not be so reluctant to entertain her requests.

I have refered at the beginning of this minute to the importance, which appears to be of almost a vital character, of maintaining the integrity of the Asiastic possessions of the Turkish
Empire. Turkey's way of assuring her independence is by an
alliance with us or by an undertaking with the Triple Entente. A
less risky method would be by a treaty or Declaration binding all
the Powers to respect the independence and integrity of the present
Turkish dominion, which might go so far as neutralisation, and
participation by all the Great Powers in financial control and the
application of reforms.'[99]

The memorandum makes it quite plain that in June 1913
Britain was only concerned with the situation in Europe. As a result
her policy towards the Young Turks had become most compromising.
She had become extremely cautious about arousing the suspicion of
the other Powers. No longer did she encourage the Young Turks to
look exclusively to Britain for sympathy and inspiration. Her policy
had the limited aim of keeping Turkey neutral.

The man chosen to execute this policy was Sir Louis Mallet,
who went out as ambassador to the Sublime Porte in October 1913.
Unlike Lowther, Sir Louis was not a professional diplomat but a
member of the Foreign Office staff. He had been private secretary to
Sir Edward Grey in 1905-1906, Senior Clerk in the Foreign Office
1906-1907, and Assistant Under-Secretary of State for Foreign Affairs,
1907-1913. Only recently he had taken part in the negotiations with
Hakkı paşa in London, and 'His Majesty's Government now desired
to have a representative in Turkey who could express their policy with
full knowledge of what had passed in London.'[100]

Mallet seems to have been the very antithesis of his predecessor.
Sir Andrew Ryan who served both ambassadors describes him as 'a
bachelor, very much a dilettante in appearance, very quizzical, highly

---

99 Sir Louis Mallet's Minute, in F.O. 371/1826/28098.
100 Ryan, n. 27, 83-4. For the negotiations with Hakkı Paşa, February to 2 July, 1913, see B. D. x, Part ii, 90-183.

intelligent, as supple as his predecessor had been unbending, and intent on conciliating the Young Turk leaders by friendliness and charm.'[101] Significantly Mr. Fitzmaurice, who had been Lowther's 'alter ego', and Mallet were not congenial to one another.[102]

Sir Louis Mallet's embassy had considerable success with the Young Turks. On the eve of the war relations between Britain and Turkey seemed healthier than they had been for some time past. This is borne out by the apparent strength of the British position in the Empire. A British admiral commanded the Turkish fleet. Mr. Crawford was still an influential figure in the financial and customs administration. Other British advisers, headed by Sir Robert Graves, a former member of the Levante Service, had recently been given employment under the Ministry of the Interior. As late as June 1914, Orme Clerk was appointed Inspector-General to the Ministry of Justice.[103] On June 26, two days before the assassination of Arch-Duke Ferdinand at Sarajevo, the Porte had shown its goodwill towards Britain by allowing the British Commander-in-Chief in the Mediterranean to pass the Straits in a cruiser, instead of the customary yacht.[104] But in spite of such auspicious signs in favour of Great Britain, a few months later the Porte signed an alliance with Germany and fought against Britain and the Triple Entente.

Turkey's alliance with Germany seems a paradox after all her attempts to reach an agreement with Great Britain. The alliance with Germany was not brought about by any pro-German faction among the Young Turks. If such a faction ever existed, it was among the senior officers of the army, the Şevket Paşa's and the Muhtar Paşa's. This group was virtually destroyed, by the defeats of the Ottoman army during the Balkan Wars. The main body of the C.U.P. remained

---

101 Ryan, 84.
102 *Ibid.*, 86.
103 *Ibid.*, 93, and Mallet to Grey, 5 December, 1913, B. D. x, Part i, 360.
104 Ryan, 89 and Allan Cunningham, 'The Wrong Horse? – A Study of Anglo-Turkish Relations before the First World War' in *St. Antony's Papers*, No. 17, *Middle Eastern Affairs*, No. 4, 70.

pro-Entente. In May 1914 Talât offered Russia an alliance with Turkey. Being well aware that the Porte did not want to become totally dependent on Germany, Mr. Giers, Russia's ambassador at Constantinople, knew that this proposal was a serious one.[105] The Russians however rejected it. One conjecture offered to explain russian behaviour is that Russia calculated that she could satisfy her ambition to gain Constantinople by having the Porte as her enemy and not an ally.[106] Turkey's last attempt to reach an understanding with the Entente Powers was her overtures to France. Cemal Paşa, the Minister of Marine, was sent to Paris in July 1914 for this purpose. But he too drew a blank. Negotiations with Germany had been opened while Cemal was in Paris. But it was his failure to conclude an alliance with France which gave an impetus to the negotiations. Even Cemal, who was fervently pro-French, now realised that Turkey had no other choice than to conclude an alliance with Germany.[107] On August 2, 1914, the alliance was duly signed.[108]

The victory of the Entente Powers in the First World War is sufficient vindication of British diplomacy in the decade before the war. Its only setback was the failure to keep the Porte neutral in the conflict. That it was in Turkey's own interest to remain neutral was a valid and logical conclusion for the F.O. to draw from the situation prevailing in the Ottoman Empire. After the disastrous defeats in the Balkan Wars, Turkey needed nothing more badly than peace in order to recuperate. Neutrality would also enable her to exploit her geographical situation in order to obtain the best terms from both sides should a

105 Serge Sazanov, *Fateful Years*, 1909-1916, London, 1928, 138-9.
106 M. N. Pokrovski, *Pages d'Histoire*, Paris, 1929, 128-32, cited in H. Butterfield, 'Sir Edward Grey in July, 1914', Irish Conference of Historians, *Historical Studies*, 5, London, 1965, 5 and W. Langer, n. 73, 335, also Philip E. Mosely, 'Russian Policy in 1911-12', *The Journal of Modern History*, xii, 1940, 71-4.
107 Cemal, n. 56, 117-29 and Djemal (Translation), 103-15.
108 'The Germans were equally uneasy at the possibility of having Turkey as an ally requiring defence against Russia.' Butterfield, n. 96, 5 and J. C. Hurewitz, *Diplomacy in the Near and Middle East*, 194-1956, ii, New York, 1956, 1-2.

major war break out. Such was the logic of the situation. But the mood in the country was very different, and a rational policy of this sort was out of the question. The Foreign Office did not take this mood into consideration. They underrated the Young Turks' fear of a war with Greece or their appreciation of Russian aggression. The Young Turks were far too conscious of their isolation, and sought in an alliance with either bloc of Great Powers security from attack. When their overtures to the Entente Powers did not bear fruit, the Young Turks turned to Germany. The German alliance was a gamble and the outcome of the war proved that they had backed the wrong horse. But events had shown that they had had no other horse to back.

The Search for Ideology in Kemalist Turkey, 1919-1939[*]

A lmost everyone who writes about the transition from single-party to multi-party politics in 1945 attributes this momentous change to President İsmet İnönü's statesmanship. Some claim that it was he who realised that the time had come for Turkey to begin its experiment with parliamentary democracy and join the Western world. Others argue that the factor which nudged Turkey in the direction of pluralist politics was the defeat of the single-party fascist régimes and the triumph of the democracies. This victory demonstrated the superiority of the democratic model and Turkey's ruling classes were quick to take note and make the necessary adjustments.

Both arguments are valid and deserve our full attention. But there is more to the political transition than the foresight of an individual, or the impact of external factors. On the contrary, an examination of Kemalism from its earliest years suggests that the transition to competitive politics was built into the ideology. That does

(*) The research for this paper was facilitated by a grant from the Social Science Research Council for the year 1983-4.

not imply that the transition was in any sense inevitable; it did mean that if the aims of Kemalism were to be fulfilled, it would be through the establishment of a democratic régime, defined in a rather broad and general way. The national and democratic strands in Kemalism were partially the legacy of Wilsonian principles which were expected to provide legitimacy for the new Turkish state in the post-war world. But, as we shall see below, the determination to carry out a bourgeois revolution in which nationalism and democracy were expected to play important roles preceded President Wilson's contribution.

The régime established by the Kemalists in 1923 was not democratic in any accepted sense of the word. For example, that peculiar and characteristic feature that is generally associated with Western democracy, that is to say the existence and acceptance of élites or classes and the presence of open political competition between them, was absent virtually throughout the period under discussion. Given the prevailing internal and external circumstances during these years, it would be rash to expect such a régime. The Kemalists were in the process of carrying out a revolution against the old order and one could perhaps anticipate democracy at the end of it. But by the mid-twenties, they had only acquired political power and succeeded in securing it by expelling the leadership of the former régime, and silencing the opposition within their own ranks. But they still had to cope with a latent opposition as well as a suspicious, sullen, and resentful population unable to comprehend the emerging new order. Despite its exclusiveness, the deposed Ottoman ruling class had not lived in total isolation from the rest of society, especially with regard to ideology. During the long centuries of its rule, it had created a vast network of institutions and loyalties, particularly religious loyalties, among almost all social groups. Not even a revolution could destroy these overnight. A Kemalist ideologue noted that "the monarchy and the Caliphate could be abolished by an act of parliament. But in order to be completely safe from the threat of these institutions, it would be necessary to struggle for many years against the ideas and activities which gave them strength."[1]

Given such circumstances, there was no question of the republicans introducing competitive politics. That would have been a great risk and even threatened the very existence of the régime. Instead, the Kemalists set up a single-party government which, faced with the Kurdish rebellion in the east (1925-6) and opposition within the movement, had to resort to "a drastic law for the Maintenance of Order" which gave "extra-ordinary and, in effect, dictatorial powers to the government for two years."[2] These powers were renewed in 1927 and finally expired in March 1929. In order to compliment these powers, special "Independence Tribunals" were set up in the east to deal with the rebellion, and in Ankara and İzmir to crush the opponents of the régime. The report of the Ankara tribunal led to the dissolution of the Progressive Republican Party on 3 June 1925, marking the virtual end of the brief interlude in multi-party politics. The Communist Party, which had been destroyed in 1921, was also outlawed in 1925.

But the expiration of this extra-ordinary law was followed by political liberalisation and led to the founding of an opposition party in August 1930. This suggests that Mustafa Kemal's commitment to pluralism was genuine and sincere and was seen by many as such. However, the popular anti-government response aroused by the opposition, leading to strikes and disturbances, again raised the spectre of counter-revolution. The Free Republican Party was dissolved and Turkey had to wait another fifteen years before the experiment in political competition could be renewed.

If there is an almost total absense of formal democracy in Turkey during Mustafa Kemal Atatürk's tenure as president, is it valid

---

1   Falih Rıfkı [Atay], 'Osmanlılık Geri Gelemez' (Ottomanism Cannot Return), *Cumhuriyet*, 19 Nov. 1924. The name in square brackets was adopted as the surname after the "Family Name Law" was passed on 2 July 1934.

2   B. Lewis, *The Emergence of Modern Turkey*, 2nd ed., 1968, 266.

to talk of a democratic strand in the Kemalist ideology? The answer is a tentative 'yes' if we see the Kemalists (as they saw themselves) as the founders of a transitional régime whose goal was to raise Turkey to the level of contemporary Western civilisation. We may define this goal by simply equating it with 'modernization' or 'westernisation'. But if we try to be more specific, for the Kemalists it meant establishing an order that was capitalist and therefore democratic. At that time, and until quite recently, the myth prevailed that the development of capitalism led to the establishment of democracy, eliminating on its way political instability rooted as that was in the weakness of the economy. Thus democracy was seen as the method of political organisation peculiar to capitalism which was by definition competitive, and a competitive parliamentary system was the only political régime compatible with capitalism. This line of thought had been sanctioned by westen intellectuals like Max Weber and Harold Laski, and the Kemalists, in the process of carrying out their bourgeois revolution, had implicitly accepted this equation. Thus Burhan Asaf [Belge] argued that "Democracy was not something which existed in its own essence or had its own meaning, it emerged from the political and administrative mould of capitalism."[3]

It was also possible to have capitalism and autocracy, as the Germans had demonstrated until their defeat in 1918. In fact, the Young Turks had experimented with this model during the years 1914-1918.[4] But the inferiority of this model had been established by defeat in war. Moreover, the Turks, ever conscious of the successes and failures of western régimes, were not about to adopt a formula the Germans had themselves rejected, if only temporarily.

---

3   "Rejimler Nasıl, Niçin Değişiyor?" (How and Why are Regimes Changing?), *Kadro* 1/12, Dec. 1932, 28.

4   Feroz Ahmad, 'Vanguard of a Nascent Bourgeoisie: the Social and Economic of the Young Turks 1908-1918', in O. Okyar and H. İnalcık (eds.), *The Social and Economic History of Turkey 1071-1920*, Ankara, 1980, 329-50, and Zafer Toprak, *Türkiye'de "Milli İktisat" (1908-1918)*, 1982.

In actual fact, nothing would have been easier for the Kemalists than to set up a military dictatorship. The army had emerged with great prestige, having played a vital role in the national struggle. Had Kemal Paşa chosen that path, there was nothing to prevent the army from assuming power. But he rejected this easy way and insisted on removing the army from politics, stipulating that officers who wished to be active in politics surrender their commissions. Such was the Kemalist concern about military interference in the affairs of state that a soldier on active duty was not even given the right to vote. Morris Janowitz has noted that the Kemalist model is in this respect virtually unique.[5]

Establishing a military dictatorship would certainly have proved more convenient in the short run, as the example of neighbouring Iran under the Pahalavis demonstrates. Such a régime would not have been transitional; instead of preparing the ground for pluralism and democracy, it would have actually hindered this process by blocking social and political developments. The Kemalists seemed determined to avoid this trap.

If we accept, *the principle* of popular participation as an important element in democratic practice, then this principle had become and integral part of Kemalism from the earliest days of the national struggle. The key words in the ideological struggle against the Sultan-Caliph were "people" *(halk)* and "nation" *(millet)*. They found expression in the National Pact signed at the Erzurum Congress on 17 August 1919. Later Mustafa Kemal Paşa explained the significance of these concepts for the new ideology as it took shape:

> "I think the fundamental reality of our present day existence has demonstrated the general tendency of the nation, and that is populism and people's government. It means the passing of government into the hands of the people."[6]

---

5   *The Military in the Political Development of New nations: an essay in comparatice analysis*, 1967, 104-5.
6   Kemal Atatürk, *Atatürk'ün Söylev ve Demeçleri*, 1, 1945, 87. The translation is Lewis's, op. cit., 256.

Or again:

> "... Our point of view, which is populism, means that power, authority, sovereignty, administration should be given directly to the people, and should be kept in the hands of the people."[7]

These quotations speak for themselves and require no comment. There may be a touch of rhetoric in them but they are far from insincere. They very use of the terms 'people' and 'populism' was revolutionary in a social and political setting in which these terms carried a pejorative association among the élite. For most members of the Kemalist élite populism was a form of political barbarism or luddite political activity in which the people were manipulated in order to prevent progress.

The concept of populism may have entered the late Ottoman Empire via Russia and the Narodnik movement which idealized the peasant. The Kemalists may have in turn idealized the peasant of Anatolia. But their use of the term 'people' was broader than Narodnik usage. Its defination was closer to that of the 'Third Estate' during the early phases of the French Revolution, whose influence on modern Turkish political thought remains to be studied. Thus 'people' implied the coalescing of the various social forces against the old order. The principal task of this collective was to defeat and destroy the old order and then create a new one. Since this task required cohesion and unity among all the components of this entity, 'halk', there was no room for conflict of interest (i.e. class conflict) amongst them.

In France, the leadership of the Third Estate had passed into the hands of the bourgeosie. In Turkey, there was no such class to seize the initiative. Therefore, the Kemalists, who were autonomous of all class interests, assumed the task of carrying out a bourgeois revolution by proxy.[8]

---

7   *Ibid.*, 97-8.
8   For a more detailed argument of this point see my paper, 'The Political Economy of Kemalism' in Ali Kazancıgil and E. Özbudun (eds.), *Atatürk: Founder of a Modern State*, 1981.

The Kemalists knew that political democracy had been an essential part the bourgeois revolution in Europe and that the process would have to be created in Turkey. Mahmut Esat [Bozkurt] argued this point in a series of articles he wrote in the official daily, *Hakimiyet-i Milliye* (National sovereignty) in November-December 1921. He wrote that

"... the fundamental law [or constitutionalism] acquired its significance from the Bourgeois Revolution of Europe. The history of this law, the application was attempted in Turkey, originated in Europe. Thus it may said that its *raison d'être* may be explained by the "Bourgeois Movement" in Europe and the economic and social situation of the bourgeoisie. However, in our case there was no class whose economic interests could be described by the adjective 'bourgeois', or which could be differenciated as a social class standing between the people and the aristocracy *(soylular)*. There was in fact no aristocracy. In Turkey, there was only the people and the Palace."[9]

He then observed that

"... The 1908 revolution was only able to establish a state resting on the principle of class rule in this country. That was an absolutely vital contribution. As is the case everywhere in today's world, the system based on a written constitution did not have any quality other than its ability to create class rule.

"... The constitutional régime prior to our on Law on Fundamental Organisation [a reference to the 1921 Constitution] was heading towards class rule under a sultan and the creation of a bourgeoisie which our country still did not recognise."[10]

Then commenting on the situation of the various social groups encountered by the Kemalists during the national struggle, Mahmut Esat was thankful "that in our country our intellectuals, merchants,

---

9 15 Nov. 1921. Mahmut Esat was an important ideologue and politician of the Kemlist movement, representing its radical wing. The series was entitled 'The Meaning of the New Turkey in the Light of Political History and Public Law.'

10 *Ibid.*

farmers and peasants, and officials are not members of different social groups. There are not even deep economic differences amongst them. Everyone is a producer and of the people."[11]

During the struggle itself, the Kemalists began to confront the problem of how "to put an end to this period of slavery." Mahmut Esat says that a number of radical proposals were put forward to deal with the crisis. Until they had won the war, the Kemalists decided not to reveal their intentions lest they divide the movement by alienating the conservative–religious groups. But to a large extent, their freedom of choice had been 'determined by the socio-economic situation they had inherited from the Young Turks. The Kemalists therefore opted for continuity. They, like the Young Turks before them, decided to continue the process of creating a bourgeoisie and establishing its rule, once it was strong enough, under a republic rather than a constitutional monarchy.

The time required to complete this process was never specified; it would be completed only when the class in question had grown and matured sufficiently to take control. The historic task of Kemalism was to create the proper environment for the bourgeoisie to grow, as well as the other conditions necessary for pluralist politics, thereby making the single-party régime redundant. This was the theory; but it was in this sense that the Kemalist régime was transitional.

While laying the foundations of the new Turkey, the autonomous Kemalist state often acted against the short terms interests of the infant bourgeoisie. This class would have settled for an American mandate, and preferred a moderate constitutional monarchy with a traditional religious ideology to the ideology of a radical, secular republic. But such a class, even in alliance with landed interests, lacked the power to influence let alone determine Kemalist policy. The Kemalists differed from their ward in so far as they had a long-range vision of a society in which industry would be an essential com-

---

11 *Hakimiyet-i Milliye*, 16 Nov. 1921.

ponent. Like Stalin, they were convinced that if they failed to establish an industry of their own, they would be "wiped off the face of the earth."[12] The bourgeoisie, on the other hand, viewed the situation from its own narrow perspective; it was happy to profit from the role of commercial intermediary in a country run by a mandatory power.

As one would expect, in a society which was pre-modern and pre-capitalist modern classes such as a bourgeoisie, commercial farmers, and workers, existed only in a rudimentary form. Far from being in a position to influence state policy, these classes depended on the state to protect and to mature them. That is precisely what Kemal Paşa told the Soviet ambassador accredited to the Nationalists:

> "In Turkey there are no classes... There is no working class as there is no developed industry. As for a bourgeoisie, it is necessary to raise it to the level of a bourgeoisie. Our commerce is extremely weak because we have no capital..."[13]

The government had to give priority to the development of "national trade, open factories, bring underground wealth to the surface, aid the merchant of Anatolia and make them wealthy. These were the problems facing the state."[14]

Thus the task confronting Kemalism was not that of abolishing classes but of developing them by destroying the fetters of the old regime which continued to inhibit this process. At the same time, the new régime took active measures to create a modern state structure

---

12 Stalin's remark to Prime Minister İsmet [İnönü] and Foreign Minister Tevfik Rüştü [Aras] in Moscow, 6 May, 1932, *International Affairs*, (Moscow) no. 2, Feb. 1969, 113.

13 S. I. Aralov, *Bir Sovyet Diplomatının Türkiye Hatıraları*, 1967, 234-5. Celal Nuri [İleri] said much the same thing as Atatürk, but added: "Had there been a middle class in the Ottoman world, it would undoubtedly have captured the state and forced it to serve its interests. However, in time government became the monopoly of the sultan and the bureaucracy. Naturally such a government cannot be involved with economic development. We are now suffering the consequences." See 'Biraz İktisadiyat' (A Little Bit of Economics), in *Türk İnkılabı*, 1926, 219-26.

14 Aralov, 234-5.

which, according to Yusuf Akçura's criteria, ought to enjoy the rule of law, be national and sovereign, liberal (i.e. *hürriyetperver* or more literally 'freedom caring') and democratic, that is to say where the people are sovereign.[15] Some of these ideas had been taken directly from President Wilson's Fourteen Points which *Hakimiyet-i Milliye* (21 Feb. 1920) had described as "the principles of the century."

The Kemalists tried to accomplish this by carrying out the radical reform programme of the twenties. Thus the constitutions of 1921 and 1924 guaranteed amongst other things, the supremacy of parliament acting as the representative of the people and the nation, the subordination of the bureaucracy to the government, the independence of the judiciary, the supremacy of the Rule of Law and the inviolability of the constitution. Section V of the 1924 Constitution guaranteed 'The General Rights of the Turks' and provided all those rights that have come to be associated with liberal régimes.[16]

It may be said that the Kemalist régime was liberal in its juridical system and ideological discourse but not democratic in so far as it did not permit direct mass participation in politics because of the two-tiered electoral system. It sanctioned by law the equality of citizens, safeguarded their basic freedoms (thought, speech, worship, etc.), adopted enlightened legal codes and jurisprudence, guaranteed personal property, established a free market in labour, adopted positivizm, and regarded secularism as a vital weapon against the anti-capitalist forces of the old order.

The Kemalists resorted to extra-ordinary methods such as the "Law for the Maintenance of Order" when they felt threatened by counter-revolution. Once such threats were over, as they seemed to be by 1929, liberalisation followed. Even ex-communist intellectuals like

---

15 Akçuraoğlu, Yusuf (Yusuf Akçura after 1934), 'Asrı Türk Devleti ve Münevverlere Düşen Vazife' (The Contemporary Turkish State and the Obligations of the Intellectuals), *Türk Yurdu*, II/13, Oct. 1925, 1-16.

16 An English translation of the 1924 constitution may be found in G. L. Lewis, *Turkey*, 3rd ed., 1966. For the reforms of the twenties see Bernard Lewis, op. cit., *passim*.

Vedat Nedim [Tör], Şevket Süreyya [Aydemir], and Burhan Asaf [Belge] were incorporated into the Kemalist network and permitted to play a role in defining ideology as it evolved.

In keeping with the promises of the constitution, liberalisation was extended beyond the Kemalist network and a literary-political journal like *Resimli Ay* was allowed to appear in 1929. Founded by Sabiha and Zekeriya Sertel, it included on its editorial board the unrepentent communist poet, Nazım Hikmet. Its contributors included such distinguished writers as Sabahattin Ali. Ironically, neither such journals nor such writers were allowed to publish in the multi-party Turkey of 1945-1960. Allowances may be made for the Cold War raging during these years. Nevertheless, Kemalist Turkey seems to have been, until about 1938, a more open society which permitted greater intellectual freedom than the period that followed.[17]

What has been said so far is valid only for the twenties; in the thirties there was a sharp turn in Turkey's ideological orientation. The advent of the worldwide economic crisis in the late twenties discredited the capitalist, democratic West and had a great impact on Turkish thinking. But the régime had already become disenchanted with its indigenous capitalists. Instead of investing in the economy, they had not behaved as they were expected to. Instead of investing in the economy, they had exploited the provisions of the Treaty of Lausanne stipulating low import tariffs and hoarded cheap foreign goods before the term of the treaty expired in 1929. Such behaviour was regarded as 'selfish' and 'anti-national; and diametrically opposed to the Kemalist policy of establishing a national economy. Even had the world crisis not intervened', the government would have had to reconsider its policy of free enterprise, given the complaints against the private sector. The crisis clinched the issue in a number of ways.

---

17 This was also the opinion of the leftist writer Vâlâ Nurettin who lived through both periods. See Vâ-Nû, 'En Hür ve En Sıkı Devir' (The most Free and the Most Controled Period), *Cumhuriyet*, 24 Nov. 1954.

Firstly, the régime decided to experiment with the two-party system as a way of easing political tensions in the country and providing a consensus which facilitated (badly-needed financial and economic reform). The Free Republican Party was founded in August 1930 by Fethi [Okyar], a close associate of Kemal Paşa from his war college days. It was expected to provide mild liberal opposition to the nationalist ruling party, the Republican People's Party (RPP), and improve Turkey's standing in the West, especially in financial circles. The régime was so completely out of touch with the masses that it sincerely believed that the new party would require state protection when its leaders criticised the government publicly. In fact, the people were so alienated from the ruling party that they responded with great fervour to the appeals of the opposition.

The demonstrations in favour of Fethi Bey in İzmir in September 1930, which were followed by strikes, and the reactionary incident in Menemen in December, led to the dissolution of the Free Republican Party by its founders. The experiment in multi-party politics had been a failure, but the significance of this experience was not lost on the RPP. The leadership realised that the Turkish masses could not be taken for granted, that they had been alienated by the reforms of the twenties which had never been explained to them, and that the party would have to launch an ideological offensive in order to win their allegiance.

By 1930, liberalism and democracy had been discredited in the eyes of many Kemalists. The single-party régimes, especially the fascists in Italy, offered an attractive alternative. There was sympathy for the Bolsheviks, but their ideology was thought to be inappropriate for Turkey because the country lacked the necessary conditions of class formation. Moreover, communism was anti-religion and international while one of the pillers of the new Turkey was nationalism. Thus while Turkey, like the rest of the post-war world, was moving towards the left, it would not become communist.[18]

---

18 Hüseyin Ragıp [Baydar], 'Sağdan Sola Doğru' (From the Right to the Left), *Hakimiyet-i Milliye*, 28 March 1921.

Fascism, on the other hand, was nationalist and patriotic and therefore more suitable for the régime in Ankara. Like Kemalism, it believed that class conflict brought only harm to the nation and therefore had to be avoided. Fascism had succeed in Italy during a most critical period after a difficult and dangerous struggle, and could therefore be an example for Turkey in crisis.[19] But more than ideas, it was the role that the state played in the organisation of society in the single-party régimes which appealed to the Kemalists. They even thought that Roosevelt's New Deal Administration fit into this pattern, describing it as a statist economy. They were impressed by state intervention in the economy, resulting in a balance impossible to achieve in the liberal system. They marvelled at the disciplined youth organisations and the sense of harmony compared to the anarchy of the capitalists world. It was argued that if Kemalist Turkey adopted these methods, it too would achieve salvation.

This pro-fascist climate prevailing within the Kemalist elite was undoubtedly influential in the demise of the Free Republican Party. The *Hakimiyet-i Milliye* had been arguing that fascism did not permit opposition parties but allowed criticism within the ruling party. However, no fascist party would allow its fundamental principles to be criticised.[20] There were now signs that the Kemalists were also considering establishing a régime in which party and state would coalesce. The emphasis was on adopting fascist-communist methods of organisation rather than pure fascist ideology, on 'revolutionary' *(inkılapçı)*

---

19 Abdullah Suphi [Tanrıöver]'s speech in *Ayın Tarihi*, May 1930, 6201-5. He was the president of the nationalist Turkish Hearths organisation. There was much discussion about the fascist state in the press of the period and the long article in the official 'History of the Month' gives a good idea about Kemalist thinking on the matter. See Nusret Haşim, 'Faşizm ve Korporatif Devlet: Nasıl Doğdu? - Nedir? - Ne Olabilecektir?' (Fascism and the Corporate State: how it was born, what it is, and what it will become), *Ayın Tarihi*, Oct.-Dec. 1930, 6718-30 and Jan.-Feb. 1931, 6983-98.

20 Zeki Mesut [Alsan], 'Tek Parti ile Murakebe', *Hakimiyet-i Milliye*, 4 Dec. 1930 cited in Çetin Yetkin, *Türkiye'de Tek Parti Yönetimi*, 1983, 31-3. This is one of the best evaluations of the period.

methods rather than bureaucratic ones.[21] However, ideology would now emanate only from one source, namely the party.

The first victim of this policy was the Turkish Hearth organisation, thus far the principal source of nationalist ideology. It was closed down in April 1931 and its property taken over by the RPP which set up 'People's Houses' *(Halkevleri)*. The aim was to reach people in town and country and explain the Kemalist revolution to them. In May, the third party congress adopted six principles – Republicanism, Nationalism, Populism, Statism, Secularism, and Revolutionism – and officially launched Kemalism as ideology. Recep [Peker], who both represented and articulated the single-party mentality, was elected the party's general secretary, a post he held until June 1936. For the next four years, the party continued to strengthen its hold on the state. Finally, in 1935, following the example of the Nazis in Germany, the RPP congress passed a resolution uniting party and state, taking what seemed like the final step towards establishing a party dictatorship in Turkey.

Despite the admiration for Rome and Berlin among certain Kemalists, often expressed in glowing articles in the press, the régime never tried to adopt fascism as ideology. There were a number of reasons for this. For one, the private sector was constantly expanding and becoming politically influential around Celâl Bayar and the *İş Bankası* (Business Bank) group, founded in 1924. These people had no objection to dictatorship but preferred the Yugoslav variety to that of Rome or Berlin. They disliked the excessive state controls associated with fascism which became noticeable in the early thirties. They resisted these trends and were sufficiently influential to bring about the fall of Mustafa Şeref, Minister of National Economy, in September 1932. He was replaced by Celâl Bayar, the founder of the

---

21 Falih Rıfkı, 'İnkılapçı Metodları' (Revolutionary Methods), *Hakimiyet-i Milliye*, 19 Nov. 1930 cited in Yetkin, 34-7 and 41-2. The ideas were developed by Falih Rıfkı in booklets like *Yeni Rusya*, 1931 and *Moskova-Roma*, 1932. Yunus Nadi argued the same thesis in his paper *Cumhuriyet*. For references, see Yetkin, 38-9.

Business Bank, who because responsible for implementing statism until 1939.[22]

This group, which came to be associated with liberalism within the RPP, also diskliked the extreme interpretation of populism which denied the existence of all classes and defined society in corporatist terms. That might eliminate class conflict, which the group welcomed, but it also prevented the growing bourgeoisie from organising and becoming more influential. (It is not surprising that when the single-party period came to an end in 1945, one of the main demands of Bayar's Democrat Party was the freedom to organise on the basis of class). Throughout the thirties, the Bayar group resisted the policies of the extreme statists around Recep Peker. As a result, Ankara never rejected liberal principles , even though it did not practice them – or the idea of progress. It continued to recognise the rule of law and the importance of the constitutional state. It never denied the universality of civilisation, as did the fascists, or rejected rationalism, individualism, and the fundamental equality of man and ethnic groups. There were signs of anti-Semitism in 1934, but the government was quick to take counter-measures.[23]

From the left wing of Kemalism, represented by the monthly *Kadro*, came a more interesting rejection of the equation between fascism and Kemalism. *Kadro*, which had been founded by some ex-communist and radical intellectuals, began publication in January 1932. One of its main aims was to produce an original ideology for the régime in Ankara. The editorial in the first issue noted that "Turkey is in revolution, but it still has not produced a system of thought that can act as an ideology for the revolution."[24] *Kadro* then tried to produce an ideology which would be applicable not only to Turkey but also to the colonies and the semi-colonies which were expected to liberate

---

22 *The Times* (London), 10 Sept. 1932, and Yetkin, 34 and 122-3.
23 *Ibid.*, 4, 5, and 16 July 1934, and for the response of the Turkish press see *Ayın Tarihi*, Aug. 1934, 78-80.
24 *Kadro*, I/i, Jan. 1932, 3.

themselves in the near future.[25] Here we can see the genesis of the concept of 'third worldism'.

It is possible to follow *Kadro*'s line of thought from the polemic it engaged it with Italian fascist intellectuals who claimed that Kemalism was a copy of their fascism. *Kadro* and other Kemalist publications vehemently denied this claim. Burhan Asaf [Belge] wrote an article, "Fascism and the Turkish National Liberation Movement" in which he outlined the basic differences between fascism and Kemalism.

Fascism, he argued, was a movement whose aim was to save a semi-capitalist Italy from the contradictions of capitalism and from domestic anarchy born out of these contadictions. These were reflected in the demogogic and bureaucratic administrative apparatus as well as in democracy and parliament. With corporatism, fascism was trying to make class contradictions harmless instead of finding a permanent solution for them.

The Turkish national revolutionary movement, on the other hand, was marked by the creation of an independent Turkish nation according to the historical conditions of the day, replacing the semi-colonial Ottoman Empire. Since the Turkish nation began its revolution with a national structure which had no classes, it was continuing to take measures which rejected class formation and made it an impossibility. The state's appropriation of the great enterprises of production, and the acceptance and codification of a progressive and planned statist economy resulted from this. (Burhan Asaf was not being completely candid. The state may have rejected class conflict but not class

---

25 'Şevket Süreyya Aydemir'le Bir Konuşma', *Yön*, 20 Jan. 1967, 7. Responding to Italian propaganda, Zeki Mesut wrote: "The salvation of Asia lies not in the claims of Rome or the principles of fascism, but in its own environment, in its own soil, in the intelligence of its own children, and in the experience of its own history. If Young Asians want inspiration and an example from life, let them investigate more deeply the Turkish revolution and its unique character and initiatives. Revolution, independence, and civilisation are the products of the race and nation itself. They can neither be exported nor imported, let alone borrowed", *Hakimiyet-i Milliye*, 13 Jan. 1934 (İtalya ve Asya).

formation; it was doing little to prevent the emergence of a bourgeoisie!)

Continuing his attack on Dr. Ettoro Rossi, who had initiated the polemic, Burhan Asaf noted the demographic pressure forcing Italy to pursue colonial dreams despite the decline of colonialism after the war. Kemalism, on the other hand, was a revolt against colonialism. It had fought against colonialism and its external and indigenous lackeys, namely the Greek army, the Palace and the Galata bankers, concluding the struggle at Lausanne in 1923.

> "Having symbolised, with all its conscience, the reaction to colonialism, Kemalism remains sincere about its statism in both its domestic and foreign economic relations. It has rejected both internal and external contradictions, that is to say the contradiction between classes and among nations."

There were other points to be scored. Fascism, claimed Burhan Bey, suited only semi-capitalist structures; it was unsuited to societies which were either fully capitalist or pre-capitalist (like Turkey). It had not succeeded in Spain. In Germany it had been forced to change its character, a reference to the "socialist" element in National Socialism. Kemalism, however, represented a source of permanent ideals and ideology for nations which had yet to realize their national aspirations, a reference to counteries like India and China, and the Arab states in the Middle East.

Two false assumptions, concluded Burhan Asaf, had driven Dr. Rossi to error: Firstly, the assumption that Turkey was on the same old path of westernisation, so familiar in the nineteenth century. That was not the case. Secondly, he had reached conclusions about some aspects of the Kemalist programme without investigating it as a whole or studying the historical conditions which inspired it.

If there was any similarity between Kemalism and fascism, or between Kemalism and capitalism (and democracy which was its political expression), that resulted from "the common historical needs of all the nations after the war" and not from an attempt to copy. To deny that is to deny "the original character of our revolution... The Turkish Revolution... claims to be the most just and the most progressive phenomenon in the post-war national and international scene. If that fact has been obscured upto the present moment, that is due to the innate qualities of the Turkish nation and may be attributed to its disklike for humbug and boasting."[26]

In 1932 when this polemic was written, Turkey was enjoying a sense of self-confidence it had not enjoyed for at least a century. There was pride also about Turkey's stable economy, at least relative to that of the West which was in deep crisis.[27] Writing about the crisis in Germany which resulted in Hitler's rise to power, *Kadro* quoted the economist Werner Sombart who lamented the fact that his country also needed a "man of will" *(irade adamı)* – like Gazi Mustafa Kemal, Lenin, or Mussolini – to lead it out of chaos. Such statements were a source of great pride for the Kemalists, adding to their sense of purpose and making them feel optimistic about the future. Here was Germany, a great European power, envious of the new Turkey because of its leadership. In times of severe crisis, observed *Kadro*, "Humanity longs for the enterprising hero and not the cunning politician."[28]

Rome's thesis and Ankara's rejection of the thesis that Kemalism was a copy of Italian fascism was also dictated by foreign policy considerations. Italy had ambitions in the region which Turkey found alarming, motions she could not ignore while the Italians occupied the Dodocanese islands off the western coast of Anatolia. The *Kadro* article was thus Ankara's rejection of Italy's attempt to establish her ideological hegemony; it was the first step in the struggle to ward off fascist imperialism. Mussolini's speech of 18 March 1934,

---

26 'Faşizm ve Türk Milli Kurtuluş Hareketi', *Kadro* I/8, Aug. 1932, 38-9.
27 See the speech of Rahmi Bey at the opening of the Third National Industrial Exhibition in İzmir. He was deputy for İzmir and the general secretary of the Society for the National Economy and Savings. *Kadro* I/5, May 1932, 47.
28 *Kadro* I/5, May 1932, 3.

claiming that Italy's historical mission lay in Asia and Africa forced Turkey to take active measures to meet the challenge.[29]

Italy became the principal factor in Turkey's foreign policy and the government began to diversify its diplomatic relations.[30] It continued to strengthen its links with the Soviet Union but, at the same time, it began to seek the support of the two great naval powers in the Mediterranean, Britain an France. The fact that both were parliamentary democracies also influenced Ankara's ideological thinking. By May 1934, Turkey began to propose the need to remilitarize the Straits and that led to the signing of the Montreux Convention two years later. She became a supporter of collective security within the League of Nations and a critic of appeasement. She supported the Ethopians against Italian aggression and the Republicans in the Spanish Civil War. Such was Turkey's record that "In the years 1935-9, when almost any ally against Fascism seemed acceptable [wrote George Orwell], left-wingers found themselves praising Mustafa Kemal..."[31] The İstanbul correspondent of *The Times* noted that Turkey's foreign policy which had relied on Moscow, and after 1936 on London and Paris, depended on having a régime at home which did not have a fascist colouring.[32] Precisely in 1936, President Atatürk began to take measures to change the régime's 'fascist colouring' even though the single-party régime remained intact.

Despite the response to Mussolini's adventurism, the success of fascism in Itay and Germany did unfluence a group within the ruling

---

29 *The Times* (London), 7 April 1934. The text of the speech in Turkish translation is in *Ayın Tarihi*, April 1934, 299-307, with press comment on 308-20. Mussolini tried to calm Turkish fears by informing the ambassador in Rome that Turkey need not worry since it was a European and not an Asian/African state.

30 For Turkey's foreign policy during these years, see the perspective article by Selim Deringil, 'Turkey's Diplomatic Position at the Outbreak of the Second World War', *Boğaziçi Üniversitesi Dergisi*, vols. 8-9, 1980-1981, 63-87.

31 'Who are the War Criminals?', *Tribune*, 22 Oct. 1943, in S. Orwell and I. Angus (eds.), *The Collected Essays, Journalism and Letters of George Orwell*, vol. 2, Penguin ed. 1970, 367. I owe this reference to Dr. Naim Turfan.

32 *The Times*, 25 May 1937.

party. This influence was reflected partly in the desire to establish state instead of liberal capitalism and partly in the hostility to liberalism. Recep Peker, who led this wing of the party, often attacked liberalism, forecasting its imminent doom which would be followed by the universal reign of statism.[33] Peker's attitude had already alienated the Business Bank group in the party and they had long campaigned against him. But his dismissal as the party's general secretary on 15 June 1936 suggests that it was foreign policy concerns which dictated Atatürk's personal intervention and not the pressure of any lobby. The negotiations at Montreux were reaching their climax and a significant gesture was needed to rally support. Peker's dismissal would strength the liberals at home and that would please Britain, alarmed by the growth of German influence in Turkey. The Convention was signed on 20 July, bringing about an Anglo-Turkish rapprochement which was sealed by King Edward VIII's visit to Turkey in September.[34] Political and economic liberalisation continued into 1937, the most significant event being the resignation of İsmet İnönü in October and the appointment of Celâl Bayar as prime minister.

This liberal interlude could not last long given the growing crisis in Europe. The power and prestige of Nazi Germany, its economic policy which drew Ankara into its commercial sphere despite British counter-measues, also influenced politics and ideology. By 1938, the régime had become more autocratic and borrowed legislation freely from the fascist states. The death of Atatürk in November 1938 accelerated this process. İsmet İnönü's presdency saw the establishment of a régime based on the fascist slogan "One Party, One Nation, One Leader". Such was the impact of foreign relations on ideology. This trend lasted until the Nazi defeat at Stalingrad in 1943. Thereafter,

---

33 See, for example, his speech of 22 April 1936 in *Ülkü*, May 1936, 161-2. Later, speaking on the Labour Law on 8 June, Peker observed that "This new law is a régime law. It is against liberalism because liberalism puts workers against employers." *Ülkü*, July 1936 quoted in Yetkin, *Tek Parti*, 102.

34 *The Times*, 2-7 Sept. 1936.

Ankara began to retrace its steps away from single-party autocacy towards liberalism, culminating in the restoration of multi-party politics in 1945. This time, however, the process of liberalism and democracy would be distorted by the politics of the Cold War.

The Political Economy of Kemalism

The ideology that came to be described as Kemalism was unveiled in 1931 at the congress of the Republican People's Party (RPP). It was defined in terms of six pinciples, namely nationalism, republicanism, populism, secularism, statism and revolutionism, which would thenceforth guide the destinies of the Turkish nation. They were first made part of the party's programme, and then in 1937 inserted into the constitution and institutionalised. Though unveiled only in 1931, Kemalism had been evolving throughout the previous decade, in fact ever since the start of the national struggle in 1919, re-adjusting to event and circumstances. However, if we consider the late nineteenth – and early twentieth-century trends of Ottomanism, Pan-Islamism, and Pan-Turkism, the search for ideology was much older. But these were limited ventures with aims which hardly went beyond the search for identity for the Muslim-Turkish community; they did not seek to provide an ideological framework for the development of state and society as a whole. Kemalism, on the other hand, not only provided an identity defined by the revolutionary concept of nationalism, but the other five principles became the basis for the new regime and the society it set out to create.

Despite the original character of Kemalism, it did have antecedents for both its ideas and its social foundations. It would be unhistorical to conceive of such an ideology without recognising the contribution of the Young Turk era (1908-18), when some of the ideas refined by Mustafa Kemal were first put forward and discussed. Nor must we forget that Kemal Paşa played an active role during the decade when the Ottoman empire was undergoing a most rapid and radical transformation. He witnessed and engaged in the debates of the period, and later some of the most prominent intellectuals and ideologues – Ziya Gökalp and Yusuf Akçura, to mention only two of the most important – joined the Kemalist movement and participated in the development of its ideology.[1]

Perhaps even more important than ideas was the social and political transformation of the Young Turk era. Not only did the old ruling class of the Palace and the Sublime Porte lose much of its power, but the Young Turks began to take active measures to create a new social basis for the Turkish polity. Modernisation and westernisation were now defined as the establishment of capitalism with all the features of a capitalist society, and no longer as the implementation of institutional reforms. That meant creating a class capable of sustaining capitalism – the bourgeoisie – without which, Yusuf Akçura warned, 'the chances of survival of a Turkish society composed only of peasants and officials will be very slim.'[2] By the end of the war, such a class, still very much in its infancy, had begun to emerge, as had a new but small group of capitalist farmers. Both groups had acquired great wealth through wartime profiteering encouraged by the Young Turk government, and were more confident of the political role they would play. As a result, by 1919 when the national struggle was

---

1   Yakup Kadri Karaosmanoğlu, *Atatürk*, İstanbul, 1961, 64, claims that Kemalism was totally originall, and he does not think that these thinkers, whom he names specifically, influenced Atatürk.

2   From, *Türk Yurdu*, no. 14, 12 Aug. 1333 (1917), quoted in Niyazi Berkes, *The Development of Secularism in Turkey*, Montreal, McGill University Press, 1964, 426.

launched, Turkish society was no longer composed only of peasants and officials, though they were still numerically dominant. The journalist Falih Rıfkı Atay, a spokesman for the Kemalists, might well ask in 1922: 'The bourgeoisie? I wonder, where is this Turkish class?'[3]

The question of Turkey's political economy, however, ought not to be considered merely in terms of numbers. It is true that there was hardly a strong indigenous business or industrial class – capitalists or workers – worth talking about: in the 1915 industrial survey, only 284 workplaces employed more than five workers, of which 148 were in İstanbul, 62 in İzmir, and the remaining 74 in western Anatolia. Of the capital employed in these ventures, 85 per cent was Greek, Jewish, Armenian or foreign.[4] The situation improved in the years 1915-18 but not in the sense of bringing about a numerical breakthrough or a take-off to bourgeois industrial society. Nevertheless, psychologically there was an important change in attitude during the war years;[5] there was a realisation within the Turkish ruling étite that without the reorganisation of social and economic life, it would not be possible to modernise the political and cultural life of Anatolia or gain the acceptance of Europe. The first step in this direction was the abolition of the capitulations in September 1914; this, *inter alia*, permitted the Turks to raise tariffs on imported goods so as to be able to protect and develop local commerce and industry. The existence of free trade had not only been a factor in discouraging the growth of local industry, it had also provided a small segment of the commercial community, predominantly non-Muslim, with better opportunities for money-making by handling foreign trade rather than by trying to develop local markets and manufactures. The Kemalist, who succeeded the Young

---

3   F. R. Atay, *Eski Saat*, İstanbul, 1933, 95, quoted by Taner Timur, *Türk Devrimi ve Sonrası 1919-1946*, Ankara, 1971, 21.
4   See Timur, *op. cit.*, 21.
5   See Feroz Ahmad, 'Vanguard of a Nascent Bourgeoisie, the Social and Economic Policy of the Young Turks 1908-1918' in Osman Okyar and Halil İnalcık (eds.), *Social and Economic History of Turkey (1071-1920)*, Ankara, 1980. Yıldız Sertel, *Türkiye'de İlerici Akımlar*, 1969, 17, gives figures for the workforce in 1921 which suggest an increase from that figures for 1915.

Turks, accelerated the protectionist trend and accomplished what may perhaps be described as a bourgeois revolution from the top or, stated in another way, a bourgeois revolution by proxy. This was often done against the wishes of the infant class which seemed to prefer the easier route of foreign collaboration to Kemalist autarchy. But it sill lacked the power to influence state policy, directed as the latter was by an élite of autonomous vested interests.

This is not to suggest that the Kemalists set out consciously to carry out a revolution; in a sense such a process had already been set in motion by the Young Turks, and the Kemalists were partly carried along by the momentum thus created. The collapse of empire and foreign occupation of the most valuable parts of Anatolia brought into question the very existence of a Turkish nation and state, even while these were mere ideas waiting to be translated into reality. Thus in the summer of 1919 it was conceivable that Anatolia might go the way of Greater Syria and be partitioned into small states for the convenience of Western control. There were local groups of notables organising themselves to safeguard their own interests, and they seemed willing to do this by compromising with one great power or another, accepting its tutelage and, if necessary, agreeing to sacrifice other parts of Anatolia. In their minds, the notion of a national struggle was of secondary importance. Such were the 'Defence of Right Societies' founded in Thrace and İzmir and then in other parts of Anatolia.[6] In the capital, the Sultan and his entourage, who might have provided the focus for national resistance, threw themselves upon the mercy of the Allied powers, especially Great Britain. They accepted, under protest, any outcome that was decided for their future so long as they were permitted to retain the trappings of power. In their minds there was no concept of nation or national sovereignty, let alone national economy; on the contrary, they found the idea of national sovereignty subvert-

---

6 On these societies, see T. Z. Tunaya, *Türkiye'de Siyasi Partiler 1859-1952*, İstanbul, 1952, 481ff.

sive, for it challenged the very basis of their power, based as it was on archaic tradition. İstanbul therefore resisted the national movement in Anatolia with cunning and fanaticism. But once the capital had been occupied by Allied troops on 16 March 1920, that was the *de facto* end of the Ottoman state and the Sultan's claim to lead the people as the 'shepherd leads his flock.'[7]

It is instructive to examine the social groups which either actively supported the Sultan, or sat on the fence waiting to see whether he would succeed in retaining control of the delicate situation. As one would expect, die-hard support for the Sultan came from his palace entourage as well as from the high bureaucrats of the Sublime Porte, who had sided with the pro-British liberals during the Young Turk era. The Sultan had everything to lose if the nationalist ideas of sovereignty and populism were allowed to prevail. The men of the Sublime Porte, like Tevfik Paşa and Ali Kemal, depended on British support to maintain a reformed traditional order in which a monarch, restrained by constitutionalism, would reign while they, the high bureaucrats, ruled. Such a formula meant political and economic subordination to Britain. They were willing to accept that, as were the bourgeoisie who were content merely to replace the ousted Christian minorities in the economic order. These Turkish groups were rather like the liberal faction in the Indian National Congress in the same period who preferred dominion status within the British empire to full independence. They were willing to settle for a British mandate so long as it guaranteed a viable Ottoman-Turkish state; others among them believed that an American mandate would be better suited to Turkey's needs. All the pro-İstanbul factions were convinced of the need for a period of foreign tutelage before Turkey could stand on its own feet.

Even as Mustafa Kemal Paşa began to give shape to a nationalist movement at the Sivas Congress in September 1919, he heard voic-

---

7   One the role of the İstanbul governments in this period see Sina Akşin, *İstanbul Hükümetleri ve Milli Mücadele*, İstanbul, 1976. For the Sultan's claim to be the 'sepherd of his flock' see Şevket Süreyya Aydemir, *Tek Adam: Mustafa Kemal (1919-1922)*, vol. 2, İstanbul, 1966, 226.

es among his supporters favouring a mandate. This was partly a symptom of general demoralisation caused by all the setbacks the empire had suffered, ever since it was described by Europe as 'the sick man' whose demise was a matter of time. It was also due to the belief among the bourgeoisie and the landlords in the nationalist camp that the Allies might permit the creation of a nationalist Turkey if they, in turn, were permitted to enjoy economic privileges. Thus Bekir Sami Bey, the Kemalist foreign minister at the London Conference in 1921, made substantial economic concessions to the European Powers whereby 'the French were to have preference in enterprises for the economic development of districts evacuated by France, as well as the provinces were to be granted mining concessions in Ergani, etc. ...'[8]

Italy agreed to support Turkish claims at the conference for the restitution of Thrace and İzmir, and in return the nationalists would cede to Italy the right to exploit the regions of Antalya, Burdur, Muğla, Isparts, as well as parts of Afyonkarahisar, Kütahya, Aydın and Konya. Bekir Sami went as far as to agree to cede to Italian capitalists those enterprises which could not be carried on by the Turkish government or by Turkish capital, as well as to transfer the coal mines of Ereğli to a Turco-Italian company.[9] Bekir Sami was convinced that the agreements he had signed were in accord with the highest interests of the nation. He appealed to the National Assembly to support him, arguing that 'while the opportunity is still given us, prudent policy might save the country from the abyss into which it has fallen. ... If this is not done, none of us will be able to withdraw from the responsibility imposed upon him before history and the nation. ...' The continuation of the national struggle, he contended, 'will destroy and annihilate our country to such a degree that its existence as well as that of the nation will be jeopardised.' He advised Kemal Paşa to take

---

8   *A Speech delivered by Mustafa Kemal Atatürk 1927*, Ministry of Education Printing Plant, İstanbul, 1963, 498. This is an improved edition of the English translation, published in Leipzig in 1929; it is certainly more readily available.

9   *Ibid.*

this opportunity to make peace on the terms he had negotiated, his conclusion being that the Allies would give nothing better.[10]

Mustafa Kemal described Bekir Sami as 'an adherent of peace at any price.' The terms he was asking the Assembly to accept were the same as the ones the 'powers had concluded among themselves, under the name of the "Tripartite Agreement" and which divided Anatolia into three spheres of influence.' The Kemalists found such terms totally unacceptable, for they contradicted the very principles of the national movement. As a result of these differences, the foreign minister was forced to resign.[11]

Bekir Sami's views, however, were shared by significant factions in the bourgeoisie and among the landowners. Such groups viewed the national struggle as primarily a struggle for political sovereignty and control of the state. Economic sovereignty was not of such significance since both groups believed that they had much to gain from economic subservience to Europe. Its capital investment was expected to develop the infrastructure while its factories would supply goods for the Turkish market. In return, Turkey would export agricultural goods and raw materials. But the Kemalist made no distinction between political and economic sovereignty, arguing that the one could not exist without the other. The Minister of the Economy, Mahmut Esat, stated this quite categorically in his speech before the Economic Congress of Turkey: 'I understand national sovereignty to be national economic sovereignty', he declared. 'If that is not the case, then national sovereignty becomes a mirage."[12]

In the early years of the national movement, the emphasis of the Kemalist leadership was on change even revolutionary change. There was an acute awareness that the Turks were in the process of making a fresh start and abandoning their decadent Ottoman past. This attitude was in keeping with the influence of the French revolutionary tra-

---

10 *Ibid.*, 500-1.
11 *Ibid.*, 498.
12 A. Gündüz Ökçün (comp. and ed.), *Türkiye İktisat Kongresi 1923-İzmir*, Ankara, 1968, 259.

dition on radical thought in Turkey. Thus the Allied occupation of İstanbul in March 1920 was seen as not merely the *de facto* end of the Ottoman state but the beginning of a new age marked by what Mustafa Kemal described as the 'first national year' or *'birinci millî sene'*.[13] This fresh start was expected to lead to the creation of a totally new state and society. In order to carry out this metamorphosis, the Kemalists realised that they would have to create even 'a new type of Turk very different from the "Ottoman".'[14] Given this propensity for revolutionary change, the dependent political economy of the old order would have to be the first to go. This becomes quite clear if one reads contemporary nationalist writings.

In his speech before the Grand National Assembly in March 1922, Kemal Paşa noted that the Turkish economy had been unable to defend itself against European competition ever since free trade was permitted by the 'Reorganisation' or *Tanzimat* regime (1839-76). To make matters worse, the competitive edge had been blunted even more 'by the claims of economic capitulatons'.[15] After this period, foreign capital had acquired an extraordinary position in the empire reducing Ottoman state and government to the status of 'the gendarmes of foreign capital.' The Ottoman empire was now nothing more than 'a colony of the foreigners.' Turkey, like any other new nation, concluded Kemal Paşa, could not consent to the continuation of such a state of affairs.[16] It was true that they were now living in a different age, but in many respects the situation remained unchanged. Mustafa Kemal noted that there were millions of unemployed in Britain and that they would influence Britain's policy towards Turkey. Britain would try to

---

13 Kemal Paşa uses this term at least three times in his speech opening the new session of the Grand National Assembly. See Kazım Öztürk, *Cumhurbaşkanları'nın T. Büyük Millet Meclisi'ni Açış Nutukları*, İstanbul, 1969, 105, 108 and 113. The analogy with the fall of the monarchy in France in 1792 seems obvious.
14 See Vedat Nedim Tör, *Kemalizmin Dramı*, İstanbul, 1980, 20.
15 Kemal Paşa's Assembly speech of 1 March 1922 in Öztürk, *op. cit.*, 86.
16 Kemal Paşa's speech inaugurating the Economic Congress of Turkey, 17 February 1923, in Ökçün, *op. cit.*, 248 and 253.

establish open markets in order to solve the problem of unemployment created by the general post-war economic crisis prevailing in Europe.[17] Turkey therefore had to be on her guard and insist on the right to impose tariffs, without which the creation of industry would be virtually impossible. The Kemalists differed from their bourgeois supporters insofar as they had a long-term vision of a new Turkey, of which industry was an essential component. The bourgeoisie, on the other hand, viewed the situation from their own narrow perspective, content to profit from the role of commercial middlemen in an economy controlled by Europe.

Thus during the war of independence the Kemalist were anti-imperialist, not only because they wanted to prevent the partition of Anatolia, but also because they refused to allow the new Turkey to remain an economic colony of the West. This aspect of the struggle is sometimes lost sight of because some critics have cast doubt on Kemalism's anti-imperialism, claiming that the Kemalists were making concessions to foreign capital while indulging in rhetoric against it at the same time. Such critics miss an important point about the political economy of Kemalism, namely that it was capitalist yet at the same time anti-imperialist. There was no contradiction in this policy, though it was undoubtedly most difficult to follow. It became the stated policy of almost all the new nation-states in the period of de-colonisation. Foreign capital was welcome so long as it did not come with political or economic strings. It was realised that Turkey, ravaged by war and starved of capital, would have to rely on foreign investment if it were to build an infrastructure for a modern economy. Mustafa Kemal explained this to the Assembly in March 1922: 'If we want to bring happiness and prosperity to our nation in a brief period of time, we will have to obtain foreign capital as rapidly as possible, and benefit to the maximum from whatever foreign know-how is necessary to achieve our country's well-being and prosperity, and our nation's hap-

---

17 Öztürk, *op. cit.*, 103.

piness and welfare; our own present financial position is inadequate to build, install, and operate public utilities.'[18] But the representatives of the nation were quickly reminded that 'we cannot think of anything other than achieving our national goal which consists of guaranteeing, before all else, our life and liberty; ... the aim of our present crusade is total independence. Total independence is possible only with financial independence.'[19]

Perhaps nothing illustrates the aspirations of Kemalist political economy better than the proceeding of the Economic Congress of Turkey, held in İzmir in February 1923. The war of independence was over and peace was in the process of being negotiated in Laussanne. The nation's boundaries, stipulated in the National Pact of 1919, had virtually been won on the battlefield, but the struggle for economic sovereignty was still being waged at the negotiating table. One aim of the Economic Congress was to show the world that there was a unity of purpose between the political leadership and the various economic groups, particularly the commercial community which, in the empire, had been the instrument of foreign penetration, and whose nationalist sentiment was still suspect. But at the congress this group, represented by the 'National Turkish Commercial Union', adopted a strong nationalist platform. It demanded the right to impose tariffs against foreign goods, opposed concessions to or monopoly rights for foreign capital in Turkey, proposed monopoly-free cabotage for Turkey's coastal waters, and called for a national bank of emission to be established as soon as possible. Foreign capital would be welcomed only provided that it was deemed beneficial for the economy of the nation.[20] Almost all the measures proposed at the congress were designed to achieve one fundamental goal: to further the establishment

18 *Ibid.*, 88.
19 *Ibid.*, 89.
20 Ökçün, *op. cit.*, 406ff; and Doğan Avcıoğlu, *Türkiye'nin Düzeni*, Ankara, 1969, 229-33. By 1926, Kemal Paşa could proudly inform the Assembly that cabotage had been placed under the Turkish flag. See his speech of 1 November 1926 in Öztürk, *op. cit.*, 190.

of a national economy and to strengthen those economic forces in the country which, within a short time, would provide the socio-economic basis for the emerging republican state.

There was unity of purpose between the new state created in 1923 and the principal economic classes, the infant bourgeoisie and the landlords. But that ought not to disguise the fact that the Kemalist state was essentially autonomous, and not subservient to the dictates of those classes. That is as one would expect in a situation in which society was essentially pre-capitalist, and modern classes such as the bourgeoisie, capitalist farmers and workers existed in a most rudimentary from and were very much in the process of growth. Far from being in a position to direct the state, these classes had to be nurtured by it.

The new state was dominated by an intelligentsia *(münevverler, aydınlar)*, military and civilian in composition, which formed the hard core of the Kemalist movement. For convenience, we may appropriate Arthur Koestler's description of the intelligentsia and the historic role it has played, for it approximates closely to the role of the Turkish intelligentsia: 'The intelligentsia in the modern sense thus first appears as that part of a nation which by its social situation not so much "aspires" but is *driven* to independent thought, that is, to type of group-behaviour which debunks the existing hierarchy of values (from which it is excluded) and at the same time tries to replace it with new values of its own. This constructive tendency of the intelligentsia is its second basic feature. The true iconoclasts always had a prophetic streak, and all debunkers have a bashfully hidden pedagogic vein.'[21] By 1923, the Kemalist intelligentsia was actually in power. It was determined to replace 'the existing hierarchy of values' and take the country far beyond the vision of the bourgeoisie, let alone the landlords and the tribal chiefs. These old classes would have preferred a constitutional monarchy with its traditional religious ideology;

---

21 Arthur Koestler, *The Yogi and the Commissar*, Danube edition, New York, 1967, 73.

instead, the Kemalists established a republic which was rapidly secularised, against the opposition of even some of the most prominent leaders of the national movement. This was the logical coutcome of a struggle which had emphasised nationality and national sovereignty, as well as the striving for Western civilisation. But the old classes found the new order difficult to swallow. Nevertheless the reforms were carried out 'for the bourgeoisie in spite of itself', to corrupt the more familiar Kemalist adage. The reforms of the mid-1920s and 1930s were more acceptable to these classes for they destroyed many of the institutional and juridical obstacles of the traditional, pre-capitalist order to the emerging modern structure, while maintaining existing property relations.[22]

For the next quarter-century, the political economy continued to evolve in the shadow of the state. Aware of the weakness of the private sector as well as public interest, Kemal Paşa informed the Assembly as early as March 1922: 'One of the most important goals of our political economy is to place under state control, as far as our financial and technical ability allows, economic institutions and enterprises which directly involve public advantage.'[23] This goal remained fundamental to the economic philosophy of Kemalism and it was to become one of the main planks of the statist policy of the 1930s.

If we have emphasised the relationship between the new regime and the main urban class, the bourgeoisie, it is because the Kemalists were convinced that the urban economy would be the driving force for development while the rural sector would provide the fuel. The countryside was not being taken for granted and there were no illusions about its importance for the nation's future. 'Gentlemen, our nation is agrarian', Kemal Paşa said to the Assembly. The peasant was 'Turkey's real master and owner, and the true producer... The quintessence of

---

22 For an account of the reforms see Bernard Lewis, *The Emergence* of *Modern Turkey*, 2nd edn, London, 1968, 261-74 *et passim*.
23 Öztürk, *op. cit.*, 86-7.

our political economy is to use the results and the fruits of the peasant's labour for his own highest advantage.'[24]

These statements should not be dismissed as mere rhetoric. The Turkish intelligentsia had a genuine appreciation of the peasant's contribution to the economy – and to the army as cannon-folder – as well as sympathy for his tragic plight. The intelligentsia followed the example of the Russian *narodniks* and tended to idealise the peasantry. Influence by such sentiments, the Young Turks had intended to destroy the *status quo* in the countryside, and to save the peasant from the clutches of the feudal lords *(derebeys)*, tribal *ağas*, and notables *(eşraf)*. Despite their good intensions, they failed to carry out any measures to improve the lot of the wretched peasant; on the contrary, his situation actually became worse during the turbulent decade which ended in 1918.[25] In the Republic, the condition of the peasantry improved to some degree – the burden of the tithe was removed – but there were no structural changes in the countryside. More specifically, no land reform was carried out. We need to ask why.[26]

To begin with, the Turkish Republic was not confronted with a land question of the type which confronts so many newly-independent Third World nations, resulting from a large population and insufficient land. In Turkey, the value of land had been going up since the turn of the century, leading to increased demand. This rising demand led to some regional tensions, but in general there was sufficient land available to meet the demand. Thus, except for pockets of large holdings in parts of Anatolia, Turkey remained a land of smallholders.

The real problem of agrarian Turkey was not the shortage of land, but the shortage of labour, aggravated as it was by constant warfare and the loss of population. The shortage of farm-labour became

24 Both quotations are from the speech of 1 March 1922 in *ibid.*, 84-5.

25 See Feroz Ahmad, 'The Agrarian Policy of the Young Turks 1908-1918' published in the proceedings of the Second International Congress on the Social and Economic History of Turkey, Strasbourg University, 1-5 July 1980, edited by Irene Melikoff and Jean-Louis Bacquet-Grammont. Published as chp. 4 in this volume.

26 See Avcıoğlu, *op. cit.*, 233.

so critical during the First World War, the government was forced to institute the *corvée* so as to provide cheap labour and maintain vital farm production. By 1923, the population within the borders of the new state – and with it the productive capacity of the nation – had declined by about 20 per cent.[27] The re-distribution of land at this point would have sharply reduced the size of the agrarian labour force available to the landlords; they would have been forced to pay higher wages while land rent would have fallen. On both counts, the land-lords opposed land reform or any structural change in the countryside. Scarce and costly labour might, however, have forced the landlords to adopt modern farming methods involving the use of machines, there-by making Turkish agriculture capital-rather than labour-intensive. That is how the Young Turks, and the Kemalists after them, ensivaged solving the problem of under-population. Kemal Paşa observed: 'as our population is small in relation to the size of our country, there is a much greater need here than in other countries to use machines and scientific tools for farming.'[28] The government hoped to nudge the farmers in this direction by demonstrating the efficacy of scientific farming on some model farms. But that method did not work and mechanised farming became wide-spread only after farm machinery was imported under the Marshall Plan.

The agrarian question in Turkey was primarily political and not economic in nature. Its solution may well have depended on whether it was the peasants or the landlords who supported the national move-ment. As it turned out, it was the landlords who gave their lukewarm support while the peasants remained generally apathetic. How is that to be explained?

The peasants may have been exploited and abused by the nota-bles in the countryside, but they held the state responsible for their oppression. It was from the state that they expected succour. They

---

27 Vedat Eldem, *Osmanlı İmparatorluğu'nun İktisadi Şartları Hakkında Bir Tetkik*, İstanbul, 1970, 63.

28 Assembly, speech of 1 March 1923 in Öztürk, *op. cit.*, 128.

hoped that the revolution of 1908 would bring change to the countryside, but they were bitterly disappointed. The Kemalists simply inherited the sullen bitterness of the Anatolian peasantry. One has a sense of the peasantry's hopes and expectations, its disappointment and frustrations, from reading the reports of the journalist Ahmed Şerif from Anatolia in 1909. One report in particular which chronicles the complatints of an old peasant bears quotation at length. It describes a situation which was serious in 1909, but which must have become desperate a decade later, just as the Kemalists were preparing for their life-and-death struggle:

> Liberty was a word we only began to hear recently. From what we have heard, and from some activities, we understand that it is something worth-while. ... but we thought that everything would be rectified; taxes would be collected peacefully and justly; murderers and thieves in the village would be reformed; our children who go for military service would not be kept hungry and naked for years, but would be discharged on time; officials would not do things as they pleased and everything would be changed. So far nothing has happened. In the past some things used to even function better; today everything is in a mess. If we go to a government office we do not know who is in charge. ... The government still does not look into our problems. ... Several people hold a deed for a particular field and we are not sure whether the ground we till belongs to us or not. Because of that there are fights every day and sometimes people are killed. We go to the state office and the court but we cannot explain our problem. They think only of collecting taxes when they are due. ... We work all the year round and we pay our taxes annually; if we don't they take them by force, even selling our pots and bedding. Thus we are always in debt. During the past few years there have been many peasants in the village who have not had seed to sow. Since. There is no help from anywhere else, we have had to buy seed from the *ağa* at either 100 or 125 *kuruş* per *kile* or return him three *kile* for one. Those *ağas* became a menace; they can have a peasant beaten by their thoughs, have him jailed, or sometimes have him frightened by having the state come in. In this way they collect their debts from those who can-

not pay. As a matter of fact, the Agricultural Bank is giving loans, but that does not help us. That money runs out before it reaches our village.[29]

This long list of grievances suggests that the peasantry was more alienated from the state than from the village notables. This alienation became even more acute during the World War. The peasants saw the national struggle as a continuation of the war and having fled from one they fled from the other. The nationalists found it very difficult to recruit peasants into the army. The peasants were most receptive to the propaganda of the Sultan's government when they were told that they did not have to serve in the ranks of the nationalists. In the turmoil of those years, there was no peasant movement to seize land; most peasants remained passive, though some joined local guerrilla forces often led by bandits, already in rebellion against the state. It is difficult to see what issue the Anatolian peasantry could have been mobilised around and therefore bad history to hold the Kemalists responsible for not mobilising it.[30] Compare and contrast the situation in Anatolia with that of India. There the peasantry was so inflamed against the oppression of British rule that it was beginning to act spontaneously, crying out to be mobilised; the Indian National Congress had to restrain the peasants and channel their activities in a non-revolutionary direction through the mediation of Mahatma Gandhi and Gandhism. No such problem existed for the Kemalists.

---

29 Ahmed Şerif *Anadolu'da Tanin*, İstanbul, 1977, 46-7. The original edition was published in 1910. Earlier, on p. 25, Ahmed Şerif commented: 'What the peasant cannot understand is that even though he has been hearing a great many promises during the past year, he has not seen them kept, not even those which would have been easy to carry out. He wants to see the venal and corrupt official removed; he wants to know that there is no need to quake any longer with fear before the gendarmes whom he feeds free of charge, and provides fodder for his beasts. He wants to see those things change which seem unimportant to us but are very important to him.'

30 The unwillingness to mobilise the peasantry that would alienate the landlords is the most general cirticism of the Kemalist regime. While that may be true, the critics never establish that there was a peasantry to be mobilised through land reform. It is ironic that later, the peasantry failed to support the party which favoured land reform but voted for the party, the Democrat Party, that opposed land reform but promised to liberate the peasant from the tyranny of the state.

Had there been a peasant movement capable of being railled to the nationalist cause, it is conceivable that the Kemalists would have turned to it rather than to the landlords. At the critical juncture when the survival of the Turkish people was at stake, Kemal Paşa sought the upport of any class: one has that impression from his brief conversation with Aralov, the Soviet ambassador to Ankara: 'In Russia you have a combative and veteran working class. It is possible to rely on it and it ought to be depended on. We have no working class. As for the peasant, he carries very little weight.'[31] Does not that suggest that a politicised peasantry might have been a different story? But such a class did not exist, fragmented as it was by ethnic and religious loyalties and totally dependent for its very survival on local forces. Therefore the Kemalists had no choice but to reach the peasants through the agency of their traditional leaders, the local notables and the men of religion, the *ülema*. These people were often the local landowners and they exerted a strong pressure to increase the size of holdings as much as possible. The Kemalists succumbed to such pressures as though to a natural process, just as they might have succumbed to the peasantry's demand for land. The price of the collaboration between the Kemalists and the notables was the tacit agreement to maintain, and even strengthen, the *status quo* in the countryside. This was done through the formation of the People's Party in which the landlords were a powerful element, by an electoral law which guaranteed the existence of an effective landlords' lobby in the Assembly, and by the inclusion of Article 74 in the new constitution which virtually closed the door to land reform.[32] Thereafter, the government tried to improve the lot of the peasantry through education, hoping that in time general enlightenment would transform the situation in rural Anatolia.

The origins of Kemalist political economy are to be found in the social structure the new regime inherited, and the way in which it

31 S. I. Aralov, *Bir Sovyet Diplomatının Türkiye Hatıraları*, İstanbul, 1967, 92.
32 See Avcıoğlu, *op. cit.*, 235.

defined this social reality. The new state was described as 'a People's State, the State of the People' *(Türkiye Devleti Bir Halk Devletidir, Halkın Devletidir)* while its predecessor, the Ottoman state, had been 'a personal state, the state of individuals' *(Müessesatı maziye ise bir şahıs Devleti idi, eşhasın Devleti idi).*[33] During the national struggle, the people or *halk* came to be identified by the Kemalists as all those who supported the nationalist cause against the imperialist powers and the old order. Like the Third Estate in France before the 1789 Revolution, the term *'halk'* included the vast majority of the nation, with an array of socio-economic groups and only members of the old order excluded. The principal task of this collective was to defeat the old order and its allies and to create a new order of their own. Above all else, this task required solidarity and united action by all the components of this entity, the people. Class conflict was therefore implicitly excluded.[34]

The problems that the Kemalist faced and the revolutionary solutions they proposed arose out of the national struggle against imperialism and the cosmopolitan institutions of the Ottoman-Islamic structure, rather than out of class struggle. These struggles, especially against the latter, implied stressing the unity of the people as a nation rather than the conflicts and the differences that divided them. That explains why the Kemalists attacked the universalist ideology of the old regime which paralysed and froze all classes, rather than act on behalf of the oppressed against their oppressors. To have done both would have been to court disaster; Mustafa Kemal was too astute politically to fall into that trap.

The Kemalists denied the possibility of class struggle in Turkey at that stage of development, precisely because there were no developed classes in the country capable of waging such a struggle. When he discussed this question with Kemal Paşa, Ambassador Aralov was

---

33 Kemal Paşa's Assembly speech of 13 August 1923 in Öztürk, *op. cit.*, 166.
34 Kemal Paşa's speech at the Economic Congress in Ökçün, *op. cit.*, 255-6. This speech may also be read in *Atatürk'ün Söylev ve Demeçleri*, vol. ii, Ankara, 1959, 112.

told: 'In Turkey there are no classes... there is no working class as there is no developed industry. As for our bourgeoisie, it is necessary to raise it to the level of a bourgeoisie. Our commerce is extremely puny because we have no capital. ...' The government would give priority to the development of 'national trade, [it would] open factories, bring underground wealth to the surface, aid the merchant of Anatolia and make him wealthy. These are the problems facing the state.'[35] Initially, therefore, the aim of Kemalist political economy was to create a nation with a class structure worthy of a modern capitalist society. When that had been accomplished and class conflict ensued, the state would then step in and mediate.

If the Kemalists did not recognise the existence of developed classes in Turkey, they were aware that interest groups were quite capable of organising political parties and indulging in activities detrimental to the nation's interest. The country had suffered from chronic instability during the Young Turk period caused by the activities of political parties. The new regime refused to permit such activities and declared that the new Turkey would be served by a single party, the People's Party, which 'includes within it the whole nation, and not just a section.'[36] This was yet another sign of the Kemalist regime's sense of autonomy *vis-à-vis* classes, as well as its paternalism, based on the belief that it was the impartial guide of the people and knew what was best for them.

Throughout the 1920s, Turkey experimented with the free-enterprise economic model, constrained as it was by the temporary limitations imposed by the Treaty of Lausanne. During these years the government played an important role in the economic reconstruction of the country, and members of the Kemalist elite participated in eco-

---

35 Aralov, *op. cit.*, 234-5 (both quotations).
36 Kemal Paşa's Balıkesir speech delivered from the pulpit of the Paşa mosque, 7 February 1923, in *Atatürk'ün Söylev ve Demeçleri*, vol. ii, 97. With this sentiment prevailing, the two brief experiments with multi-party politics were bound to fail. See Walter Weiker, *Political Tutelage and Democracy in Turkey*, Leiden, 1973.

nomic ventures like the founding of major institutions such as the Business Bank *(İş Bankası)*, which remains to this day the largest commercial enterprise of its type. The government's aim was to create an infrastructure without which the internal market would remain pitifully undeveloped.

Perhaps this experiment with economic liberalism would have continued for longer if the great depression had not had an immediate effect on Turkey, where the economic crisis in the capitalist world, ushered in by the Great Crash of 1929, gave a sharp impetus to state intervention. The impact of the depression on the economy was sufficient to force the government to take counter-measures. The crisis came to be seen as a failure of the free-enterprise system, identified with Western capitalism. The Soviet Union, with its system of state controls, seemed to have escaped the crisis. It was therefore seen by the Kemalists as a model that might be usefully copied in certain areas of the Turkish economy.

State intervention in economic affairs was in no sense a novel experience for the Turks. It had been tried during the First World War when it was described as 'state economics' or *devlet iktisadiyatı*; in the 1930s the term was streamlined and called statism or *devletçilik*. But its fundamental features remained virtually unchanged: to help the private sector to grow and mature by showing the way and by carrying out economic measures it was too weak to carry out for itself.[37] This time, however, the policy was soon institutionalised; this alarmed Turkish business circles. Statism became one of the 'six fundamental and unchanging principles' adopted by the Republican People's Party in 1931 and incorporated into the constitution in 1937. These six principles defined the ideology of Kemalism, and thus its political economy; they therefore deserve to be quoted at some length.

---

37 The early definition of statism is from Tekin Alp, 'Harbden Sulha İntikal İktisadiyatı – Devlet İktisadiyatı' in *İktisadiyat Mecmuası*, vol. 2, nos. 62 and 64, 16 Aug. and 14 Sept. 1917, 1-3. For a later discussion of statism see Korkut Boratav, *Türkiye'de Devletçilik (1923-1950)*, Ankara, 1962.

It is one of our main principles [read the 1935 Congress minutes] to consider the people of the Turkish Republic, not as composed of different classes, but as a community divided into various professions according to the requirements of the division of labour for the individual and social life of the Turkish people.

The farmers, handicraftsmen, laboures and workmen, people exercising free professions, industrialists, merchants and public servants are the main work groups constituting the Turkish community. The functioning of each of these groups is essential to the life and happiness of the others and of the community.

The aims of our Party, with this principle, are to secure social order and solidarity instead of class conflict, and to establish harmony of interests. The benefits are to be proportionate to the aptituted and to the amount of work.

Although considering private work and activity a basic idea, it is one of our main principles to interest the State actively in matters where the general and vital interests of the nation are in question, especially in the economic field, in order to lead the nation and the country to prosperity in as short a time as possible.

The interest of the State in economic matters is to be an actual builder, as well as to encourage private enterprises, and also to regulate and control the work that is being done.

The determination of the economic matters to be undertaken by the State depends upon the requirements of the greatest public interest of the nation. If the enterprise, which the State itself decides to undertake actively as a result of this necessity, is in the hands of private enterpreneurs, its appropriation shall, each time, depend upon the enactment of a law, which will indicate the way in which the State shall indemnify the loss sustained by the private enterprise as a result of this appropriation. In the estimation of this loss the possibility of future earnings shall not be taken into consideration.[38]

Despite the corporatist rhetoric evident in this document and influenced by the prevailing fascist mood of the 1930s, the Kemalist denied any affinity with fascism. Unlike the regime in Rome and

---

38 The quoted passage is an excerpt from the official translation of the programme of the RPP, reproduced in Donald Webster, *The Turkey of Atatürk*, Philadelphia, 1939, 308-9.

Berlin, Ankara accepted liberal principles and the nineteenth-century idea of progress. It recognised the rule of law and the importance of the constitutional state. Unlike fascism, there was no denial of the universality of civilisation, nor a rejection of rationalism, individualism, and the fundamental equality of man and ethnic groups. The Kemalist regime continued to be transitional in character, preparing the ground for a liberal political and economic system which would replace it in the near future.

In the early 1930s, there was a danger that the bureaucratic elements in the state and the party might become dominant and strive for state rather than liberal capitalism. The 1935 Congress, whose minutes are quoted above, reflected this danger. This bureaucratic threat was most real under the influence of the journal *Kadro*, which was patronised by premier İsmet İnönü. But strong and determined opposition led to the closure of this journal in late 1934. Meanwhile Celâl Bayar, the leader of the Busines Bank group, was appointed minister of the economy in 1933, suggesting the regime's opposition to extreme statism. Bayar held this portfolio until 1937 when he was made prime minister. Although a committed liberal, he recognised the weakness of the Turkish bourgeoisie and the need for the state to play the leading role in the economy. Bayar feared that under the extremists, statism might assume such proportions as to lead to the eclipse of the emerging private sector. He warned against that and pleaded that private enterprise be given a larger share of the national economy. Thus if there were any controversy, it was over the state's failure to define the extent of its intervention to the satisfaction of Turkey's business community.[39]

The businessmen need to have worried, for prime minister İnönü reassured them that state intervention was only designed to create a viable industrial base, something the bourgeoisie was incapable

---

[39]   Korel Göymen's, interview with Celâl Bayar, 2 March 1970, cited in his article 'Stages of Etatist Development in Turkey', *Gelişme Dergisi/Studies in Development*, no. 10, Winter 1976, 91.

of doing on its own.[40] Most of the measures of this period – the first five-year plan for 1934-8, the founding of Sümerbank in 1933 and Etibank in 1935, for example – were designed to achieve this purpose, and directly benefited the private sector.[41] The state was still playing its autonomous role of behalf of the bourgeoisie, despite the latter's fears and criticsm.

In these years of controversy, the trend towards a mono-party state, in which party and state coalesced, it worth noting. This trend, which derived from the example of the fascist states, was favoured in the RPP by a faction led by the party's secretary-general, Recep Peker. This faction railed against liberalism, forecasting its imminent doom which would be followed by the universal reign of statism. Although their voice was loud and alarming, their following in the party was limited. They succeeded in alienating the business community as well as many influential republicans. As a result, President Kemal Atatürk intervened and Peker was forced to resign in 1936 for trying go gain control of the party and for holding extreme views on all subjects, including economics.[42] The following year, the economy was liberalised and this trend continued until it was halted by the pressures of wartime neutrality.

The success of Kemalist political economy was seen only after 1945 and the triumph of the liberal democracies. It was marked in Turkey by the establishment of multi-party politics and a mixed economy in which the state sector was subordinated to the private. The infant bourgeoisie, which according to Kemal Atatürk had to be nurtured to the level of the bourgeois class, had grown strong enough to challenge the ruling party and defeat it in the first honest general election. Thereafter this class continued to grow, enlarging both the commercial and the industrial sector of the economy, creating at the same

---

40 Başvekil İsmet, 'Fırkamızın Devletçilik Vasfı', *Kadro*, no. 22, Oct. 1933, 4-6.
41 Göymen, *loc. cit.*, 97ff; and Z. Y. Hershlag, *Turkey: the Challenge of Growth*, Leiden, 1968, 61ff.
42 Göymen, *loc. cit.*, 105.

time the other class of capitalist society, the proletariat. Even the countryside, which the Kemalist regime had neglected for political reasons, was affected by the post-war transformation and integrated more rapidly into the expanding market economy. Yet whenever the country ran into a structural crisis – as in 1960, 1971 and 1980 – the interim regime which seized power invariably spoke of returning to the path of Kemalism. This suggests that ever since the Second World War, the political economy of Turkey has lacked firm ideological foundations. The search for those foundations continues.

The Times (London) and the Kemalist Revolution, 1930-1939

*T*he Times (London) used to be one of the great newspapers of the world, reflecting the power of the British Empire over which the sun was never said to set. The American journalist, William Shirer described it as "one of the chief glories of English journalism." The poet and writer Robert Graves claimed that the paper held an "unchallenged position as the best-informed and most independent journal in England... accepted as gospel... a semi-official journal." The *New Statemen and Nation* (5 January 1935) made an assessment with great foresight when it wrote that: "The power of *The Times* will remain just as long as England continues to be ruled by an intelligent upper-middle class which has been dominant since the Reform Bill (of 1832). It exactly reproduces the merits and defects of the British governing class. It is as safe as that class, as safe as the monarchy with which *The Times* has been so often compared, as safe as the British Empire, as safe as, and no safer than, the capitalist system of England."[1]

---

[1]   Quted in Magraret George, *The Warped Vision*, British foreign policy, 1933-1939, University of Pittsburg Press, 1965, p. 139.

The Times was the eyes, ears, and voice of the British ruling class, read religiously by its members at home and abroad. Its columns were read with equal attention by foreigners who desired to know about London's unofficial or semi-official view of the world. The Turks were no exception, especially after the revolution of 1908 when the press was again free to report and discuss the political situation at home and abroad. One gets a good idea of what Turkish journalists thought of *The Times* from their enthusiastic response to the special supplement the paper published called "The New Turkey" on 9 August 1938. "What the greatest newspaper in the world thinks of us" wrote *Journal D'Orient*. Ahmed Emin Yalman described *The Times* as "The best living representative of the ideals of integrity and responsibility in world journalism." "*The Times* writes what the average Englishman thinks and the average English thinks what *The Times* writes", noted *Kurun Haber* on 11 August 1938.[2]

As a result, *The Times*'s interpretation of the situation in Turkey soon became the dominant view in British ruling circles and in the world dominated by Great Britain. That is why the paper's coverage of Turkey in any period is both important and interesting, though we ought to be clear that it tells us more about how a few Englishmen saw Turkey than about actual reality. I have chosen to concentrate on the years 1930 to 1939 because the paper's views were now more flexible and in a state of flux, reflecting the uncertainties of the thirties. From 1908 to 1930, except for a very brief period of honey-moon immediately after the Young Turk Revolution of 1908, *The Times* was invariably hostile to the regimes in İstanbul and Ankara. First it was the Committee of Union and Progress (1908-1918) which bore the brunt of its criticism, then the Nationalists during the national struggle (1919-1923), and finally the Republican government in Ankara. All the criticism was consistent with British policy during these years, as was the change which one begins to notice during the early thirties.

---

2   *The New Turkey* was published as a book later in 1938.

The man who covered Turkey for *The Times* during all these years was Philips Perceval Graves. He was born in 1876, educated at Haileybury and Oriel College, Oxford before joining *The Times*. By 1906, he had become assistant to Valentine Chirol, the foreign editor, and two years later he was sent to İstanbul as correspondent, a position enjoying great prestige. Graves arrived in Turkey just before the outbreak of revolution and seems to have remained there until World War II, with a temporary absense during the 1914-18 war. In 1912, he established an intimate relationship with the Anglo-Levantine community of İstanbul by marrying Leila Millicent Knox, daughter of Gavin Gilchrist of Kadıköy. This must have given him a sense of belonging to the decaying and decadent Turkey of the capitulations- the unequal treaties between the European powers and the Ottoman Empire – and the religious communities, the *Millets*.

One would expect such a person to have acquired a deep and intimate knowledge of the country after such connections and long residence. And perhaps Graves did. But he does not seem to have out- grown the prejudices of the class to which he belonged and for which he wrote. During the Young Turk period his sympathies were with the old ruling class and the Ottoman liberals, symbolized by Kamil Paşa and the Liberal Union. The Unionists were seen as upstarts, totally unfit to takeover from the established ruling circles. This is exactly how *The Times* and the conservatives felt about the Labour Party in Britain! Yet, Graves was a perceptive observer; within a few months of his arrival in İstanbul he had noted quite accurately that while the notion of European classes was not altogether applicable to Ottoman society, the Young Turk movement was essentially middle class. "The high officials, generally speaking, were hostile to the movement... The lower classes... were, as a rule, indifferent. It was among the junior officers of the army and navy, the middle and lower grades of the civil service, the professional classes, and the *ulema*, that the movement for reform carried all before it."[3]

---

3   *The Times*, 24 Aug. 1908 quoted in Feroz Ahmad, *The Young Turks*, Oxford, 1969, p. 18.

Francis McCullagh, journalist and Graves's contemporary in İstanbul, noted *The Times*'s anti-Unionist bias when he wrote: "The alleged disklike of *The Times* and the British Embassy for the Committee since Kamil Paşa's fall (in February 1909) was also utilised to the full by the anti-committee press." Later, when the Unionists were overthrown during the counter-revolution of April 1909, *The Times*, observed McCullagh, "almost rubbed its hands in its satisfaction at being able to say: 'I told you so'."[4] The hostility of the paper increased sharply after the counter-revolution had been crushed and turned to enmity in 1914 when Turkey entered the war against Britain and the Triple Entente. After Turkey's defeat in 1918, the hostile attitude of *The Times* was transfered to the nationalists. This hostility persisted throughout the twenties, becoming bitter during periods of Anglo-Turkish tension, especially during the tension over the Mosul question. Only after this question had been resolved in Britain's favour did London begin to adopt a new attitude towards Turkey, and *The Times* fallowed suit.

But before examining the paper's attitude in the thirties we ought to briefly examine the basis of this attitude towards Turkey and the Turks. It is worth noting that the attitude was formed during the age of imperialism and made respectable by being defined in the psuedo-scientific terms of vulgarised Darwinism, commonly known as social Darwinism. Thus the world was divided hierarchically between rulers and ruled, defined racially with the white races at the top and the black races at the bottom, the Turks coming somewhere in the middle. When this formula was applied to the Ottoman Empire by *The Times*, a similar picture emerged. The Turks were considered more advanced than the Muslim Arabs and Kurds but more backward when compared with the Christians of the Balkans, the Greeks, the Armenians, and the Jews. "What I blame the Turks for is their persistence in attempting the impossible" wrote Graves.

---

4   Francis McCullagh, *The Fall of Abd-ul-Hamid*, London, 1910, pp. 58-9.

"'Ottomanization' under Turkish auspices is an impossibility. Will 1,000,000 moderately progressive Rumeliotes (i.e. Turks of Europe) and 7,000,000 or 8,000,000 backard Anatolians be able to impose their will on the non-Turks?"[5] Even after the republic was established, these old attitudes persisted and provided the backdrop to *The Times*'s reporting on Turkey throughout the thirties. It is to these years that I now turn.

The formation of Fethi Bey's Free Republican Party-*Serbest Cumhuriyet Fırkası*, described by *The Times* as the Liberal Republican Party-provides as convenient starting point. It provided the paper with an opportunity to look closely and critically at the Kemalist regime which was described, rather simplistically, as a "military autocracy" under the cloak of a "democratic republic." It was said to be controlled by two men: Mustafa Kemal and İsmet; later a third figure-Fevzi Paşa-was added and the regime described as a triumvirate,[6] reminiscent of the Young Turk triumvirate of Enver, Cemal, and Talât. The deputies, *The Times* wrote, were nominated by the government with a show of popular elections and there was neither freedom of press nor full freedom of speech. But there was tension between "nationalists" and "liberals" and the need for financial and economic reform had prompted the political change which would provide an outlet for the liberals (9 and 11 Aug. 1930).

For *The Times* all this seemed a replay of politics in the Young Turk period with the Republican People's Party (RPP)'in the role of the Committee of Union and Progress (CUP) and the Free Republican Party in that of the Liberal Union (*Ahrar* and *Hürriyet ve İtilâf Fırkası*). Fethi Bey was expected to lessen state controls over the economy through economic and financial reform and permit freedom of thought and the press. But more importantly, he was expected to work for closer collaboration with Europe and be more

---

5   Philip P. Graves, *Briton and Turk*, London, 1941, p. 155.
6   "The Triumvirate in Turkey: Soldiers All", *The Times*, 9 July 1931.

tolerant towards foreign capital (11 and 14 Aug. 1930). Editorially the paper applauded the decision to permit an opposition. The 1927 election results "gave the impression that he (Mustafa Kemal) had definetely decided to follow the example set by Russia, Italy, and China, where various forms of dictatorship are based on the support of assemblies composed of members of a single party... His decision is exceptionally interesting in days when it is fashionable in many quarters to assert that 'one-party' Governments are the last word in efficiency" (15 Aug. 1930).

The paper continued to be most sanguine and laudatory about Fethi Bey, describing him as an "experienced politician and diplomatist with a European outlook" (16 Aug. 1930). He was said to be popular in the advanced regions of İstanbul and İzmir while backward Anatolia supported İsmet Paşa. The Armenian, Greek, and Jewish minorities were behind the Free Republican Party which called for collaboration with them, while the RPP argued against (11 Oct. 1930). In the opinion of *The Times*, Turkey's interests were best served by the liberal policies of the Free Republican Party as they had been in the past by the liberal parties of the Young Turk period. But this time when the experiment in multi-party politics failed and the Free Republican Party was dissolved, the paper did not attack the ruling party as it had done the CUP. This time, the responsibility was placed squarely on another group, "the communists and the Turkish Bolsheviks."

The Times had reported with some alarm the success of the communist movement in Russia and the spread of its influence into Asia. There was even a conviction that the Ankara regime was sympathetic to Moscow and the Soviet-Turkish Treaty-sometimes described as an alliance-was important for the expansion of Soviet influence in the region (29 July 1930). But there was a sense of relief whenever the paper was able to report the arrest of Turkish communists; cordial relations with Moscow did not necessarily mean communism at home (4 Sept. 1930).

The demonstrations and violence which coincided with Fethi

Bey's visit to İzmir in September 1930, and which led to the decision to dissolve the Free Republican Party were blamed on the communists. "The Symrna riots in September were, it is said, instigated by Communists and in other parts of the country Bolshevist propaganda has been seduously spread among the officers, State employees, and workmen... İsmet Paşa has hinted that Fascist methods may have to be employed if law and order are to be maintained (3 Nov. 1930).

This analysis of events is very interesting-especially the rumours about attempts to subvert the army and the bureaucracy-and perhaps represents İstanbul opinion close to the correspondent. Perhaps the strikes in İzmir, which he didnot mention rather surprisingly, were described to him as the work of communists; otherwise, the reporting in *The Times* is not borne out by either contemporary journalism or modern research.[7]

The closure of the Free Republican Party was a turning-point in the ideological development of the Turkish Republic. The surprisingly large support for Fethi Bey, the outburst of anti-reformist and reactionary activity in Menemen and the Manisa region, and signs of communist influence among students and young professionals was most alarming for the RPP. It journals, reported *The Times*, proposed dealing with this problem by reorganising and disciplining the youth of Turkey. "Fascist and Communist regimes and methods are quoted as examples of what can be done; and it is argued that a similar regime, under the name of Kemalist, must be introduced in Turkey. It is, however, made clear that Communism would not be welcome in Turkey" (20 Dec. 1930).

This concern regarding communism and its influence remained a constant theme in *The Times* of the thirties. It may have been the result of the concerns of the paper's editor in London, for Geoffrey Dawson and his Conservative patrons were extremely anti-Soviet and firm believers in an Anglo-German rapprochement.[8] But by the early

---

7   See, for example, Çetin Yetkin, *Serbest Cumhuriyet Fırkası Olayı*, İstanbul, 1982.
8   See George, n. 1, who provides an excellent analysis of this period, especially pp. 141-6 and *passim*.

thirties, Graves was doing his best to calm these phobias. For example, in 1933, as the Kemalists began to implement statist policies and threatened to take over foreign trade, the paper asked rhetorically if Ankara was going the way of Moscow and Teheran (9 April 1931). Soon after, it reported that the Ministry of National Economy had denied any intention of establishing a state monopoly on foreign trade and noted the satisfaction with which this announcement was received by Turkish trading and banking circles (21 April 1931). *The Times*'s man in İstanbul kept an eye on all such developments as they were bound to be of great interest to the British business community faced with a shrinking world market. That is why the ideological tendencies of Ankara were analysed with care.

After Prime Minister İsmet Paşa's visit to Moscow and Rome in April-May 1932, Graves was able to reach some tentative conclusions about the character of the new Turkish nationalism. The Kemalists' "avowed intention" he wrote, "Is still to foster a species of nationalism which is neither Fascism nor Bolshevism, though it may have certain characteristics of both." Kemalism is based not on any ideological imperative, he suggested, but "on the character of the Turkish people, who have always been submissive and well disciplined, but lacking in a spirit of initiative"; thus the one-party regime, the lack of freedom of speech, the state's interventionism. It is not necessary to note falacy in his argument, but simply to quote his conclusion: "The present system is perhaps not ideal, but under it the Turkish nation is progressing towards a higher form of civilization and standard of life; and from that alone it compares more than favourably with every other form of goverment previouely experienced" (3 June 1932).

By 1934 *The Times* had become more sympathetic and understanding towards Turkey. The growing threat of Mussolini's Italy in the Mediterranean and the region as a whole was bringing London and Ankara closer together. The embassy of Sir Percy Loraine, who presented his credentials to Gazi Mustafa Kemal on 15 February

1934, undoubtedly speeded up the process. *The Times* made its own contribution to the Anglo-Turkish rapprochement.

The adoption of a planned economy, with the First-Five-Year Plan and the Soviet loan to implement it, must have alarmed capitalist circles in Britain, leading them to believe that Turkey too was following in Moscow's footsteps. *The Times*, however, explained the logic of Turkish statism: Turkey's handicrafts had been eliminated from the world market by industrial goods from the West and her exports had been confined to agricultural goods and raw materials. Post-war conditions and the economic depression had so reduced the value of these exports that the balance of trade could no longer be maintained by a policy of free trade. High protective tariffs and a system of barter had provided temporary relief but industrialization was considered the remedy (10 June 1934).

What was needed was understanding not alarm. "The announcement last year that Turkey was embarking on a five-year plan at once gave rise to the belief that she had become a slavish disciple of her friend and neighbour Soviet Russia; ..." However, there was a major difference between the two regimes which needed to be understood: "... whereas the Russian plan primarily represents an attempt to socialize the state still further, the Turkish industrial movement is a more modest affair inspired by a desire for economic independence and national security" (26 Jan. 1935).

The growing sympathy of Great Britain and *The Times* for Kemalist Turkey may best be explained by the rise of Nazi Germany as an economic power bent on spreading its influence in the Middle East. The suspicion against communist penetration remained strong; but the fear that Ankara might be absorbed into Berlin's sphere of influence now became dominant. Thus, by the time Dr. Hjalmar Schacht, President of the Reichbank and Acting Minister for Economic Affairs, visited Turkey in November 1936, Turkey had become the Third Reich's best trading partner. *The Times* noted that Berlin was buying Turkish goods at prices above the world market prices, thereby making Ankara a captive supplier who was losing her other markets. Schacht was believed to be working hard to counteract Britain's growing influence and, at the same time, seeking to replace Moscow by having Berlin play the major role in the second five-year plan (16 Nov. - 21 Nov. 1936).

For the next three years, *The Times* reported German moves to consolidate their economic and political position in Turkey (see, for example, 1 April 1937; 5, 8, 10, and 12 Oct. 1938; and 21 Jan. 1939). Dr. Funk, the German Minister for Economic Affairs who visited Turkey in October 1938, was quoted as saying: "Our trade in the Balkans and Turkey will make up for our loss in the U.S., because these agricultural and raw material producing lands yield nearly all German needs. Moreover, through increasing their production by placing bigger orders and sending bigger quantities of industrial products, Germany is improving the buying power of these peoples and raising their standard of living" (21 Jan. 1939).

The Times also reported that Turkey was trying to diversify its commerce so as not to become a satellite of Germany. She had been alarmed by Italy's expanionist aims in the region, in the Adriatic, the Mediterranean, and in Africa, notably Ethiopia. But Ankara was most shocked by the Anglo-French policy of appeasing the Fascist dictators, Hitler and Mussolini, a policy which soon came to be described as Appeasement with a capital A. The paper under Dawson gave this policy its full-hearted support.[9]

Appeasement, according to Graves, reminded the Turks of Great Power policy towards the late Ottoman Empire. "In private conversation", he wrote, "Turks generally point out that the new (Anglo-French) proposals... (for solving the Ethiopian crisis) savour rather of the methods so well known to the Turks in past, when kind words and high-sounding formulas led to the break up of the Ottoman Empire. It is considered that if the (League of Nations) enforces the

---

9   *Ibid.*

Anglo-French proposals it will be merely playing the part formerly played by the concerted European Powers, which the Turks cannot easily forget."[10]

In the thirties, Turkey became a firm and vocal supporter of the league of Nations and collective security. She supported the Republicans in Spain, which is understandable given Italy's role in the civil war. *The Times* does not mention any Turkish reaction to the annexation of Austria but it does tell us how the Turks felt about the dismemberment of Czechoslavakia. There was a deep sense of shock because that country had given up its independence without a struggle, bringing to mind Turkey's own struggle for survival. The *Cumhuriyet* was qouted as saying that the situation would not have been worse if Prague had fought the German army. But Britain was blamed for Czech passivity because her Prime Minister, Neville Chamberlain, had signed the Munich Agreement (20 March 1939).

I have dwelt on the theme of Anglo-Turkish relations to highlight *The Times*'s reporting on Turkey because it seemed to me to be the most illustrative. But there was much else in the paper about Turkey. In fact, the breadth and quality of reporting in *The Times* of the thirties was better than one finds in contemporary Anglo-American journalism. A great deal was reported about everyday politics, though not always with precision. For example, when the paper wrote that the six principles of Kemalism were being written into the constitution, it said that "Thereafter the Turkish State will be democratic (i.e. Halkçı), Statist (implying State Socialism or control) (i.e. Devletçi), evolutionist (i.e. İnkılapçı), nationalist (i.e. Milliyetçi), republican (i.e. Cumhuriyetçi), and secular (i.e. laik) (19 May 1936). Why did Graves make such inaccurate interpretations regarding halkçılık, devletçilik, and inkılapçılık? Perhaps, that is how the circle

---

10 The Anglo-French proposals refer to the notorious Hoare-Laval Pact signed in December 1935 surrendering Ethopia to Mussolini. See George, p. 68-9. On the relations between Europe and the Ottoman Empire, see a recent study, Marian Kent (ed.), *The Great Powers and the End of the Ottoman Empire*, London, 1984.

of Turks he moved in interpreted these words for him. His friends and contacts were likely to be either westernized, liberal Turks or local Levantines who, if not actually hostile to Kemalism were probably lukewarm towards it. They must have spoken to Graves in terms he was familiar with. It is also unlikely that Graves learned much Turkish despite his long residence in the country, or bother to follow the vernacular press closely. However, as we shall see below, he did learn sufficient Turkish to enjoy bargaining in the bazaar.

The Times interpreted the new Turkey from İstanbul, that ancient and cosmopolitan city where its correspondent continued to reside despite the move to the new capital in Ankara. He lived in a city whose old elite despised the new regime, a sentiment reciprocated by the Kemalists; Mustafa Kemal refused to enter the city for eight years, having left it in May 1919. Like the members of this old, anachronistic elite, Graves too, must have hankered for the past with its capitulations and genteel "old Turks." He seemed to write much of the time for old Turkey hands leading retired lives sitting in their London clubs, reminiscing while reading *The Times*. One senses this from reading obituaries in the paper and finding detailed accounts of the lives of former paşa's like Ahmed İzzet, Ahmed Tevfik, or Mahmut Muhtar. These are even obituaries of "Carasso Efendi: A Parasite of the Young Turks" (8 June 1934), and Dr. Lewis Mizzi, a Maltese who had owned the *Levante Herald*, described as a "leading European lawyer in İstanbul" (14 Aug. 1935). That he had been in the pay of the British government while he edited the *Levante Herald, The Times* does not mention. Such lives could have meant something only to old Turkey hands, or perhaps to future students of the Young Turk period, for whom *The Times* is indeed a valuable source of information.

There is no real attempt to understand the Turkey of Mustafa Kemal. How could there be while the correspondent resided in İstanbul while the heart of the new Turkey was in Ankara? There is no empathy with the spirit of the age bent on creating a modern society; only talk of "the Turkish character, more open to change during the past decade than at any other period of its history, retaining something of its Oriental langour..." (6 Dec. 1934). I have already quoted *The Times* as stating that Kemalism was based "on the character of the Turkish people, who have always been submissive and well disciplined, but lacking in a spirit of initiative" (3 June 1932). All these attributes are questionable, but they fit snugly into a stereotype about Turks and Turkey which persists even today.

However, it must be said that *The Times* was never dull to read. Occasionelly it featured articless by "a Special Correspondent" which were much better than anything written by the regular correspondent. The article "Emancipation in Turkey-A Contrast to the Harem" is a good example of what I mean (23 May 1935). After giving a brief but objective survey of the situation of women in the Ottoman Empire, he described the Kemalist reforms with sympathy and understanding. But it is his concluding paraghaph, giving reasons for the emancipation legislation, which is of interest to the reader and therefore worth quoting:

> "It is from the recent economic development of Turkey that the freedom of her women has come. Women are wanted in Turkey not only on the land but in the towns. The pace of industrialization increases. The cotton factories plan an output for 1937 of 150,000,000 yards of yarn and piece goods. Cigarettes, silk, woolens and carpets, spirits, sugar, and shoe leather plants, all major industries in Turkey, are to a great extent using the labour of women. These women, as well as girl shop workers and typists, may not actually demand representation, but the part they are now playing in the industrial life of the country justifies a new political status."

The paper sometimes featured a variety of amusing, off-beat stories such as the government's ban on Christmas trees. This was done firstly to protect trees, and secondly to stop Turks from giving parties at Christmas (29 Dec. 1931). The law banning porters or *hamals* was attributed to a "rather high conception of the modern Turk's dignity which has prompted the Turkish Government to abolish the *hamal* by legislation (2 Mar. 1937). The banning of the British comedy "The Geisha" was said to be due to the fact that an Oriental people, namely the Japanese, was presented as inferior to western nations. But *The Times* also noted that the government refused to show films about the defeated Greek army (12 Mar. 1937).

However, it was the law banning bargaining between customers and shopkeepers which made *The Times* man a little sad." "Shopping in the bazaars of İstanbul will thus lose most of its charm, for no longer will the buyer have the thrill of making a purchase, often after weeks of bargaining, at half the price originally demanded..." (21 April 1938). The editor lamented: "one more mark distinguishing East and West obliterated; shopping will be carried out Occidental fashion." The last comment, in a sense, summed up *The Times*'s attitude towards Kemalist Turkey.

War and Society Under the Young Turks, 1908-18

I

Anyone seeking an appropriate period in order to study the impact of war on society is unlikely to find one more suitable for this purpose than the decade 1908-18 in the history of the late Ottoman Empire. This decade witnessed political strife, violence, and war on an unprecedented scale; throughout these ten years, and beyond to at least 1922, there was hardly a year when the empire was at peace. The Turks were no strangers to warfare, having built their state and empire on the foundations of conquest extending to three continents. Later, they were forced to engage in a long rear-guard action as European armies pushed them back towards the borders of their original state in Asia Minor. In a sense, Ottoman society was already organized as a military society and therefore one should not expect any substantial impact during the decade under discussion. In fact, there was a dramatic difference in the way society was mobilized for war by the Young Turks, reflecting the radical character of the new regime spawned by the constitutional revolution of 1908. The impact of the new regime is almost comparable to that of the revolutionary governments in France after 1789, especially the Jacobins. In any case, the most radical wing of the Young Turks, the Unionists – members of the Committe of Union and Progress (CUP) which led the constitutional movement – were deeply inspired by the Jacobin example and tried to emulate their policies, though not with similar success.

Following the establishment of a constitutional regime by the Young Turks in July 1908, they were confronted with a number of crises which threatened the new regime. Bulgaria threw of the authority of the Sultan and declared itself independent on September 5, 1908; next day, Austria announced the annexation of Bosnia and Herzegovina, provinces she had occupied in 1878. On the same day, Crete announced its decision to unite with Greece. There was little that the Sublime Porte could do but protest to the Great Powers who had signed the Treaty of Berlin in 1878, since the first two acts were a violation of that treaty, while the status of Crete was also guaranteed by the Powers. The Powers, however, informed İstanbul that they would not interfere on behalf of Turkey. As a result, the Turks were forced to fend for themselves. In the next three years there were rebellions in the Yemen, Macedonia, and Albania requiring military intervention. By 1911, the Turks were at war with Italy in Libya, abandoning that province to Rome when they were attacked by a coalition of Balkan states in October, 1912. The Balkan Wars of 1912-13 were a disaster on a scale that neither the Ottoman general staff nor the people had imagined possible. Not only did the Ottoman Empire lose virtually all its European possession to the enemy, but invading armies penetrated to the outskirts of the capital and threatened the very existence of the Empire.

İstanbul did not fall, and the Turks even regained some territory in Thrace in the second Balkan War. But it is impossible to exaggerate the impact of these military and diplomatic disasters on the Young Turks. Some amongst them had become so demoralized and so full of despair that they were convinced that the Empire could survive only under Western tutelage. Others, notably the Unionists, believed that the Empire could be saved through a program of radical reform.

They were also convinced that, in order to buy time to implement such a program, the Porte had to become a member of one of the two alliances that divided Europe, preferably the Triple Entente. Neutrality meant isolation, and isolation, as the Porte's experience during the Balkan Wars had demonstrated, would spell total disaster in another major conflict. Therefore, the Young Turks tried to end their diplomatic isolation by seeking alliances in Europe during the brief interlude without war between the summer of 1913 and August, 1914. With great difficulty, they finally managed to sign an alliance with Germany on August 2, just as the First Would War broke out. Initially, İstanbul observed a precarious armed neutrality which lasted three months; by November, she was forced by circumstances, not completely in her control, to enter the war. For the next for years. Turkey was engaged in a struggle that required the mobilization of all its resources, human and material.[1]

II

Confronted with such a series of crises, any regime would have been hard put to provide suitable responses. The old regime of the sultan would have succumbed to partition under international pressure after making token protests, and would have accepted the *faith accompli*, so long as the regime was permitted to survive in some form or other. Its interests were restricted to those of the Ottoman family and a very small elite that monopolized power in the Palace and in the upper reaches of the civil and military bureaucracy. The Unionists, who constituted the most radical wing of the Young Turk movement, represented what may be described as Gramsci's "subordinate class." In the late Ottoman Empire, this class had become politically organized and articulate, demanding a place for Ottoman Muslims in the social and economic structure, a constitutional state, and a new intellectual and

---

1   For the diplomacy of this period see Kent (1984), Heller (1983), Trumpener (1968), Weber (1970), and Ahmad (1966).

moral order to go with it. Thus, immediately after the constitution was restored, the Unionists began to discuss the need to carry out a social revolution. They talked about transforming their society to bring it to the level of advanced societies of the West or Japan which had become a source of inspiration for them. They were proud to consider themselves as the "Japan of the Near East" (Ahmad, 1969: 23, n.1). The setbacks they suffered as a result of the crises and the defeats in war forced the Unionists to push for reform. Only after they had seized power during the Balkan Wars through the *coup d'état* of January, 1913 could they implement a program of reform and reorganization. Even then, they could not go very far without running into the barrier of the capitulations, unequal treaties which restricted Ottoman sovereignty and which the Great Powers refused to abrogate. The outbreak of war in 1914 provided the Porte with the opportunity to abrogate the capitulations unilaterally without the fear of intervention from Europe. These hated treaties were abolished in September, 1914, and the Turks were finally masters of their house, free to guide their own destiny.

Even before they had acquired the power and the autonomy to transform their society, the Unionists introduced new methods into politics. The restoration of the constitution had been marked by an explosion of popular sentiment for the new regime. Some of this may have been spontaneous, but much of it was organized by the CUP wherever it had its clubs. Thereafter, organized crowds and mass meetings, addressed by popular figures in the Committee, such as Hüseyin Cahit, the journalist, Rıza Tevfik, the "philosopher", or Halide Edip, the feminist novelist, soon came to play an important role in the political activity of the CUP. This was especially true during crises and in wartime.

The Unionists used urban masses for the first time when they organized boycotts against Austria's annexationist policies and Greece's union with Crete (Quataert, 1983; Yavuz, 1978). Later, during the Balkan Wars, organized demonstrations were used to keep off balance a government hostile to the CUP. Finally, a popular demonstration was organized against the anti-Unionist government of Kâmil Paşa (thought to be arriving at a consensus to sign an ignoble peace with the victorious Balkan coalition) in preparation for the coup of January 23, 1913.

It is worth emphasizing that the initiative to mobilize urban crowds and use them for political ends came from the Committee of Union and Progress and not from the government. In fact, the governments of the period were opposed to popular participation in politics, fearing that such activity might provide the foreign powers with the pretext to intervene. Nevertheless, the CUP organized boycotts against Austrian and Greek enterprises, and the boycott of Austrian goods played a significant role in forcing Vienna to pay compensation for the territories it annexed.

Defeat in war, or even a major diplomatic setback, forces the defeated society to assess its strengths and weaknesses. There is a tendency to try to make better use of existing resources, to remove defects in the internal fabric – in the social structure, in the instrument of power, and, above, all, in the armed forces. Talk of reform becomes the order of the day. Defeat can also trigger an imperialist response as a way to seek compensation in another area. This was the case with Russia after the Crimean War, and with France under the Third Republic. In Turkey, too, the rise of an aggressive nationalism which took the form of pan-Turkism or pan-Turanism, may be seen in similar terms. But it was a weak impulse and did not dominate politics, except briefly in 1917-18 during the revolution in Russia, simply because the Ottoman state lacked the power and the means necessary to implement an aggressive policy. Instead, defeats, first in the Balkan Wars and then during the World War, led to the rise of a populist movement inspired in part by the Russian Narodniks. This movement, known as "To the People" *(Halka Doğru)*, began to emphasize a Turkish nationalism rooted in Anatolia rather than the Balkans, so recently lost, or Central Asia, under Russian occupation.

III

After this brief introduction, it is time to look more closely at how the Young Turks responded to the problems of mobilizing society for actual war. The Turco-Italian conflict broke out on September 29, 1911. The government of İbrahim Hakkı Paşa was taken by surprise and resigned. The new government responded in the usual bureaucratic manner: it tried to parry the Italian blow "by raining telegrams upon its ambassadors and diplomatic notes upon the Powers" (Pacha, 124: 136). But, as ussual, the European powers refused to lift a finger in defense of Ottoman sovereignty.[2]

Meanwhile, the CUP had been making preparations to hold its annual congress in Salonica, the site of its headquarters until the city was lost to Greece in 1912. One the day the Italian ultimatum was delivered (September 28), delegates from all over the empire had begun to arrive. The issue of war naturally became the principal concern of the Congress. On October 5, after days of heated discussion, the Committee issued a manifesto inaugurating the Committee of National Defense (CND – *Müdafaa-i Milliye Cemiyeti*). This body was composed of eight members from the Salonica CUP, the organization that had provided the leadership of the constitutional movement both before and after 1908. Generally speaking, the CND's main function was to aid the war effort in any possible way. But it was an unofficial body, acting independently of the government in İstanbul, which soon became openly hostile to the CUP. The inspiration for this populist method of mobilizing for war came directly from the example of the Jacobin Republic of 1792-94. However much the Unionists may have wanted to emulate the Jacobins, their actions could only be superficial. They lacked the support of any independent mass organization like that of the *sans-culottes*, though they did use the guilds, like those of the porters and the boatmen, to build the semblance of a popular power base. More importantly, they did not attempt to win over

---

2 Only the International Socialist Bureau tried to mobilize European public opinion against Italian aggression, but with no success (see Haupt, 1972: 56-68).

the peasantry by distributing land as the Jacobins had done, thus rejecting the classical path of the bourgeois revolution, of which the French Revolution was the archetype (Soboul, 1965: 163-64).[3]

Nevertheless, the analogy o the French Revolution and the Jacobins continued to be applied to Unionist methods of mobilization, especially after they seized power in January, 1913. The British ambassador observed in his dispatch of February 5:

> I have the honour to note that the Committee of Union and Progress, which styles the Mahmut Şevket Paşa Cabinet as the "Cabinet of National Defence", has also formed a committee of national defence on the lines of the French revolutionaries of 1793 and the Communists in 1870. They have issued rousing appeals to the "nation" and all parties to rally to the cry of the "country in danger", and have declared the whole Ottoman nation in a state of mobilization. ... The committee of national defence... is raising subscriptions and organising the country for a "last ditch" effort. ... The new Sheik-ul-Islam [Esat Efendi] has sent a religious appeal, for the defence of the Moslem fatherland, to his subordinates in the provinces, while committee agents have been preaching a holy war in Saint Sophia and other mosques (Pacha, 1924: 136).[4]

The Committee of National Defense remained an unofficial body, without any power, until the Unionist coup. In late 1912, the position of the CUP, which won the fraudulent election in the spring, had become so precarious that it was threatened with destruction by an opposition movement with support in the army. The disaster of the Balkan War gave the CUP a new lease of life, enabling it to appear as the only body with a program and the will to fight.

---

3 On the reason for Unionist failure to carry out a radical policy towards the peasants see Feroz Ahmad (1983).
4 Lowther to Grey, no. 92 con., Constantinople, 5 February 1913, F.O. 371/1788/6200. The American Embassy also described the Committee of National Defense in similar terms as *Comité de Salut Public*. See the dispatch from Constantinople, February 13, 1913, 867.00/485 no. 412. Some documents on the CND may be found in Tarık Zafer Tunaya's invaluable study *Türkiye'de Siyasi Partiler* (1984: 448-57). See also *Tanin*, Jan. 30, 31, Feb. 1, 1913.

On Friday, January 31, 1913, a week after the Unionists formed the cabinet with General Mahmut Şevket Paşa as grand *vezir*, they held a meeting at the *darülfünun*, the university in İstanbul, to formally establish the CND. Prior to the meeting, the CUP had issued a proclamation inviting the opposition as well as the Armenian political organizations – the Dashnaks and the Hunchak – to cooperate in the defense effort, declaring that the entire nation had to be in a state of total mobilization in order to meet the threat from the enemy. The formation of the CND under these circumstances suggests that the Unionists intended to undertake tasks that would touch upon almost every aspect of Ottoman society. The primary goal was to raise volunteers for the army and money for the war effort, but sub-committees were formed to take charge of sanitation and health or to carry out propaganda. Thereafter, sub-committees were created on an ad hoc basis to meet new needs and solve problems as they arose. During the First World War, some of these committees became deeply involved in economic activity in order to create what was described as a "national economy."[5]

It should come as no surprise to us to find that the inevitable outcome of the CUP's involvement in the economy was widespread corruption. Patronage was one way to reward and enrich loyal party members and to create the bourgeois class missing from the Ottoman-Muslim social structure. It would be more accurate to say that rather than creating a new class out of nothing, the Unionists were providing economic opportunities for established groups and attempting to instil in them the spirit of capitalism. Being a Unionist naturally improved one's chances of benefitting from patronage. A reading of the diary of an American diplomat in wartime İstanbul gives us an idea of what was going on in this sphere. On August 6, 1915, Lewis Einstein noted that, "The Committee of National Defense is now making money

---

5   One the question of "national economy" see Toprak (1982). This must be the last word on the subject. See also Ahmad (1980).

rapidly by its monopolies of sugar and petrol *et cetera*. Their declared intention is to accumulate a capital which they can afterwards use to get the trade of the country in Moslem hands." On the 17th, he observed that "The Committee ... has monopolized all commodities and doles them out at enormous profit" (1918: 218, 243).[6]

The corruption and profiteering led to tension between Şeyhülislâm Hayri Efendi and İsmet Bey, Prefect of İstanbul. The cause seems to have been the scarcity of bread in the capital while the sub-committee responsible for this commodity was said to be making "four thousand [Turkish] pounds daily." Şükrü Bey, the Minister of Education, was asked to investigate the matter, but it seems that he too was involved in the profiteering! (Einstein, 1918: 247). Not missing a trick, the CND ordered M. Weyl, director of the French Tobacco Regie, to sell tobacco to the Ottoman army through the agency of the committee. Weyl complied. But instead of the tobacco being sold to the army at regulated prices, it ws sold in the towns at great profit. The army blamed M. Weyl whom the CND denounced as a French spy, forcing him to leave the country (Einstein, 1918: 260-61).

Wartime necessity forced the Unionists to be creative and rational in regulating the affairs of state at every level. Money was raised at home and abroad, and missions were sent off to distant India and Egypt for this purpose. At home, the most common method was public collection, which not only raised substantial sums of money for various purposes, but also raised public consciousness about politics and foreign affairs. For example, the Fleet Committee *(Donanma Cemiyeti)* was reinstituted in February, 1914; it had been originally set up in June, 1909 in response to the crisis with Greece over the island of Crete. But it became defunct and was revived in order to collect funds for the purchase of ships to meet the Greek naval challenge in

---

6   Such a work has a tendency to belittle the Turks since it was obviously published as a part of the U.S. propaganda campaign against Turkey. But Einstein is quite accurate about the corruption prevailing in the capital at the time. Plenty of other sources could be cited.

the Aegean Sea. Branches were set up in almost every town, and government officials were expected to give up a month's salary for the cause. Even European companies were being asked to contribute, and those with business interests in the Empire did so. Much of the money used to order the two battleships from British shipyards came from public subscription. That is why Great Britain's decision to confiscate these vessels on July 31, 1914, before the outbreak of war and before the signing of the alliance with Germany, aroused great indignation among the Turkish people who saw it as "an act of piracy" (Gilbert, 1971: 193).[7] After this event, it was easier to manipulate public opinion against Great Britain and in favor of Germany, and the "purchase" of the two German ships, the *Goeben* and the *Breslau*, was greeted with jubilation, as though an insult had been avenged.

Propaganda and intelligence came to be taken more seriously as a result of war. The *Teşkilât-ı Mahsusa*, or the "Special Organization" had been set up by the CUP in 1911 and had played an important role in organizing resistance to the Italians in Libya. This body continued to grow during the war in the Balkans and came into its own after the Unionist seizure of power. On the advice of Rıza Bey, the former *mutasarrıf* of Gümülcine, a town recently lost to the Serbs, the functions of this organization were broadened. Guerilla bands were formed from the local Muslim population of Macedonia, very much in keeping with the tradition of the region, as a way of keeping up resistance while İstanbul negotiated. The *Teşkilât* became more active in collecting intelligence, reconnoitering, and carrying out acts of sabotage, even assassinations. The CUP had used assassins in order to achieve its political aims both before and after 1908; that too was in keeping with the political traditions of the Balkans where the Committee was born. When Noel Buxton, President of the Balkan

---

7   The *Donanma Cemiyeti*, modelled on the German "Flotten Verein" and the British "Navy League", was founded on June 9, 1909 according to its proclamation, given to me by Dr. Aydoğan Demir of İzmir University, to whom sincere thanks. However, Fahir Çoker, a retired admiral and naval historian, gives July 19, 1909 as the date (1965).

Committee, arrived in Sofia in mid-September, 1914, the İstanbul press became paranoid, convinced that he had come to intrigue against the Porte. There was speculation that London, using the good offices of the Balkan Committee, was attempting to resurrect a new Balkan alliance against İstanbul, hoping to purchase Bulgaria with the offer of Edirne and Thrace. The Unionist responded by dispatching a Special Organization assassination team to kill Buxton, "whose name is enough to spell hostility to Turkey", *Tasvir-i Efkâr* had noted on September 17, 1914. The attempt on Buxton's life failed and he was only wounded; but *Tasvir-i Efkâr*, believing that Buxton was dead, opined that "he had received his punishment", marking "the end of an enemy of Islam" (Oct. 16, 1914).

During the period of armed neutrality, the CND was placed under the supervision of the War Ministry under Enver Paşa, no doubt to strengthen the hand of the war minister against his civilian rivals within the CUP. This body was no longer to concern itself with any-thing prolitical; instead, it was to devote all its efforts to advancing agriculture, industry, commerce, and education. And as though to add prestige to this body, the Sultan was made president, and the heir apparent a member of the board of directors in İstanbul (*Tanin*, Aug. 1, 2, 1914). Throughout the war, the Committee of Union and Progress, using a variety of affiliates of the CND, continued its efforts to organize the Ottoman Muslim masses and introduced all sorts of innovations to Turkish society.

The CND, working with the Red Crescent, the Muslim coun-terpart of the Red Cross, organized orphanages in Anatolia to teach trades and modern farming methods to the ever-increasing number of war orphans. In June, 1915, the government passed a law to establish educational institutions, scientific and technical, to meet the needs of orphans. The budget in these institutions was to be met by taxes on alcoholic beverages and tobacco, as well as by taxes on letters and telegrams. War also caused much destitution among the families of soldiers killed in battle. An association of women was set up to help such families, and its president was the wife of a prominent Unionist, İsmail Canbolat. Members of the committee included the daughter of the German general, Liman von Sanders, as well as the wives of other Unionists and high officials. Whatever the committees may have lacked, they did not lack prestige, provided in abundance by members of the Unionist elite!

IV

It is not at all clear how much solace such organizations brought to the population suffering from the hardships of war. But one may conclude from all these initiatives that the Young Turks recognized the need for social peace if the empire was to survive a long and terrible war. The situation of the Ottoman Empire was in many ways far worse than that of any of the other belligerents, and it was least equipped to wage war on such a scale. The Turks may have had an empire, but it was an empire dominated and exploited by all the Great Powers of Europe and totally dependent on them. The dependent character of the Empire was soon exposed in a dramatic manner as Europe prepared to go to war in August, 1914; the Ottoman economy was completely paralyzed.

The first consequence of the outbreak of the crisis in Europe in late July, 1914 was the closure of the foreign-controlled bourse in İstanbul and İzmir, with disastrous effect on the commerce of both cities. There was panic on the market, and the Porte was forced to intervene on July 31, suspending all transactions in transferable commodities. Foreign-owned shipping companies, operating in the coastal waters of the Empire, suspended their services, disrupting all imports and exports. Insurance companies, again all foreign-owned, refused to insure goods that they believed might be confiscated as contraband of war by belligerent powers. The premium for goods that they were willing to insure rose sharply, naturally affecting prices for the consumer. All these factors led to shortages and an explosion in prices; to make matters worse, the situation was exploited by merchants and traders who were still predominantly non-Muslim. This aggravated the chauvinism among Muslims and Turks.

The outbreak of war between the Great Powers during the first week of August increased the panic in İstanbul. There was a run on the banks – again all European – which were rapidly running short of cash because no money was available from their headquarters in Europe. The people with money stopped making deposits, aggravating the crisis. On August 4, the government intervened, and a moratorium on payments went into effect.

People in the cities, especially in the capital, speculated that there would be shortages of all commodities and began to hoard, as did the shopkeepers. Naturally prices rose out of control, particularly food prices; by August 5, the price of bread in İstanbul had risen from 5 to 55 para.[8] Faced with shortages in the capital, the Porte began to requisition grain in the provinces and made arrangements to import wheat from Rumania. The social-democrat revolutionary, Alexander Israel Helphand, better known as Parvus, who was residing in İstanbul at the time, is said to have made a fortune by organizing the import of Romanian grain for the Porte.

The government tried to regulate prices and stamp out hoarding, but with little success. Despite raids by the police in the capital, the press continued to complain that shopkeepers were charging whatever they wished. There are reports of fines being imposed, but that did not deter the profiteers. Apart from the price of bread, which kept rising, the price of potatoes rose 40% during the first week of August; sugar imported from Austria rose 200%, and kerosene 100 per cent. If the price of imported commodities rose sharply, that of local products that could neither be exported nor brought to the capital fell equally sharply. The fruit harvest was bountiful in the Marmara-Aegean region that summer, but it remained unsold. Bursa peaches and İzmir grapes rotted for the want of buyers. The silk industry of Bursa suffered a similar fate.

---

8 10 *para* were worth roughly one cent.

The situation in the capital may have been bad. But it seems
that the situation in the provincial towns, about which there is a
dearth of information because the local press has yet to be studied,
was much worse. But the consular reports of the foreign powers provide a sketch of the provincial scene. There too, the European crisis
and the out-break of war led to economic paralysis. In Baghdad,
where Anglo-Indian trade was dominant, all business came to a stand-
stil. The same was tue for towns in Syria as well as Anatolian commercial centers such as Adana. Money was in such sort supply in the
provinces that even the staff in a number of American consulates could
not be paid their salaries. The situation of the treasury in İstanbul was
equally critical; the French loan of TL 35,200,000, negotiated earlier
in the summer, had been virtually exhausted, and the Finance Ministry
was left with a mere TL 92,000 as petty cash on August 3, 1914. The
bankruptcy of the treasury became an important factor in bringing
about Turkey's entry into war on the German side three months later.

The Turks had long been aware of their total dependence on,
and subordination to, the Great Powers. The outbreak of war served
only to confirm the depth and extent of their subjugation. Western
domination over the empire was maintained through the institution of
unequal treaties known as the capitulations. The Sublime Porte, especially after 1908, had made great efforts to negotiate the abrogation
of these treaties, but with no success. Whatever their differences, the
Powers were unanimous about maintaining their control over the
Turks. The outbreak of hostilities prevented them from intervening in
Turkey's affairs and provided the Unionist government with the
opportunity to denounce unilaterally the hated capitulations. Thus, on
September 9, 1914, the ambassadors of all the Powers received a note
informing then that privileges acquired through the capitulations
would no longer be recognized on October 1. The Ottoman Empire
had become a sovereign state at last.[9]

---

9   It is worth quoting the note of the Turkish ambassador in Washington, Ahmed Rüstem Bey, to

V

One has only to read the Turkish press of the period to sense the great psychological impact of this unilateral act on the population at large. It seemed as though Turkey, far from being an empire, was a country that had just been liberated from generations of colonial rule; that is how oppressive the capitulations had been. There was a feeling of euphoria which the Unionists exploited by organizing marches and rallies, and making patriotic speeches in the main squares of the capital. September 9 came to be regarded as a national holiday and was given the same status as July 23, the day the constitution was restored. Here was another event – the recapture of Edirne and the "purchase" of the two German ships being earlier occasions – that enhanced the collective charisma of the Committee of Union and Progress and increased its popularity among the Muslims of the empire.

Freed from the restraints of the capitulations, the Unionists set about the task of nationalizing or Turkifying their state and society by eliminating cosmopolitan elements. Ironically, this process gathered momentum precisely at a moment when the empire was threatened with destruction by Allied forces at Gallipoli and the Russian army in eastern Anatolia. Just to give a few examples of this process: the official news agency was described as "national" rather than "Ottoman"; Turkish was prescribed as the language to be used by the post office, as well as the language to be used in all communications with the Ministry of Finance. This was followed by a decree requiring all shop signs to be in Turkish. These messages helped to instil a sense of national awareness in the population. But some ideologues among the

the Secretary of State to have a sense of what the capitulations and their abolition meant to the Turks.

Sir: I have the honor to inform you that by Imperial trade the Ottoman Government has abrogated as from the first of October next the conventions known as the capitulations restricting the sovereignty of Turkey in her relations with certain powers. All privileges and immunities accessory to these conventions or issuing therefrom are equally repealed. Having thus freed itself from what was an intolerable obstacle to all progress in the empire, the Imperial Government has adopted as basis of its relations with the other powers the general principle of international law (U.S. Government, 1914: 1090).

Unionists understood that Turkish nationalism without strong socio-economic foundations would be a futile experiment. In August, 1917, Yusuf Akçura, one of the most important nationalist thinkers of the period, again issued the warning to the Turks that if they failed "to produce among themselves a bourgeois class by profiting from [the example of] European capitalism, the chances of survival of a Turkish society composed only of peasants and officials [would] be very slim" (quoted in Berkes, 1964: 426).[10]

This warning had been heeded, and towards the end of the war, thanks to a variety of wartime measures to encourage commercial and industrial activity, it was possible to observe the emergence of a "national economy." Not only was there a nascent Turkish bourgeoisie to complement this development, but also a small working class. The author of an article entitled "The Phase of Capitalism is Beginning" noted this fact and remarked that "this state of affairs could not fail to provoke conflict between capital and labor in our country" (*İktisadiyat Mecmuası*, Nov. 8, 1917: 1-2). There may be some exaggeration in this observation, but it aptly describes the great transformation that had taken place in Turkish society during this brief period of ten years. Since 1914, the government's principal concern may have been the war, but its preoccupation with economic matters was never far behind.

Anyone persuing the press of wartime İstanbul is bound to be struck by the amount of column space that was devoted to social and economic issues. Despite the war, or perhaps because of it, the problems of agriculture, commerce, or industry were always in the forefront; in fact some journals were founded specifically for this purpose, *İktisadiyat Mecmuası (Journal of Economics)*, published in February, 1915, being the most notable. Alongside articles on the military situation, there were invariably articles on all sorts of issues that affected the economic life of the country and the war effort. The size and qual-

---

10 A French translation of this article, which was originally published in *Türk Yurdu* (No. 140, 12 Aug. 1333 [1917]), is available in François Georgeon's excellent monograph on Yusuf Akçura.

ity of the harvest in various provinces was always worthy of attention; so were the measures taken by the peasants, the authorities, or even experts brought from Germany or Austria-Hungary to combat vermin, which seemed a constant threat to crops and cattle. There are reports of meteorological stations being set up in the capital and in the provinces for more accurate forecasting, and discussions of new laws for the preservation of forests. Chambers of commerce were being founded by the "new bourgeoisie" in towns around Anatolia and organizations set up to promote this or that industry. One also reads reports of local fairs where peasants were shown new implements and encouraged to adopt modern techniques. In the past, students had been sent to Europe to acquire a western education; during the war, workers were also being sent to Germany to learn to use modern machines. From all this evidence, it is no exaggeration to conclude that wartime Turkey was in the process of a social and economic renaissance.

[handwritten margin note: Turkey of 1908-1918 attempting to quick-fix and modernise its nation despite financial and social upheaval]

VI

Ottoman-Turkish society paid a heavy price for this renaissance, though the burden was shared unequally by the various segments. A small minority, the "nascent bourgeoisie", derived almost all the benefits of this transformation, retaining the lion's share of the wealth accumulated from wartime profiteering. It is no coincidence that the Koç family, still the owner of the foremost commercial-industry holding company in Turkey today, traces its rise from modest circumstances during the First World War.[11]

The people who bore the heaviest burden were the urban consumers and the peasants. The consumers paid exorbitant prices for shoddy goods and enriched the new class of war profiteers; the *332 tüccarı* or "the merchants of 1916", as they were called, became notorious for their exactions. Such was the popular outcry against their

---

11 See Vehbi Koç's autobiography *Hayat Hikâyem* (1973) and the more entertaining but historically-accurate fictionalized account by Erol Toy (1973).

activities, the government was forced to set up commissions of investigation and pass laws to control prices. The peasantry, on the other hand, having no collective voice that could be heard in the capital, suffered silently, though not without bitterness and hatred towards the state.

The wars had the most detrimental effect on agriculture. Not only were the peasants conscripted and sent off to fight, but their animals – buffaloes, donkeys, and horses – were also requisitioned. Thus the task of tilling the soil became even more formidable. Ottoman agriculture had suffered, not from the lack of land, but from the scarcity of labor, and constant warfare made the problem more acute. There was great disruption in the countryside during the Balkan Wars, and again in August, 1914 when the Porte declared general mobilization. Once Turkey became a belligerent and had to prepare to fight a long war, the Unionist government responded by virtually legalizing forced labor in order to maintain agricultural production, enforcing these measures ruthlessly throughout the war. With the men being killed and wounded in the different theaters of war, women and children were forced to assume some of the heaviest tasks on the home front. One cannot talk about the "liberation" of peasant women because they always worked, though perhaps not as hard as they were forced to work during the war. But there was a certain amount of "liberation" – if "liberation" is the appropriate term – for urban Turkish women, especially in the capital, as a result of war.

Ever since the revolution of 1908, the Young Turks had attempted to involve Turkish middle-class women in activity outside the home. There was a conviction, often expressed in polemical articles, that Turkish society could not be transformed until women were permitted to play an appropriate role. The new regime had tried to improve the situation, but with limited success in the major cities like İstanbul and İzmir. The government opened schools, trained women teachers, and prepared better text books. The liberal Islamic establishment close to the CUP interpreted Islam progressively for this purpose. Supported by

How so

Sultan Mehmet Reşad and the Şeyhülislâm, the *ulema* – the doctors of Islamic law and theology – argued that Muslim women were not being treated as the Prophet Muhammad had intended them to be, and that he had also opposed polygamy, as quotations from the *Quran* demonstrated. But Turkish-Muslim society as a whole remained conservative, and in some towns of Anatolia a man speaking to a woman in public was still liable to be fined and the woman flogged.

Wartime necessity forced Turkish society to utilize female labor on a substantial scale. Women began to work in factories, and middle-class women in offices or establishments like the new telephone exchange, until then the domain of non-Muslim women. Women had become such an active part of the labor force in the greater İstanbul region that an organization, whose name may be translated roughly as "The Society for Muslim Working Women", was set up in the capital in August, 1916. It had three branches: in İstanbul, Pera, and Üsküdar; which gives us some idea where their working places were concentrated. Its president, no doubt serving in an honorary capacity, was Enver Paşa's wife, Naciye Sultan, while the Paşa himself was listed as a patron.[12]

The İstanbul daily, *Tanin*, commenting on the founding of this body, noted that thousands of women were doing jobs they had never conceived of doing before the war. This was especially true in İstanbul. The object of this society was to publicize this activity, to give it official support in order to make it more acceptable – thus the patronage from the highest circles of Turkish society – and to organize and promote work for women by opening more work places (Aug. 12, 1916). The initial aim was to provide work for another ten thousand women.

Peasant women played an even more vital role, particularly during the harvest of 1916. Tekin Alp eulogized their contribution, observing that:

---

12 *Kadınları Çalıştırma Cemiyet-i İslâmiyesi* translated in French as "Société du travail des femmes mussulmanes", *İktisadiyat Mecmuası*, vol. I, no. 23, 10 Aug. 1916: 2-3 and vol. I, no. 25, 31 Aug. 1916: 7. For women's organizations in this period see Tunaya (1984: 476-82).

> While the men found themselves at the front struggling heroically for the very life and existence of the country, the women have remained at home struggling equally hard with all their might to provide food for the country and guaranteeing its economic future. In several places, women have succeeded through their labour in not allowing the shortage of men to be felt.
>
> This activity of peasant women [he observed] is to be noted above all in the province of Konya. Semih Bey, the *vali* of Konya, had decided to build a monument to perpetuate the memory of this noble activity by Turkish women during the historic epoch through which we are passing (1916: 1-2).[13]

Despite the imposition of forced labor and the massive contribution of peasant women to agriculture, the area under cultivation continued to decline throughout the war. When the Chamber discussed a new law for compulsory agricultural service in February, 1917, the minister reported that the area under cultivation had declined dramatically from 60 million *donums* in 1913-14 to 30 million in 1914-15, and to 24 million *donums* in 1916. The government hoped to restore cultivation to 30 million *donums* in 1917.[14] The Unionist intended to meet the acute shortage of labor by mechanizing agriculture, and farm machinery as well as Austrian and German experts were imported for this purpose. This was bound to have a great impact on peasant society in Anatolia.

The Unionists were in fact trying to carry out a structural change in agriculture, which undermined the position of the small

---

13 On Tekin Alp see Landau (1984). A telegram from İstanbul published in the *Rheinisch Westfalische Zeitung* (n.d.) and quoted in *The Near East* (London), reported that: "Women are being admitted to the Turkish army. The Ottoman Association for Women's Work publishes a call to all women between 18 and 30 to join the recently created Women Workers's Battalion. The battalion was to be attached to the First Army Corps and would work eight hours daily behind the front. The overseers and officers would first be men, but would gradually be replaced by women" (Feb. 22, 1918: 153).

14 *Echo de Bulgaria*, Mar. 1, 1917, excerpted in War Ministry (London), *Dail Review of the Foreign Press (DRFP)*, Mar. 17, 1917; Novichev (1935: 19-20). Novichev provides a most interesting account of wartime Turkey.

peasant. In 1916, the government passed a decree introducing the regimentation of farming. The German economic review, *Wirtschaftszeitung der Zentralmachte* wrote that:

> The farmers will not be able to sow and work as they please, but everything will be done in common under State supervision. The State will supply all appliances, manure, and other necessaries in sufficient quantities, and even labour where required. By this means one of the greatest drawbacks of Turkish agriculture, "small farming" as it is called, will be abolished. In Anatolia the land is very much broken up among small owners, hence intensive cultivation is difficult, but it will, now be made possible by the nationalisation of agriculture and the joint cultivation of the soil (Oct. 16, 1916; quoted in *Dail Review of the Foreign Press*, Oct. 28,1916).

Thus, despite the exploitation of the vast majority of the peasantry, a small class of prosperous "middle peasants" began to emerge, at least in western Anatolia where capitalist agriculture was most developed. An interview with Dr. Nazım, a high-ranking Unionist, provides an illustration of this phenomenon.

Dr. Nazım, who had just been instrumental in setting up an association in İzmir for "the moral and physical improvement of the peasantry", claimed that the War had enriched the population of Turkey, and this was especially true of the region around İzmir.

> In nearly all parts of the town one can see traces of our economic revival. The coffee-houses which used to line the quayside before the war have made way for shops. Wherever you look you see signs of newly formed limited companies. The value of money has fallen to such an extent that our peasants, who have made fortunes through the unwarranted rise in the price of food..., can pay three liras for a pair of stockings for their daughters" (1918: 2-3).

Wartime policies resulted in strengthening the position of the landlords who had emerged as a political force following the Land Code of 1858. Their position was further bolstered by the newly created "middle peasant". Both groups benefitted by acquiring lands left vacant by peasants killed in war, and by the expulsion and massacre of Greek and Armenian peasants. However, most of the vacated land was resettled by Turkish peasants fleeing from the Balkans and the Caucasus.

In contrast, the position of the Turkish peasantry as a whole deteriorated sharply. How did they respond to their increasing exploitation and oppression? In most cases they seemed to bear their lost with a large dose of fatalism. But sources also reveal a massive increase in banditry and brigandage, not new phenomena in Anatolia. News about this activity is abundant in the press of wartime İstanbul, especially after political and military censorship was lifted in June, 1918. Thereafter, the press carried reports of bandits who were hampering the vital activity of the summer harvest as the peasants were constantly threatened by marauding bands.[15] Many of the brigands were deserters from the army, and there are reports of Turkish deserters seeking refuge with Greek bands in the Black Sea region. By 1918, brigandage *(eşkiyalık)* had become so widespread that small provincial towns were insecure, and public life was threatened.

The situation became sufficiently serious for the Talât Paşa government, which came to power in February, 1917, to oppoint İsmail Canbulat, a retired officer and dedicated Unionist, Minister of the Interior. He was expected to deal with this problem energetically, but he too failed to crush the bands. He resigned in September, 1918 after bandits had attacked the train at Bandırma for the second time. He complained that the government was simply not strong enough to cope with the situation (Cavit, 1945). After the War, the nationalist movement inherited the problem of a disgruntled and alienated peasantry and therefore had to rely on the traditional notables to mobilize the countryside. This proved to be an unfortunate legacy for the

---

15 Ahmed Emin [Yalman] writes that in many regions: "peasants had to pay regular tributes to brigands in addition to their official contribution to the Government" (1930: 80).

republican regime ater 1923, as it prevented virtually any reform that threatened the interests of the landlords from being passed in the Assembly.

Another important contribution made by wartime Unionist practices to the Republican regime was the role that the state began to play in social and economic engineering. The Young Turks, including the Unionist wing, intended to follow, as closely as circumstances permitted, the path of individual initiative and free enterprise in creating a modern capitalist economy. But the situation created by a long war forced the state to intervene in order to guarantee the very survival of its people. The ruling party – the Committee of Union and Progress – and the state become involved in every sphere of social and economic activity, from organizing companies to protecting consumers. The proponents of capitalism, inspired and reassured by Germany's wartime example, recognized the necessity of state intervention in a backward society. They began to talk of a "new" economic model, which was described as *devlet iktisadiyatı*, or state economy, in which the state would assume those responsibilities that private enterprise could not or would not. These ideas were adopted by the republic in the 1930's, becoming *devletçilik* or *étatisme*, one of the "six arrows" of Kemalist ideology.

One must also consider how and to what extent the mentality of Turkish Muslims was altered by the events of this decade, especially under the impact of war. This matter needs to be studied and, like so many topics in modern Turkish history, awaits its historian. For the moment, one can only note the observations of a contemporary. Dr. Rıza Nur, who played a very active oppositional role in the Young Turk period and was also an acute observer of events and trends, remembered how conservative his society had been as the constitutional period commenced. When Rıza Tevfik proposed in parliament the introduction of European time, the conservatives came out in opposition claiming that "the abolition of our time [based on the movements of the sun] will mean the end of prayer." When the voters of Samsun saw a picture of their deputy in a hat, they said reproach-fully: "The deputy for Samsun went to Europe and wore a hat. He became an infidel. The dirty pig." Ten years later, in 1919, Rıza Nur returned to his old constituency, Sinop on the Black Sea, after his long exile in Europe. He was apprehensive about his reception, especially as he now had a European wife. But he was pleasantly surprised when people asked: "Did you wear a hat, did your wife move around with-out a veil?" Rıza Nur noted that ideas had changed greatly in the ten years and remarked how attendance to the Alaettin Mosque in Sinop had dropped sharply" (Nur, 1967: 281-82). One can see how the ground had been prepared for the reforms of Mustafa Kemal Atatürk.

VII

Such, in broad outlines, is the sketch of war and society during the Young Turk decade. Despite the great transformation that took place during this brief period, the historian must resist the temptation to exaggerate the accomplishments of the Young Turks. Much of Anatolia and Turkish society remained unchanged, indeed untouched, by the reforms, because of the failure to ameliorate the lot of the peas-antry, the vast majority of the population. Nevertheless, the reform of society was sufficient to create classes, both in the towns and in the countryside, with a strong commitment to the survival of a Turkish nation state in Anatolia, "discovered" during the War. These classes sided with the nationalists in the struggle against imperialism and in the civil war against the old regime. They were the dynamic element in Turkish society, the creation of wartime policies. The *Tanin* recog-nized this and acknowledged the benefits war had brought, liberating the Turks from the straight-jacket the Powers had forced them to wear (Sept. 19, 1917). A German journalist, who spent the years 1915-16 in İstanbul, provides a fitting conclusion to a discussion of the impact of war on Turkish society:

> The war with its enormous intellectual activity has certainly

brought all the political and economic resources of the Turks... to the highest possible stage of development, and we ought not to be surprised it we often find that measures, whether of a beneficial or injurious character, are characterised by modern exactness, clever technicality, and thoroughness of conception. ... No one can doubt that it will enormously intensify zeal in the fight for the existence of the Turkey of the future, freed from jingoistic outgrowths, once more come to its senses and confined to its own proper sphere of activity, Anatolia, the core of the Empire (Stuermer, 1917: 1-2).

REFERENCES

Ahmad, Feroz (1966). "Great Britain's Relations with the Young Turks, 1908-1914", *Middle Eastern Studies*, II, 4 July, 302-29.

— (1969). *The Young Turks*. Oxford: Clarendon.

— (1980). "Vanguard of a Nascent Bourgeoisie: The Social and Economic Policies of the Young Turks, 1908-1918", in Osman Okyar & Halil İnalcık, eds., *Türkiye'nin Sosyal ve Ekonomik Tarihi (1071-1920)*, Ankara: Meteksan, 329-50.

— (1983). "The Agrarian Policy of the Young Turks, 1908-1918", in Jean-Louis Bacqué-Grammont & Paul Dumont, eds., *Economie et sociétiés dans L'Empire Ottoman (fin du XVII-début du XXe siècle)*. Paris: Ed. du. C.N.R.S., 275-88.

Cavit, Mehmet (1945). "Meşrutiyet Devrine Ait Cavit Bey'in Hatıraları", *Tanin*, Aug. 2.

Çoker, Fahri (1965). "Donanma Cemiyeti İhyası mı?", *Cumhuriyet*, May 3.

Einstein, Lewis (1918). *Inside Constantinople*. New York.

Emin, Ahmed [Yalman] (1930). *Turkey in the World War*. New Haven.

Georgeon, François (1980). *Aux origines du nationalisme turc – Yusuf Akçura (1876-1935)*. Paris: A.D.P.F.

Gilbert, Martin (1971). *Winston S. Churchill*, III. Boston: Houghton Mifflin.

Haupt, Georges (1972). *Socialism and the Great War*. Oxford: Clarendon.

Heller, Joseph (1983). *British Policy towards the Ottoman Empire, 1908-1914*. London: Frank Cass.

Kent, Marian, ed. (1984). *The Greek Powers and the End of the Ottoman Empire*. London: Allen & Unwin.

Koç, Vehbi (1973). *Hayat Hikâyem*. İstanbul: s.n.

Landau, J. M. (1984). *Tekin Alp, Turkish Patriot, 1883-1961*. Leiden: Brill.

Novichev, A. D. (1935). *Ekonomika Turtsi v period mirovoi voiny*. Leningrad.

Pacha, Mahmoud Moukthar (1924). *La Turquie, l'Allemagne et l'Europe depuis le Traité de Berlin*. Paris.

Quataert, Donald (1983). *Social Disintegration and Popular Resistance in the Ottoman Empire, 1881-1901.* New York: New York Univ. Press.

Soboul, Albert (1965). *A Short History of the French Revolution, 1789-1799.* Berkeley: Univ. of California Press.

Stuermer, Harry (1917). *Two War Years in Constantinople (Sketches of German and Young Turkish Ethics and Politics).* London.

Tekin Alp (1916). "Bu Seneki Mahsulümüz", *İktisadiyat Mecmuası.* Vol. I, July 21/27, 1-2.

Toprak, Zafer (1982). *Türkiye'de "Milli İktisat" (1908-1918).* Ankara: Yurt.

Tunaya, Tarık Zafer (1984). *Türkiye'de Siyasal Partiler.* Vol. I, *İkinci Meşrutiyet Dönemi.* İstanbul: Hürriyet Vakfı.

Toy, Erol (1973). *Imperator.* İstanbul: May Yayınları.

Trumperner, Ulrich (1968). *Germany and the Ottoman Empire, 1914-1918.* Princeton: Princeton Univ. Press.

United States Government (1914). *Foreign Relations of the United States, 1914.* Washington.

Weber, Frank (1970). *Eagles on the Crescent.* Ithaca: Cornell Univ. Press.

Yavuz, Erdal (1978). "1908 Boykotu", in Orta Doğu Teknik Üniversitesi, *Gelişme Dergisi.* Ankara: Özel Sayısı-Türkiye İktisat Tarihi Üzerine Araştırmalar, 163-81.

The Kemalist Movement and India

"If the British had been driven out [of India] in 1957 (wrote V.G. Kiernan, the distinguished historian) the history of the world, not of Britain and India alone, would have gone differently."[1] They survived "the first massive revolt of Asia against Europe",[2] but it left deep scars on both the victors and the vanquished, especially the Muslims of India. The British never quite recovered from the trauma and continued to live in the shadow of another rebellion which never materialised. The Muslims, upon whom the British placed principal responsibility for the event they described as a "mutiny", became even more alienated from their foreign rulers. They tried to find psychological relief by giving their sympathy to the Ottoman Empire, the last independent Islamic state to survive in the age of imperialism. The relationship between India and Ottoman Turkey began in the last quarter of the nineteenth century and concluded with the Kemalist episode in the first quarter of the twentieth.

---

1   V. G. Kiernan, *The Lords of Human Kind*, Boston, 1969, p. 32.
2   *Ibid.*, p. 46.

It is possible to isolate the final episode and examine it on its own. However, such an analysis would tend to be superficial and would tell us little about the motivations of the movement either in Turkey on in India. At this level, we might note that the names Ghazi, Mustafa, and Kemal became popular among the Muslims of India as a result of the Kemalist anti-imperialist struggle, just as the names Niyazi, Enver, Talât, and Cemal had been a symbol of Young Turk popularity in the Muslim world, including India. (In the early sixties, there was a Pakistani student at the Middle East Technical University who was named Mustafa Kemal Paşa, much to the astonishment of Turkish students). At that level of influence, Kemalist Turkey continued to be an inspiration in the Indian sub-continent into the 1940s and beyond.

One could also cite the praise that contemporary Indians – both Muslims and Hindis – showered upon Gazi Mustafa Kemal and his regime. Articles by Indian and Pakistani scholars read at conferences to commemorate the centenary of Atatürk's birth in 1981 tend to rely on such writing in order to make their case. After the Kemalist victory in 1922-3, and especially after Atatürk's death in November 1938, there were numerous glowing tributes to the achievements of the great man published in India, along with the rest of the world.

Throughout these years, the admiration was genuine as Indian leaders watched the new Turkey in the process of transformation. Writing in the early 1930s, Jawaharlal Nehru asked rhetorically "May we not envy the lot of other countries where education, sanitation, medical relief, cultural facilities, and production advance rapidly ahead, while we remain where we were, or plod wearily along at the pace of a snail." Nehru was thinking primarily of Stalin's Russia though he also observed that "Backward Turkey, under Atatürk, Mustafa Kemal's leadership, has taken giant strides toward widespread literacy."[3] He was equally impressed with Turkey's – and Soviet

---

3   Jawaharlal Nehru, *Toward Freedom the Autobiography of Jawaharlal Nehru*, New York, 1941, p. 279.

Central Asia's – success in adopting the Latin script though he did not believe that it would be possible (or desirable) to in introduce such an innovation into India's cultural environment.[4]

Though the two nationalist movements – the Turkish and the Indian – made political use of each other against British imperialism, their aims were exclusive and contradictory and were even at cross purpose. Thus there was no question of one influencing the other. The Turks under Mustafa Kemal fought for national self-determination with the goal of establishing a modern nation state. Their Indian supporters – Muslim and Hindu – wanted the Turks to retain a multi-national Islamic state under the Sultan-Caliph. For the Indian National Congress national self-determination strictly defined and narrowly applied could mean that the Indian sub-continent would be fragmented like the Balkans, and therefore had to be discouraged and fought against. For Indian nationalists, there was also the psychological factor which made the success of the Turkish struggle an important element in their own fight against the British. Clearly, defeat of Turkish nationalism at the hands of Western imperialism would demoralise anti-colonial national movements throughout Asia and Africa, setting them back decades. As we shall see, both the British and the Indians were aware of this factor and, for the Indians, it became fundamental in their relationship with the Kemalists. There was an historical basis to this factor which needs to be examined.

The relationship between the late Ottoman Empire and Indians began on the basis of Islamc solidarity. The retreating Ottoman Empire under Sultan Abdülhamid II (1976-1909) tried to exploit pan-Islamic sentiment around the world to control the growing appetite of the European imperialist powers. The Muslims of India, on the other hand, sought psychological relief for the rapid decline of their fortunes following the great rebellion of 1857 by identifying with, and taking an active interest in the affairs of their co-religionists in İstanbul. The

---

4   *Ibid.*, pp. 286-7.

Hindoo Patriot remarked during the Balkan crisis of 1875-1878 that the Muslims [of India] had been utterly indifferent when the integrity of the Turkish empire was threatened prior to the Crimean War. But in the crisis of 1875-1878, they took an active interest in Turkish politics, wrote petitions to London appealing for the protection of the Sublime Porte, raised funds to help the Turks, and keenly watched the manoeuvres of the Great Powers.[5]

At first, such interest on the part of British India's Muslim population suited the policy being persued in London and the Muslims were therefore encouraged in their pro-Ottoman proclivities. Muslim demands coincided with Britain's policy of "maintaining the integrity of the Ottoman Empire" from the encroachments of her imperial rivals, Russia, France, and Germany after her unification. Support for the Sultan-Caliph during the last quarter of the nineteenth century won England the loyalty and gratitude of her Muslim subjects and strengthened her position in India, especially after the founding of the Indian National Congress in 1885.

However, Indian Muslim support for Turkey in the Balkan crisis, and especially during the Russo-Turkish war of 1877-1878 soon had other implications for India as a whole. Before long, the Hindu leadership also began to support the Turks and that puzzled British observers, convinced of the permanence of the immutable religious divisions in Asia. The *Hindoo Patriot* of 27 August 1877 explained that the "Hindus had no common cultural and religious ties with the Turks, [nevertheless] they felt a sort of cosmopolitan interest in the war because the Turks were an Asian power and their achievements had some value in the eyes of all Asians. Their success in the war, despite European prognostications about imminent demise of the 'sick man', invested them with a peculiar halo in the eyes of the Hindus."[6]

---

5   *Hindoo Patriot*, 29 Jan. 1877, quoted in R. L. Shukla, *Britain, India and the Turkish Empire 1853-1882*, New Delhi, 1973, p. 111.
6   *Ibid.*, 27 Aug. 1877, in Shukla, p. 113.

If Turkey had defeated Russia in 1878, would there have been the same kind of impact in Asia as there was after the Japanese victory of 1905? We can only speculate. But we do know that Turkey's defeat encouraged the imperialist powers and demoralised Asia and Africa, thus facilitating European expansion around the world.

The English could no longer afford to be complacent about the policy of pan-İslamism which, in the hands of an anti-imperialist like Jamal al-Din al-Afghani (1839-1897), could be interpreted so as to appeal to all Asians who felt oppressed by European domination. Thus for Afghani, who was most concerned about India and its future, "... a religious link does not exclude national links with men of different faiths; in countries such as Egypt and India Muslims should cooperate with others and there should be [Afghani noted] 'good relations and harmony in what pertians to national interests between you and your compatriots and neighbours who adhere to diverse religions.' There is even a natural solidarity beyond the nation: that which binds together all the people of the east threatened by the expansion of Europe."[7]

Indian, and especially Muslim, interest in the fate of the declining Ottomans continued to grow throughout the late nineteenth century. There were even minor rebellions among the Muslim tribes of the Northwest frontier, coinciding with the growing interest in the affairs of the Muslim world stimulated by the pan-Islamic propaganda during the Greco-Turkish war of 1897. The exhortations of the Sultan's propagandists to regard the Ottoman Sultan "as the political and spiritual leader of all Muslims made Englishmen apprehensive about future Muslim loyalty to British rule."[8]

The constitutional revolution of July 1908, carried out by the Young Turks, had an immediate impact on India. This was not lost on

---

7   Albert Hourani, *Arabic Thought in the Liberal Age 1789-1939*, London, 1962, p. 118. For the political and religious writings of Afghani see Nikki Keddie, *An Islamic Response to Imperialism*, Berkeley, 1983.

8   John McLane, *Indian Nationalism and the Early Congress*, Princeton, 1977, p. 29.

the Foreign Office in London and Sir Edward Grey was quick to note that "If Turkey really establishes a Constitution and keeps it on its feet, and becomes strong herself, the consequences will reach further than any of us can yet foresee. The effect in Egypt will be tremendous, and will make itself felt in India..."[9] Grey went on to inform his ambassador in İstanbul that Turkey's success would lead to demands for constitutional rule which the English would find hard to deny. Grey was right. In India, Young Turkey's constitutional experiment was watched with both enthusiasm and expectations, by both Muslims and Hindus.

The Mussalman, an organ of the Muslim intelligentsia, noted in the issue of 31 July 1908 that "The transformation of the Turkish Empire into a constitutional Monarchy is emblematic of the fact that the Orient has awakened, that the Moslem is no longer in sleep and that the "Sick man" is convalescent. It is a matter that will inspire a new spirit in the Mussalmans of India."[10] It must be emphasized that while events in Turkey were undoubtedly an inspirations for Muslims everywhere, in India they were seen as a reflection of the awakening of Asia. Thus as M.N.P. Srivastva and others have shown, the revolution in İstanbul was celebrated by the Indian press as a whole.[11]

Ever since 1905, when the British partitioned the province of Bengal into what was essentially a Hindu and a Muslim province, the country had been in political turmoil marked by a certain amount of terrorism. The Japanese victory over Russia in the same year increased the sense of confidence among Asians and intensified Indian nationalist agitation against this measure. The government of India countered Indian protests with harsh repression, exiling such militant national-

---

9   Grey to Lowther, Private, London, 31 July 1908. The Grey Papers, FO 800/78 quoted in Feroz Ahmad, "Great Britain's Relations with the Young Turks 1908-1914" in *Middle Eastern Studies*, 2/iv, 1966, p. 303.

10 N. M. P. Srivastva, *Growth of Nationalism in India: Effect of International Events*, Delhi, 1973, pp. 33-4.

11 *Ibid.*, and Mohammad Sadiq, *The Turkish Revolution and the Indian Freedom Movement*, Delhi, 1983.

ists as Bal Gangadhar Tilak (1856-1920) to Burma in 1907. Thus the Young Turk revolution came at a time when political consciousness in India was already high and the Turkish example served to stimulate the sense of nationalism and Indian desire for self rule, if not for total independence. *The Bengalee* (Calcutta) wrote, perhaps a little prematurely, that events in Turkey had demonstrated that representative institutions were "the great solvent of administrative problems arising out of racial controversies." These were precisely the problems that plaqued the Indian subcontinent on an even larger and more complex scale than in the Ottoman Empire. Nevertheless, taking Turkey as the model, *The Bengalee* asked: "Are we not, therefore, justified in holding that self-government is the only true panacea for the widespread unrest and discontent which now prevails in India?"[12]

The western powers may have welcomed the failure of the Turkish experiment in constitutionalism; for Indians this was a disappointment and a setback marked the failure of an Asian power to cope with its problems and therefore did not bode well for Asians in general. It also allowed Europeans to gloat and say "we told you so"! But Indians tended to hold the Great Powers responsible for the setbacks in the Ottoman Empire for they had done nothing to help the new regime. Bulgaria's declaration of independence, Austria-Hungary's annexation of Bosnia and Herzegovina, Europe's harsh and humiliating conditions for loans to a virtually bankrupt Turkey suggested that the Powers were not anxious to see Turkey reformed. Public opinion in India turned sharply against the West during these years, and Italy's attack on Turkey in 1911 and its seizure of the Ottoman province of Tripoli in Libya increased the sense of hostility towards the West. Indian newspapers noted that none of the Powers had raised a finger against the aggressor. *The Mussalman* asked rhetorically: "... What would have been the attitude of [the] Powers if a European Power was going to be treated in this fashion by an Asiatic one?"[13]

---

12   *The Bengalee*, 2 Aug. 1908, quoted in Srivastva (n.10), p. 34.
13   *The Mussalman*, 13 Oct. 1911, quoted in Srivastva (n.10), p. 39.

The year 1911 was a minor turningpoint in the history of the national movement in India. The unwavering nationalist agitation against the partition of Bengal, despite governmental repression, forced the English to revoke their decision in December. While this was a triumph for the nationalists, it was a blow to Muslims with communal aspirations. This group, led by landed interests, had always looked to the British for support to satisfy their aims and aspirations. They now felt betrayed, especially after they saw the isolation of constitutional Turkey which had also sought inspiration and support from England, "the mother of parliaments." For the moment, Indian Muslims in general were alienated from the British and therefore decided that the interests of their community would be served better if they cooperated with the nationalists.

This trend of Hindu-Muslim cooperation received a boost with the outbreak of the Balkan War in October 1912; even the Muslim masses became involved in the fate of the beleaguered Ottoman Empire struggling for survival against great odds. The masses followed the progress of the war through the columns of an active Urdu-language press newly mobilized to meet the demand for fresh and accurate news. For the Muslims in India – as for the Christians in the Balkans, and elsewhere – the struggle became a religious war, a crusade being waged by the Christian West against the world of Islam. "An Islamic Power in Europe (wrote *The Mussalman*) is an eye-sore to the Christian nations of the continent and accordingly they are determined to dismember the Empire and humiliate it in every way possible."[14]

Though Indian Muslims took the initiative to organize protest meetings in support of İstanbul, they were joined by the Hindus, including radical nationalists like Bipin Chandra Pal (1858-1932). His approach to nationalism is usually identified with Hinduism. But in 1912, he was one of those who saw the Balkan War in terms of pan-

---

14 *Ibid.*, 11 Oct. 1912, quoted in Srivastva (n.10), p. 43. On the Balkan Wars as reported from the Slavic side seen Leon Trotsky, *The Balkan Wars 1912-13*, New York, 1980.

Asian nationalism rather than religion, and recognized the necessity of Hindu-Muslim cooperation in the struggle against the British.

Again funds were collected for the Turkish war effort and in December 1912, an Indian medical mission arrived in İstanbul. Despite all the pro-Turkish activity and Indian protests against British cynicism and indifference to the fate of Turkey, there was no attempt to challenge British rule in India. This should not surprise us. Even the Young Turks – including the Unionists, members of the Committee of Union and Progress – who had suffered all sorts of rebuffs and insults at the hands of Great Britain did not stop being Anglophiles. Zafar Ali Khan, who came to İstanbul to present the money collected by the Indian Red Crescent Society to the Porte, must have been surprised to find in grand vezir Kamil Paşa a man with such unabashed pro-British proclivities. Yet, Kamil Paşa was as much a creature of the British as was the Agha Khan, one of the leaders of Muslims in India, and someone the British used to further their interests in the Islamic world.

Both men believed that "Islam" could be served best by serving England. As the Turks prepared to lose the town of Edirne to the Bulgarian Army, the Agha Khan proposed to Indian Muslims in February 1913 that "now here is a good opening for the Mussalmans of India alike of serving England and Islam. Let them use all their influence through their local efforts, through their goodwill, to bring England and Turkey together and, in fact, to carry out in Asiatic Turkey the spirit of the policy of Lord Beaconsfield.[15]

The disaster of the Balkan Wars demoralized both Turks and Indians and, one may speculate, all other peoples under colonial rule. However, the hopes and expectations of other nationalities living under Turkish rule – Greeks, Armenians, and Arabs – were raised as they anticipated the collapse of the Ottoman Empire. Thus when the

---

15 *Times of India*, 14 Feb. 1913 quoted in Srivastva (n.10), p. 53. On Kamil Paşa and the British, see Feroz Ahmad, *The Young Turks, the Committee of Union and Progress in Turkish Politics, 1908-1914*. Oxford, 1969, pp. 126-130.

world went to war in August 1914, the English felt quite confident about the loyalty of their Indian subjects though they were a little apprehensive about the Muslims.[16] Indian princes – Hindu and Muslim – who had been integrated into the English imperial structure after 1858, supported the British war effort morally and materially. The high ulema also urged the Sultan-Caliph in İstanbul to remain neutral, as did the Agha Khan.[17] Given these sentiments, Sir Adam Block, president of the Ottoman Public Debt Administration in İstanbul, was able to remind Cavid Bey of "the affection Indian Muslims had for England and of their willingness to fight against Turkey, if necessary." Block's confidence was based on the profession of loyalty by Indian Muslims and the telegrams they had been sending to İstanbul advising neutrality. Cavid Bey was not convinced and confided to his diary: "I was forced to say that they [the English] were deceiving themselves and that the [pro-British] meeting being held [in India] were coerced and the telegrams that they [the English] were having written would not lead anyone to that view or that conclusion."[18]

Block was proved correct and Cavid was wrong. Indian Muslim troops did fight on the English side against the Turks on a variety of fronts. Apart from a small group of Indian nationalist revolutionaries living in exile in Europe and America before the war, the Indian national movement made no attempt to exploit the war in order to win concessions from the British, let alone fight for independence. There was no attempt to follow the Unionist lead when the latter abrogated unilaterally the hated capitulation in September 1914 and won back their sovereignty.

It is vital to understand the differences between the two movements if we are to make sense of the relationship between them. The

---

16 On British attempts to check pan-Islamic and Turkish propaganda in India during the war seen N. Gerald Barrier, *Banned Controversial Literature and Political Control in British India 1907-1947*, Columbia, Missouri, 1974, *passim*.

17 Sadiq (n.11), p. 41ff.

18 Cavid Bey's diary, 12 Sept. 1914, serialised in *Tanin*, 5 Nov. 1944.

India national movement was economically and socially more developed than its Turkish counterpart. The reasons for these differences are historical. India was incorporated into the capitalist world economy earlier and more completely than the Ottoman Empire. British rule unified the Indian sub-continent during the nineteenth century and created a "national market" with its network of roads and railways. Agriculture in many parts of India had been transformed for the production of cash crops. As a result of this process of integration, an indigenous commercial bourgeoisie and intelligentsia made its appearance in this period, the commercial elements becoming involved in industrial activity as the century progressed. Indian merchants like those belonging to the Parsi Tata family made their fortunes partly in the Chinese opium trade and later invested the capital they accumulated in industry. Such people benefited greatly from their membership in Britain's world empire and therefore had no desire for independence. All they wanted was to be treated as equals by the British and be given the status of a white dominion like Canada or Australia. But the racialist outlook of the British did not permit such concessions to a people who were not white. Yet, even when India and Pakistan became independent in 1947, both states retained their link with the British Commonwealth of Nations.

The Turkish case was very different. The Turks were also incorporated into the world economy but they produced no indigenous, Muslim bourgeoisie, this role passing into the hands of Christian merchants protected and patronized by the Powers. By the end of the nineteenth and the beginning of the twentieth century, it was clear to members of the Turkish military and civil bureaucracies, who were by now both quite numerous and influential, that the Turks had to create their own capitalist economy and society with its own hierarchy of classes. To do so, they realized that the Ottoman state would have to become independent and sovereign. It seems fair to conclude that while the Turkish national movement lagged socially and economically behind the Indian, it was more politically advanced.

In the years after 1914, in theory at least, the Turks could have been an inspiration for an India struggling for freedom, willing to take advantage of John Bull weakened by his involvement in a long and costly war. There were some Indians – Hindu and Muslim – who wanted to do just that.[19] But the leaders of the Congress and the Muslim League preferred to remain loyal to their King-Emperor. Mahatma Gandhi (1869-1948), who became the de facto leader of the national movement immediately after the war, refused to join even the reformist Home Rule League, founded in 1915 to seek self-governing dominion status within the British Empire. He refused because "he did not want to embarrass the British Government who were fighting the Germans." He said that he would wait until the war was over, confident that England, grateful for India's help in the war, would share power with Indians.[20] Such was his understanding of imperialism; but other leaders shared the same illusions. Militant members of the Muslim League, founded in 1906, wanted to support Turkey, "the Home of the Caliphate", in its struggle against England. But Mohammed Ali Jinnah (1875-1948), "the creator of Pakistan" as his biographer describes him, appealed to them to remain loyal to the crown.[21]

With such political attitudes prevailing among Indian leaders, it is not surprising that neither the proclamation of 'holy war', the *Jihad-i Ekber* by the Sultan-Caliph on 11 November 1914, nor the Seyhülislam's fetva sanctioning the *Jihad-i Mukaddes* on the 18th, nor Enver Paşa's appeal for an anti-British *ghadr* – the Urdu word for the rebellion of 1857 – had the desired effect in India. Enver Paşa's appeal appeared on 20 November in the *Jihan-i İslam*, a pan-Islamist paper published in İstanbul for the specific purpose of conducting the propaganda war against the Triple Entente. Despite all the emphasis on

---

19 Feroz Ahmad, "1914-1915 Yıllarında İstanbul'da Hint Milliyetçi Devrimcileri", *Yapıt* (Ankara), no.6, Aug.-Sept., 1984, pp. 5-15.

20 J. Dwarkadas, *Political Memoirs*, Bombay, 1969, p. 34.

21 Hector Bolitho, *Jinnah*, London, 1954, pp. 63-4.

the religious aspect of the war, Enver's appeal, it should be noted, was to Indian nationalism, to Indians – Hindus and Muslims – and the aim was the liberation of India. The appeal bears quoting:

"This is the time that the *Ghadar* (rebellion) should be declared in India, and the magazines of the English should be plundered, their weapons looted and they should be killed therewith. The Indians number 32 crores [320 millions] at the best and the English are only 2 lakhs [200,000]; they should be murdered; they have no army. The Suez Canal will shortly be closed by the Turks, but he who will die and liberate the country and his native land will live for ever. Hindus and Mohammadans, you are both soldiers of the army and you are brothers, and this low degraded English is your enemy; you should become Ghazis by declaring Jehad and by combining with your brothers murder the English and liberate India."[22]

There was no serious anti-British rebellion in India throughout the war. Major setbacks suffered by British forces at Gallipoli or Kutul Amara in Iraq did not encourage any significant uprisings; on the other hand, the fall of Erzurum to the Russians in February 1916 dampened the spirit of defiance. Lisovski, the Russian Consul-General in India, wrote that this event "created here a good impression and grander still in Afghanistan [where the Germans and Turks hoped to start the rebellion]; according to available sources, it is paralyzing the activities of the German [and Turkish] emissaries."[23]

Revolution in Russia in 1917 and the Bolshevik promise to recognize the right of all peoples to self-determination had an immediate impact all over the world. In the colonies, the hopes of peoples under foreign rule were raised and this proved embarrassing to the imperialist powers. The Unionists in İstanbul were most gratified by the atti-

---

22 The appeal is taken from Government of India, Sedition Committee Report, Calcutta, 1918, p. 169, and quoted n Srivastva (n.10), p. 69. There is a separate appeal to Indian Muslims who were fighting for the British, asking then to stop aiding the enemy of Islam; see pp. 69-70.

23 Quoted in Russian consulate reports edited by Suhash Chakravarty, *Anatomy of the Raj*, New Delhi, 1981, p. 350.

tude of the Soviet government. Yunus Nadi, deputy and journalist wrote that "the present humane government [in Russia] not only refuses to take any part in the war, but declares, as a permanent principle, the necessity of respecting the rights of every nation and of every state. The great revolution, which this new government will produce in the Near East... may be considered as good fortune for the benefit of the human race..."[24] The Western powers had to join the battle for "the hearts and minds" of all people with national aspirations and respond to the Soviet proposals. That is essentially what President Wilson did on their behalf when he put forward his "Fourteen Points" in January 1918.

The defeat of Germany and her allies in November 1918 restored some of the confidence among the victorious imperialist powers. But they still had to undermine the sense of self-assurance acquired by colonial and semi-colonial peoples like the Turks during the war if they were to restore their former hegemony. Thus Lord Curzon quoted with approval the opinion prevailing in London that "... the one thing required to convince the Egyptian [or the Indian] that he can get no help from Europe and that his connection with the Turk is severed for ever will be the disappearance of his former sovereign from the Golden Horn [İstanbul]." He asked: "If we have to face... a new form of Turkish nationalism..., will it be a more or a less formidable factor if its rallying point and inspiration is the Sultan at Constantinople than a Sultan at Brusa...?"[25]

Once again the psychological factor had gained primacy in the struggle against imperialism. The British had to humiliate the Turks, thereby humiliating all Asians and facilitating their rule in their colonies or the soon-to-be mandated territories. Indian leaders recog-

---

24 "İhtilal ve İnkılap Rusyası ve Biz" (Revolution and Reform in Russia and Us), *Tasvir-i Efkâr*, 7 Dec. 1917.

25 "Memorandum by Earl Curzon on the Future of Constantinople", 4 Jan. 1920, given in Bilal Simsir (ed.), *İngiliz Belgelerinde Atatürk (1919-1938)*, British Documents on Atatürk (1919-1938), vol. i, Ankara, 1973, p. 304.

nized the significance of this, seeing the fragmentation of the Muslim world as a precedent for India, and therefore supported the Turks. C. R. Das, one of the most prominent of the nationalist leader, had no doubt about this. In a speech celebrating Khilafat Day in Calcutta, he noted that "The dismemberment of Turkey involved two issues – political and religious. Politically writing off the Mussalman principalities [the Arab provinces] from the suzerainty of Turkey is a menace not only to India but to Asia..."[26] And so, the national movement in India supported the restoration of the Sultan's authority even as Turkish nationalists were concluding that this authority had to be terminated and replaced by the "sovereignty of the people".

In India there was little knowledge or understanding of the nationalists in Anatolia. This was understandable while the nationalists maintained the fiction that they were fighting for the same goals as the Sultan. But once the İstanbul government had denounced the nationalists as rebels and traitors whose killing was a religious duty (11 April 1920), and sentenced to death *in absentia* Mustafa Kemal and his associates (11 May 1920), it was no longer possible to maintain this fiction. Yet the leaders of the Khilifat movement continued to deal principally with İstanbul though they began to make overtures to Ankara as well.[27]

The Indian nationalist movement could hardly be influenced by the Kemalist who were engaged in an anti-imperialist war and a struggle against an *ancien régime* which refused to die. In contrast, the Indian movement under Gandhi's leadership was trying to abort such a struggle, at a time when the country was seething with discontent and capable of being mobilized for revolution.[28] The Indian movement had limited aims and resembled that wing of the Kemalist movement which would have preferred an American mandate to full sovereignty.

---

26 *The Mussalman*, 24 Oct. 1919 quoted in Srivastva (n. 10), p. 139.
27 Sadiq (n.11), p. 61.
28 R. Palme Dutt, *India Today*, 2nd, ed., Calcutta, 1970, pp. 332-53.

For their part, the Turks – the Sultan's supporters and the nationalists – were under the illusion that England would impose terms less harsh on Turkey if pressure could be brought to bear upon London from her Indian subjects.[29] They were partly correct. Pressure could have been brought to bear on the British, pressure which might have threatened the very structure of their empire. But leaders in India and the Muslim world – the Congress and the Hashimites in the Arab provinces – were not so inclined, for their own reasons, to exploit British weakness. Nevertheless, The British were aware of the danger and one can sense their apprehension from their diplomatic correspondence. A Foreign Office analysis of the alleged treaty between Sherif Feisal and Mustafa Kemal in June 1919 posed the question: "What line are the Allies to take if as an immediate result of the Treaty with Turkey, the Moslems of the Middle East [and India?] combine on religious grounds to drive out the infidel invader? We can hardly suppress them by force..."[30]

After an exhausting war, the British lacked the will and the resources to suppress determined nationalist forces as the example of Turkey demonstrated. They were fortunate in having to deal with movements led by Gandhi and Feisal, men who were willing to compromise. Again a British document reveals the extent of their dilemma. A Foreign Office offical wrote in November 1919 that "... The War Office contemplate having to hand over the Anatolian Railway to the Turks from a sheer lack of a sufficiency of men to hold it. In Mesopotamia, Egypt, Asia Minor, not to speak of India, our forces are necessarily being demobilized, and from all these places there is a con-

---

29 Vice-Admiral Sir J. de Robeck to Earl Curzon, Constantinople, 10 Oct. 1919, in Simsir (n.25), p.138.
30 Report by Commander Heathcote-Smith, Constantinople, 24 July 1919, in Simsir (n.25), p.61. Gertrude Bell reached similar conclusions about the situation. "The truth is that Asia, from the Mediterranean to the Indian frontier, is now such a devil's cauldron that it's impossible to feel convinced that we shall save Mesopotamia from the general confusion." Diary entry, 4 Nov. 1920, in Elizabeth Burgoyne, *Gertrude Bell: From Her Personal Papers, 1914-1926*, vol. ii, London, 1961, p. 181.

stant shout for more men and fresh drafts which are not forthcoming. Nor is there money to pay for more."[31]

Thanks to Gandhi's leadership at a most critical moment, the British were not put to the test in India. He called off the non-violent struggle in February 1922 precisely at the moment when it seemed to be acquiring popular and spontaneous dimensions. Nehru, a sincere and dedicated follower of the Mahatma, was in jail at the time along with other Congress leaders. None of them could understand their leader's motives in calling a halt to the struggle. Later, he expressed his feelings in his autobiography:

"We were angry when we learned of the stoppage of our struggle at a time when we seemed to be consolidating our position and advancing on all fronts... [C]ivil resistance stopped, and noncooperation wilted away. After many months of strain and anxiety the [British] Government breathed again, and for the first lime had the opportunity of taking the initiative."[32] The Indian struggle suffered a setback from which it took about a decade to recover, revived by the world crisis of the thirties.

Meanwhile in Anatolia, the Kemalists went from strength to strength after suffering setbacks on the battle field. By September 1922, they had recaptured İzmir from the Greeks, driving them back into the sea. But these successes had no effect in India, now totally demoralized and confused. One gets an idea of this confusion from reading Mohammad Sadiq's account of the "Turkish Pattern of Change and the Indian Response",[33] that is to say the response of the Khilafat movement to the abolition of the Caliphate and the secularizing reform that followed. It becomes clear yet again that the two sides were still at cross purpose as they had always been throughout their relationship.

---

31 Mr. Kidston to ir E. Crowe (Paris), F.O. 28 Nov. 1919, in Simsir (n.25), p. 246.
32 Nehru (n.3), p. 79.
33 Sadiq (n.11), pp. 104ff.

The Kemalist movement was too different from the Indian to be able to influence it. Unlike the Kemalists, the Indian National Congress was not concerned with the radical reconstruction of society. The Congress was still not united on the question of whether they were seeking dominion status or total independence. In August 1928, the All-Parties Conference accepted the [Motilal] Nehru Report in support of dominion status for India. Jawaharlal Nehru (1889-1964) and Subhas Chandra Bose (1897-1945) refused to associate themselves with this decision and came to be described as the "Young Turks" of the Congress.[34] That was the extent of Turkey's influence on India!

Nehru might envy the reforms that Mustafa Kemal carried out in the new Turkey. But he had to recognize that they were not appropriate for the conditions prevailing in India. Muhammad Iqbal, poet-philosopher, ideologue who provided inspiration for the idea of Pakistan, felt much the same. He welcomed "revolutionary reforms in the countries of the East fighting for their independence", but "he often expressed his liking for an evolutionary form of development. He had... a high regard for the activity of Mustafa Kemal and acknowledged his right to religious reform." Yet in 1930, "he did not hide his sympathies for the reformist party [Serbest Fırka], which tied Turkey's development directly to religion." Iqbal "openly expressed disagreement with Kemal Atatürk's position on the caliphate." It his 'Six Lectures on the Reconstruction of Religious Thought in Islam', he wrote: "Personally, I think it was a mistake to suppose that the idea of state is more dominant and rules all other ideas embodied in the system of Islam." Iqbal considered even a Kemal-style revolution unacceptable for India. He believed that the peoples of the Indo-Pakistan subcontinent had not yet found their own path in the struggle for the creation of an independent state.[35]

---

34 Michael Brecher, *Nehru a political biography*, New York, 1959, pp. 129-30.
35 L. R. Gordon-Polonskaya, "Ideology of Muslim Nationalism" in Hafeez Malik (ed.), *Iqbal*, New York, 1971, p. 132.

Index